Introductory Level

STANDARDS-BASED LANGUAGE LEARNING FOR WORK AND ACADEMIC READINESS

SERIES DIRECTOR
Jayme Adelson-Goldstein

Lesson Plans

Jenni Currie Santamaria

OXFORD
UNIVERSITY PRESS

198 Madison Avenue
New York, NY 10016 USA

Great Clarendon Street, Oxford, OX2 6DP, United Kingdom

Oxford University Press is a department of the University of Oxford.
It furthers the University's objective of excellence in research, scholarship,
and education by publishing worldwide. Oxford is a registered trade
mark of Oxford University Press in the UK and in certain other countries

© Oxford University Press 2018

The moral rights of the author have been asserted

First published in 2018

2023

10 9 8

No unauthorized photocopying

All rights reserved. No part of this publication may be reproduced, stored in a retrieval system, or transmitted, in any form or by any means, without the prior permission in writing of Oxford University Press, or as expressly permitted by law, by licence or under terms agreed with the appropriate reprographics rights organization. Enquiries concerning reproduction outside the scope of the above should be sent to the ELT Rights Department, Oxford University Press, at the address above

You must not circulate this work in any other form and you must impose this same condition on any acquirer

Links to third party websites are provided by Oxford in good faith and for information only. Oxford disclaims any responsibility for the materials contained in any third party website referenced in this work

ISBN: 978 0 19 474830 8

Printed in China

This book is printed on paper from certified and well-managed sources

ACKNOWLEDGMENTS
Back cover photograph: Oxford University Press building/David Fisher

CONTENTS

Pre-Unit
The First Step 2

Unit 1
Please Spell That 4

Unit 2
How Are You Feeling? 24

Unit 3
What Time Is It? 44

Unit 4
What Day Is It? 63

Unit 5
How Much Is It? 82

Unit 6
That's My Son 101

Unit 7
Do You Need Apples? 120

Unit 8
What's the Matter? 138

Unit 9
What Size? 156

Unit 10
This Is My Home 175

Unit 11
Where's the Bank? 193

Unit 12
Yes, I Can! 212

PRE-UNIT

The First Step

Lesson Overview

MULTILEVEL OBJECTIVES

On- and Higher-level: Give and follow classroom directions and introduce yourself

Pre-level: Follow classroom directions and introduce yourself

LANGUAGE FOCUS

Grammar: Imperatives *(Listen. Look. Repeat.)*

Vocabulary: *Count, listen, look, meet, partner, point, read, repeat, spell, work, write*

For vocabulary expansion, see these **Oxford Picture Dictionary** topics: Meeting and Greeting, pages 2–3; A Classroom, pages 6–7

STRATEGY FOCUS

Use the context clues from images to help you determine the meaning of new words.

READINESS CONNECTION

In this lesson, students process classroom instructions.

PACING

To compress this lesson: Practice 2D with only one partner.

To extend this lesson: Practice learning names. (See end of lesson.)

And/or have students complete **Multilevel Activities Introductory Level Pre-Unit page 13.**

CORRELATIONS

CCRS: SL.1.A Participate in collaborative conversations with diverse partners in small and larger groups.

SL.2.A Confirm understanding of a text read aloud or information presented orally or through other media by asking and answering questions about key details and requesting clarification if something is not understood.

ELPS: 1. An ELL can construct meaning from oral presentations and literary and informational text through level-appropriate listening, reading, and viewing.

Lesson Notes

Warm-up and Review
5–10 minutes (books closed)

Write the name of your class on the board and pronounce it for the students. Tell students your name. Write it on the board and help students pronounce it. Ask various students to tell you their names.

Introduction
5 minutes

1. Walk around introducing yourself to students with *Hi, I'm _____*.

2. State the objective: *Today we'll learn some classroom instructions and how to introduce ourselves.*

1 Classroom directions

Presentation I
5–10 minutes

 1. Tell students to listen and look at the pictures. Play the audio.

2. Check comprehension. Say the words and ask students to act them out.

3. Write the words on the board and help students sound out and pronounce each one. Then act out the words and have students say them.

Guided Practice I
15–20 minutes

 1. Direct students' attention to number 1. Say the letters *a* and *b*. Using pantomime, demonstrate listening and making a choice between *a* and *b* and drawing a check mark. Play number 1 and show students how the answer has already been checked for them.

2. Play the audio one item at a time and go over each answer.

Answers	
1. b	4. a
2. a	5. a
3. b	6. b

 1. Replay the audio and have students point to the pictures and repeat the words.

2. Point to each of the pictures in the activity (including the unchecked ones) and ask students to say the words.

> **TIP**
>
> For additional vocabulary practice after 1C, have students act out the words with a partner. Have one partner read the words out of the book and the other act out the word. Alternatively, have partners use Pre-unit Picture Cards FS.3–FS.10 on page 15 of *Multilevel Activities Introductory Level* as flashcards.

2 Introduce yourself

Presentation II
10–15 minutes

 Direct students to look at the pictures. Ask them to read the conversation silently.

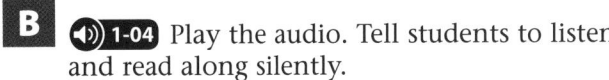 Play the audio. Tell students to listen and read along silently.

Guided Practice II
5–10 minutes

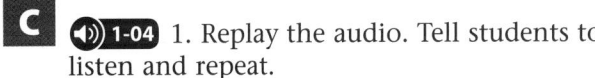 1. Replay the audio. Tell students to listen and repeat.

2. Model and have students repeat the conversation again, with a focus on friendly tone and natural cadence.

3. Conduct a choral reading of the conversation. Have half of the class be Lorena and the other half be Jin. Then switch roles.

Communicative Practice
10–15 minutes

 1. Model the conversation with a volunteer. Switch roles and model it again with another volunteer. Elicit other ways to complete the conversation.

2. Set a time limit (two minutes). Ask students to practice the conversation with several partners. Encourage pantomime and improvisation.

3. Call on volunteer pairs to present their conversations to the class.

> **EXTENSION ACTIVITY**
>
> **Learn Names**
>
> After the practice in 1D, call on a couple of students to say the classmates' names that they remember. Then have them circulate and introduce themselves to as many people as they can. Use gestures to indicate that you want them to remember the names. Set a time limit (two minutes). Call on volunteers to say other students' names and applaud the ones who remember the most names.

UNIT 1: Please Spell That

Unit Overview

This unit explores letters, numbers, writing sentences with *be*, and using spelling for clarification.

KEY OBJECTIVES

Lesson 1	Identify letters of the alphabet
Lesson 2	Identify numbers and plural nouns
Lesson 3	Use nouns and the verb *be* to talk about the classroom
Lesson 4	Use spelling for clarification
Lesson 5	Use indefinite articles; interpret a supplies checklist
Teamwork & Language Review	Review unit language

UNIT FEATURES

Employability Skills	• Communicate information • Speak so others can understand • Communicate verbally • Work with others • Understand teamwork • Read, write, and identify numbers • Identify phone numbers • Determine how to respond appropriately when you don't understand

Resources	**Class Audio** CD1, Tracks 05–26
	Workbook Unit 1, pages 2–8
	Teacher Resource Center
	    Literacy Reproducible Activities Unit 1
	    Multilevel Activities Introductory Level Unit 1
	    Multilevel Grammar Exercises Introductory Level Unit 1
	    Unit 1 Test
	Oxford Picture Dictionary Meeting and Greeting, Personal Information, A Classroom, Numbers

LESSON 1 VOCABULARY

Lesson Overview	Lesson Notes
MULTILEVEL OBJECTIVES	
On- and Higher-level: Identify letters of the alphabet **Pre-level:** Recognize letters of the alphabet	
LANGUAGE FOCUS	
Grammar: Imperatives *(Listen. Look. Repeat.)* **Vocabulary:** *Alphabet, book, paper, pen, pencil, picture, student, teacher, word* For vocabulary expansion, see this **Oxford Picture Dictionary** topic: A Classroom, pages 6–7	
STRATEGY FOCUS	
Use written and oral repetition to remember spelling.	
READINESS CONNECTION	
In this lesson, students communicate verbally as they practice the alphabet and spelling words.	
PACING	
To compress this lesson: Do 2A together as a class. **To extend this lesson:** Do a partner dictation. (See end of lesson.) And/or have students complete **Workbook Introductory Level page 2** and **Multilevel Activities Introductory Level Unit 1 page 18.**	
CORRELATIONS	
CCRS: SL.2.A Confirm understanding of a text read aloud or information presented orally or through other media by asking and answering questions about key details and requesting clarification if something is not understood. RF.3.A Know and apply grade-level phonics and word analysis skills in decoding words. Demonstrate basic knowledge of one-to-one letter-sound correspondences by producing the primary sound or many of the most frequent sounds for each consonant. L.2.A Demonstrate command of the conventions of English capitalization, punctuation, and spelling when writing. g. Spell simple words phonetically, drawing on knowledge of sound-letter relationships.	**ELPS:** 1. An ELL can construct meaning from oral presentations and literary and informational text through level-appropriate listening, reading, and viewing.

Warm-up and Review
10–15 minutes (books closed)

Write the conversation from the Pre-Unit on the board:

Hi, I'm __.
My name is __.
Nice to meet you.
Nice to meet you too.

Model the conversation with two or three of the higher-level students. Then ask students to practice it with a partner. While they are practicing, circulate and introduce yourself to any new students or students whose names you don't remember.

Introduction
5 minutes

1. Point to the letters on the board (in the conversation) and say some of them aloud.

2. State the objective: *Today we'll learn the alphabet.*

1 Learn the alphabet

Presentation I
5–10 minutes

A 🔊 **1-05** Direct students to look at the alphabet. Play the audio and have students read along silently.

TIP

During 1A, show students how to follow along with a finger on the text. Circulate and monitor. If you see students pointing at the wrong letters, stop the audio and help students find the right place.

Guided Practice I
15–20 minutes

B 🔊 **1-05** 1. Have students listen again and repeat the letters.

2. Check comprehension. Say letters out of order and ask students to point to the letters they hear. Write letters on the board and ask students to say them.

C 1. Write letter pairs on the board: a A, b B, c C. Point to the letters, lowercase first, and say "a, capital A." "b, capital B." "c, capital C."

2. Write three more pairs on the board as they are in the exercise:

___ 1. M   t

___ 2. N   m

___ 3. T   n

Point to number 1 and say, *capital M*. Ask a volunteer to point to the lowercase *m*. Write it on the line. Do the same with 2 and 3.

3. Direct students' attention to the *Need help?* box. To illustrate the point that printed lowercase *a* often looks different from the way we write it, point to some examples, such as the "a" in the author's last name on the title page and any other examples you have in the room. Then write a round *a* on the board. Use gestures to indicate that this is how students should write the letter.

4. Direct students to complete the exercise in their books.

5. While students are working, copy the exercise on the board. Have volunteers fill in the answers. Say and have students repeat each item, for example, 1. *a, capital A*.

Answers	
1. a	5. g
2. b	6. h
3. d	7. i
4. e	8. q

D 🔊 **1-06** 1. Play the audio. Direct students to listen and point to the letters they hear.

2. Copy the exercise on the board. Replay the audio and have volunteers point to the letters on the board. Have students repeat all of the letters.

Answers	
1. a	5. p
2. i	6. n
3. j	7. y
4. h	8. f

E Direct students to work with a partner to read the letters in 1D. Call on volunteers to say the letters aloud.

2 Spell words

Guided Practice II
10–15 minutes

A 🔊 **1-07** 1. Direct students to look at the pictures. Write s _ _ _ _ _ t on the board. Play number 1. Repeat the word *student* and have students spell it aloud. Show them how to write one letter on each line.

2. Copy the rest of the words (with blanks) onto the board. Play the audio in segments. After each word, stop and elicit the spelling. Complete the words on the board.

Answers	
1. s-t-u-d-e-n-t	5. p-e-n-c-i-l
2. t-e-a-c-h-e-r	6. p-a-p-e-r
3. b-o-o-k	7. p-i-c-t-u-r-e
4. p-e-n	8. w-o-r-d

B 🔊 **1-08** Play the audio again. Have students repeat the words.

TIP

For further practice with pronouncing the alphabet after completing 2B, put letters in columns on the board according to the vowel sound made when they are pronounced, for example: *a, h, j, k* and *e, b, c, d, g, p, t, v, z* and *i, y* and *f, m, n, s, x*.

C Direct students to copy the words into their notebooks. Circulate and monitor to make sure students are writing the words in a column and copying correctly.

Application and Evaluation
10–15 minutes

TEST YOURSELF

1. Direct students to look at the speech bubbles. Point to the green speech bubble and say: *student*. Point to the red speech bubble and spell out the word. Choose another word and model the activity with a volunteer. Switch roles and model it again with another volunteer.

2. Pair students. Have one pair model the activity.

3. Set a time limit (five minutes) and have the partners take turns saying and spelling the words. Circulate and monitor. Provide feedback.

MULTILEVEL STRATEGIES

Target the evaluation to the level of your students.

- **Higher-level** Direct these students to close their books as they spell the words for their partners.

EXTENSION ACTIVITY

Partner Dictation

Have students practice spelling their names for a partner. Tell one partner to spell his or her name and the other to write it. Have them check the spelling, and then switch roles.

LESSON 2 WRITING

Lesson Overview

MULTILEVEL OBJECTIVES
On-, Pre-, and Higher-level: Read and write numbers

LANGUAGE FOCUS
Grammar: Imperatives *(Write. Look. Listen.)*

Vocabulary: Numbers, *man, men, telephone, woman, women*

For vocabulary expansion, see this **Oxford Picture Dictionary** topic: Numbers, page 16

STRATEGY FOCUS
To write a list, put each item on a new line.

READINESS CONNECTION
In this lesson, students read, write, and identify numbers, including phone numbers.

PACING
To compress this lesson: Skip the evaluation. Evaluate students by monitoring class work.

To extend this lesson: Dictate numbers and classroom items. (See end of lesson.)

And/or have students complete **Workbook Introductory Level page 3** and **Multilevel Activities Introductory Level Unit 1 page 19**.

Lesson Notes

CORRELATIONS

CCRS: SL.1.A Participate in collaborative conversations with diverse partners in small and larger groups.

SL.2.A Confirm understanding of a text read aloud or information presented orally or through other media by asking and answering questions about key details and requesting clarification if something is not understood.

ELPS: 1. An ELL can construct meaning from oral presentations and literary and informational text through level-appropriate listening, reading, and viewing. 9. An ELL can create clear and coherent level-appropriate speech and text.

Warm-up and Review
10–15 minutes (books closed)

Review the alphabet. Say and have students repeat the letters. Spell out words and have students write them as a dictation: *1. p-e-n, 2. b-o-o-k, 3. p-a-p-e-r, 4. s-t-u-d-e-n-t, 5. t-e-a-c-h-e-r.* Call on volunteers to say the words and spell them back to you. Write them on the board.

Introduction
5 minutes

1. Say the numbers (1–5) as you point to them on the board.

2. State the objective: *Today we'll learn numbers.*

1 Learn numbers 0-19

Presentation I
10–15 minutes

A 🔊 **1-09** Direct students to look at the numbers. Play the audio. Have students read along silently.

B 🔊 **1-09** 1. Replay the audio and ask students to repeat the words.

2. Write the numbers on the board. Point to them in order and have students repeat them. Point to them out of order and ask students to call them out.

> **TIP**
>
> After 1B, help students with the pronunciation of numbers, especially of 3, 5, 8, 12, and 13. Show them your mouth position for each of these numbers and point out the ending sounds. For the numbers 13, 14, 15, 16, 17, 18, and 19, demonstrate how to stress the last syllable by making it longer and higher in pitch.

Guided Practice I
15–20 minutes

C 1. Direct students to read the numbers with a partner.

2. Have students point to the numbers out of order and have their partners say them.

D 🔊 **1-10** 1. Direct students to look at the telephones. Say and have them repeat the word *telephone*.

2. Play the audio. Tell students to listen and repeat the numbers.

AT WORK

Take messages

A 🔊 **1-11** 1. Write number 1 on the board. Point to *Anna Ball*. Ask: *Is this a number or a name?* [name]

2. Say: *Listen to the phone call*. Play the audio. Say: *Complete the phone number*.

3. Play the audio in segments. Circulate and monitor. Repeat segments as necessary.

4. Call on volunteers to read the completed phone numbers aloud.

Answers	
1. (212) 555-4261	5. (387) 555-2237
2. (629) 555-1964	6. (512) 555-1091
3. (748) 555-1861	7. (936) 555-8990
4. (256) 555-2490	8. (481) 555-1674

B 1. Model the activity with a student. Read one of the phone numbers and ask the student to point to the correct number. Then have the student read a number to you. Point to the number the student reads.

2. Have the students practice in pairs.

> **MULTILEVEL STRATEGIES**
>
> Adapt At Work B for your higher-level students.
>
> • **Higher-level** If students can say the numbers easily, work with them on correct phone-number cadence. Tell these students to focus on using correct cadence when they say the numbers. Model how to say the first three numbers, pause, then the next three numbers, pause, the next two, pause, and then the last two.

> **TIP**
>
> After At Work B, pair students for more practice with phone numbers. Pass out slips of paper with phone numbers on them. Direct students to take turns dictating the phone numbers to their partners. Model the activity with two volunteers.

2 Count things in the classroom

Presentation II
10–15 minutes

A 🔊 **1-12** Direct students to look at the numbers. Play the audio. Have students read along silently.

B 🔊 **1-12** 1. Replay the audio and tell students to repeat the words.

2. Write the numbers on the board. Point to them in order and have students repeat them. Point to them out of order and ask students to call them out.

> **TIP**
>
> After 2B, write these numbers on the board: 5, 10, 15, 20, 25, . . . (to 100). Point to the numbers as you count by tens, and then again by fives. Have students repeat.

Guided Practice II
15–20 minutes

 C 1-13 1. Say and have students repeat the words in 1–5.

2. Copy number 1 on the board. Play the audio. Show students how to write the number on the line.

3. Play the audio in segments. Elicit the answers after each item.

Answers	
1. 30	6. 22
2. 25	7. 56
3. 60	8. 39
4. 100	9. 120
5. 21	10. 61

 D 1. Write Classroom A and Classroom B on the board. Say: *Classroom A has 30 pencils. How many pencils are in Classroom B?* [22] Write the math problem on the board and read it aloud.

2. Ask: *How many books are in Classroom A?* [25] *How many books are in Classroom B?* [56] Write the numbers on the board and then add the plus and equals signs. Elicit the answer to the problem [81].

3. Have students work individually to complete the exercise.

Answers
1. 30 + 22 = 52
2. 25 + 56 = 81
3. 60 + 39 = 99
4. 100 + 120 = 220
5. 21 + 61 = 82

> **MULTILEVEL STRATEGIES**
>
> - **On- and Higher-level** If some students finish this activity very quickly, partner them with another on- or higher-level student. Tell them to take turns dictating three new addition problems to their partners.
> - **Pre-level** If some students are struggling with mental addition, show them how to set the problems up vertically and add one number at a time by counting.

 E 1. Point to number 1 from 2D on the board *(30 pencils + 22 pencils)*. Say: *Classroom A and Classroom B have 52 pencils.*

2. Elicit the answer to number 2 [81 books]. Have the students practice saying the totals of each item in pairs.

3. When the pairs have finished, call on students for the answers by asking the questions aloud, e.g., *How many books? How many students?*

3 Prepare to write: plurals

Presentation III
5 minutes

 A 1-14 1. Introduce the new topic: *Now we're going to write about the classroom.* Direct students to look at the pictures. Play the audio. Have students listen and repeat.

2. Check comprehension. Point to a male student and ask: *Man or men?* Point to a female student and ask: *Woman or women?* Do the same with *student/students*. Repeat several times and go over pronunciation.

Guided Practice III
5 minutes

 B 1. Copy the words on the board in a column of pairs with the singular first:

> *student, students*
> *man, men*
> *woman, women*

Direct students to write the words in their notebooks.

2. Have students practice saying the words with a partner. Monitor for spelling and pronunciation.

4 Write about your classroom

Communicative Practice
15 minutes

A 1. Direct students to look at the picture. Point out that the students are talking, not writing. Ask students to put their pencils down and work with their partners to name items and quantities in the room.

2. Call on volunteers to share their ideas.

B 1. Point out the *Writer's Note*. Say the word *list*. Check comprehension. Point to the list of words on the board from 3B. Ask: *Is this a list?* [yes] Then write a sentence: *My name is Maria.* Ask: *Is this a list?* [no]

2. Have students work individually to write a list of things in the classroom. Monitor and spot-check or collect and correct students' work.

Evaluation
10 minutes

TEST YOURSELF

1. Review the instructions aloud. Ask students to write their phone numbers on the first line.

2. Read the school phone number aloud slowly, but with a natural cadence. Repeat twice.

3. Ask a volunteer to write the number on the board.

> **EXTENSION ACTIVITY**
> **Dictation**
> Do a dictation related to the number of different items there are in the classroom. Say: *one desk, five tables, two clocks,* etc. Tell students to listen and write the words. Allow them to check their books when you've finished. Call on volunteers to write the words on the board.

LESSON 3 GRAMMAR

Lesson Overview	Lesson Notes
MULTILEVEL OBJECTIVES	
On- and Higher-level: Use subject pronouns and the verb *be* **Pre-level:** Recognize subject pronouns and the verb *be*	
LANGUAGE FOCUS	
Grammar: Subject pronouns and the verb *be* (*He is a student.*) **Vocabulary:** Classroom items For vocabulary expansion, see this **Oxford Picture Dictionary** topic: A Classroom, pages 6–7	
STRATEGY FOCUS	
Use capital letters and periods when you write a sentence.	
READINESS CONNECTION	
In this lesson, students communicate information about things and people in a classroom.	
PACING	
To compress this lesson: Conduct 1C as a whole-class activity. Assign 2C as homework. **To extend this lesson:** Have students write sentences with pronouns and *be*. (See end of lesson.) And/or have students complete **Workbook Introductory Level pages 4–5**, **Multilevel Activities Introductory Level Unit 1 page 20**, and **Multilevel Grammar Exercises Introductory Level Unit 1**.	
CORRELATIONS	
CCRS: L.1.A Demonstrate command of the conventions of standard English grammar and usage when writing or speaking. c. Use singular and plural nouns with matching verbs in basic sentences (e.g., *He hops; We hop*). g. Use frequently occurring nouns and verbs.	**ELPS:** 10. An ELL can demonstrate command of the conventions of standard English to communicate in level-appropriate speech and writing.

Warm-up and Review
10–15 minutes (books closed)

Use classroom objects and pantomime to elicit these words: *teacher, student, man, woman, pencil, pen, book, desk, clock*. Then make a two-column chart with *1* and *2* as the column heads. Write the singular words in column 1. Elicit the plural forms of the words and write them in column 2. Practice pronouncing the words in both columns.

Introduction
5–10 minutes

1. Pointing to people and objects, make statements using pronouns and the words on the board: *I am a teacher. She is a student. They are men. It is a book.*

2. State the objective: *Today we're going to learn sentences with* I am, he is, she is, it is, you are, we are, *and* they are.

1 Use subject pronouns

Presentation I
20–25 minutes

A Direct students to look at the pictures. Ask them to say what they see.

B 🔊 1-15 1. Play the audio. Tell students to listen and point to the pictures.

2. Say the words and have students repeat them.

> **TIP**
>
> For more practice with pronouns after 1B, ask several volunteers (male and female) to come to the front of the room. Point at individuals and ask: *He or she?* Point to two men and ask: *He or they?* [they] Point to two women and ask: *She or they?* [they] Point to two books and ask: *It or they?* [they] Then point to various items and people, and elicit the correct pronouns.

Guided Practice I
15–20 minutes

C 1. Direct students to work individually to circle the correct answers.

2. Call on volunteers for the answers. Write them on the board.

Answers	
1. a	4. b
2. b	5. a
3. b	6. b

> **MULTILEVEL STRATEGIES**
>
> After 1C, put students in mixed-level groups.
>
> • **Higher-level:** Have these students "test" their classmates on the pronouns by pointing to various people and items.

2 Use the verb *be*

Presentation II
10–15 minutes

A 🔊 1-16 1. Direct students to look at the pictures. Ask them to count the men and women [two men, one woman].

2. Play the audio. Ask students to point to the pictures as they listen. Say and have students repeat the sentences.

3. Write the subject pronouns on the board in a column. Write *am, is, are* in another column. Point to and say the subject pronouns and have students call out *am, is,* or *are*.

Guided Practice II
10–15 minutes

B 1. Project or copy the exercise on the board. Demonstrate how to form a complete sentence by reading number 1.

2. Tell students to work individually to match the sentence parts.

3. Have volunteers read the completed sentences. Write the answers on the board.

> **TIP**
>
> For 2B, some students may be more comfortable drawing lines to match the parts of the sentences. Allow them to work that way, but encourage them to put the correct letter on the answer line when they finish.

Answers
1. d
2. b
3. e
4. a
5. c

C 1. Read number 1 aloud. Tell students to work individually to complete the sentences.

2. Have volunteers read the completed sentences aloud. Write the answers on the board. Have the class repeat the sentences.

Answers	
1. am	5. is
2. are	6. is
3. are	7. are
4. is	8. are

> **MULTILEVEL STRATEGIES**
>
> Adapt 2B and 2C for your pre-level students.
>
> • **Pre-level** Provide these students with the answers to the exercises and have them practice reading the sentences to each other.

Lesson Plans Intro

Communicative Practice and Application
10–15 minutes

D 1. Read the sentences. Call on two or three volunteers to make statements about the class or classroom.

2. Set a time limit (five minutes). Ask students to talk about the classroom with several partners. Circulate and monitor. Provide feedback.

3. Call on volunteers to share their sentences with the class.

3 Talk about things and people in a classroom

Presentation and Guided Practice III
10–15 minutes

A 🔊 1-17 1. Introduce the new topic: *Now we're going to talk about the classroom.* Direct students to look at the pictures.

2. Play the audio. Ask students to point to the pictures as they listen.

3. Replay the audio. Tell students to listen and repeat.

4. Check comprehension. Point to items in the room and ask *or* questions: *Clock or chair? Chair or chairs?*

B 🔊 1-18 1. Play the audio. Ask students to point to the pictures in 3A.

2. Play the audio again and ask students to repeat.

Communicative Practice and Application
10–15 minutes

C 1. Point to the clock in 3A and ask a volunteer to read the example sentence: *It is a clock.* Do the same with the next two examples and new volunteers.

2. Have students work in pairs to talk about the pictures in 3A. Monitor and correct grammar.

D 1. Direct students' attention to the *Need help?* box. Copy the first two sentences on the board. Point to the capital letters at the beginning and say: *capital I, capital H.* Point to the periods and say: *period.* Write that word on the board. Point to each sentence and say: *This is a sentence.*

2. Check comprehension. Write a list on the board: *clock, teacher, table.* Point to the list and ask: *Is this a sentence?* [no]

3. Have students work individually to write sentences about three of the pictures in 3A.

4. Call on volunteers to write their sentences on the board and correct them as a class.

Evaluation
10–15 minutes

TEST YOURSELF

1. Direct pairs to look at the pictures in 1A (page 9). Ask them to work together to write four sentences.

2. Monitor and spot-check their writing.

> **MULTILEVEL STRATEGIES**
>
> Target the *Test Yourself* to the level of your students.
>
> • **Pre-level** Provide these students with sentence frames: _____ *am a student.* ____ *is a man.* ____ *is a woman.* _____ *are students.* _____ *is a book.* Write pronouns on the board: *I, he, she, it,* and *they.* Ask students to use the pronouns to complete the frames.
>
> • **Higher-level** Ask these students to write three to four additional sentences using *we* and *they.*

> **EXTENSION ACTIVITY**
>
> **Writing**
>
> 1. Put pictures on the board representing familiar vocabulary words. Include singulars and plurals, e.g., several pencils, one teacher, a clock, several students.
>
> 2. Direct students to work with a partner to write sentences about the pictures using a pronoun and the verb *be.*
>
> 3. Ask volunteers to write their sentences on the board.

LESSON 4 EVERYDAY CONVERSATION

Lesson Overview	Lesson Notes
MULTILEVEL OBJECTIVES **On- and Higher-level:** Request and use spelling for confirmation **Pre-level:** Respond to requests for spelling confirmation	
LANGUAGE FOCUS **Grammar:** The verb *be (My name is Trang.)* **Vocabulary:** *Please* For vocabulary expansion, see these **Oxford Picture Dictionary** topics: Meeting and Greeting, pages 2–3; Personal Information, page 4	
STRATEGY FOCUS When you don't understand what someone has said, you can ask him or her to spell it.	
READINESS CONNECTION In this lesson, students speak so others can understand by spelling their names.	
PACING **To compress this lesson:** Conduct 2A–C as whole-class activities. **To extend this lesson:** After completing the Evaluation, have students practice saying and spelling each other's names. (See end of lesson.) And/or have students complete **Workbook Introductory Level page 6** and **Multilevel Activities Introductory Level Unit 1 page 21.**	
CORRELATIONS	
CCRS: SL.2.A Confirm understanding of a text read aloud or information presented orally or through other media by asking and answering questions about key details and requesting clarification if something is not understood. SL.3.A Ask and answer questions in order to seek help, get information, or clarify something that is not understood. RF.2.A Demonstrate understanding of spoken words, syllables, and sounds (phonemes).	**ELPS:** 2. An ELL can participate in level-appropriate oral and written exchanges of information, ideas, and analyses, in various social and academic contexts, responding to peer, audience, or reader comments and questions. 9. An ELL can create clear and coherent level-appropriate speech and text.

Warm-up and Review
5 minutes (books closed)

Write your first and last name on the board. Have students call out the letters. Call on volunteers to say their names. Write the names and ask the class to spell them aloud.

Introduction
5 minutes

1. Write the question on the board: *What's your name?* Have students repeat the question.

2. State the objective: *Today we're going to learn how to ask for spelling of a name.*

1 Listen for spelling

Listening Extension
5–10 minutes

A 🔊 **1-19** 1. Introduce the topic: *First, we're going to listen for spelling.* Direct students to look at the names in number 1. Play number 1. Have students spell the answer aloud.

2. Play the audio in segments. Ask students to circle *a* or *b*. Ask for a show of hands to see how students answered. Repeat the segment if necessary.

Answers
1. a
2. b
3. a
4. a
5. b
6. b

B 🔊 **1-19** 1. Replay the audio and ask students to check their answers.

2. Call on volunteers to spell the answers aloud. Write the answers on the board.

> **MULTILEVEL STRATEGIES**
>
> Replay 1B to allow pre-level students to catch up while you provide a challenge for higher-level students.
>
> • **Pre-level** Have these students listen again to circle the correct name.
>
> • **On- and Higher-level** Ask these students to close their books and write the names they hear.

C 🔊 **1-20** 1. Point to the pictures and say the word *nametag*. Play number 1. Say: *Her name is Gina.*

2. Play the audio in segments. Tell students to listen and write the names on the lines.

3. Have volunteers write the answers on the board.

Answers
Gina
Jamal
Victor
Samphy

2 Practice your pronunciation

Pronunciation Extension
10–15 minutes

A 🔊 **1-21** 1. Direct students to look at the chart. Have them say *i* and *e*.

2. Play the audio. Tell students to listen and point to the words as they hear them.

3. Write *i* and *e* on the board. Say some of the words from the chart and ask students to call out the sound they hear.

B 🔊 **1-22** 1. Point out the check mark in the instructions. Play number 1. Demonstrate how to write a check mark in the correct column. Play the rest of the audio. Direct students to work individually to check the sounds they hear. While students are listening, copy the chart on the board.

2. Replay the audio. Stop after each word and elicit the correct column. Complete the chart on the board.

Answers	
i	e
1.	✓
2. ✓	
3. ✓	
4.	✓

C 🔊 **1-22** Have students listen again and repeat the words they hear.

3 Make conversation: ask for spelling

Presentation
5 minutes

A 1. Direct students to look at the pictures. Ask students to read the conversation silently.

2. Ask: *Who is the man?* [Trang] *Who is the woman?* [Marta]

Guided Practice
5–10 minutes

B 🔊 **1-23** Play the audio. Have students read the conversation silently.

C 🔊 **1-23** Play the audio again and have students repeat the conversation.

Communicative Practice and Application
10–15 minutes

 1. Model the conversation with a volunteer. Switch roles and model it again with another volunteer. Elicit other ways to complete the conversation.

2. Set a time limit (five minutes). Ask students to practice the conversation with several partners. Encourage pantomime and improvisation.

3. Call on volunteer pairs to present their conversations to the class.

> **TIP**
> Conduct 3D as a mixer. Ask students to walk around the class and introduce themselves to as many people as possible and to spell their names for each other. Challenge them to remember the names.

Evaluation
5 minutes

TEST YOURSELF

1. Model the activity, showing students that they should listen to their partners spell their names, not hand the paper over for signatures.

2. Tell them to write the names of three classmates that they don't already know in the chart.

3. As a follow-up, call on students to read one of the names on their list. Ask them to point out the person whose name it is.

> **TIP**
> After *Test Yourself*, teach students about U.S. introduction customs. Demonstrate a polite handshake. Use pantomime to show students that a limp handshake conveys indifference or dislike. Show students that both men and women may expect a handshake during an introduction, especially a more formal one.

EXTENSION ACTIVITY

Practice Spelling Names

After *Test Yourself*, help students learn each other's names. Write on the board:

I am _____. He is _____. She is _____.

Model the activity by completing the sentences with your name and the names of two students. Have students complete the sentences with their own and two classmates' names. (If your students sit in same-language clusters, tell them they must complete the activity with students from a different part of the class.) Encourage them to spell their names aloud for each other and help each other with pronunciation. Call on volunteers to read the sentences aloud.

LESSON 5 READING

Lesson Overview

MULTILEVEL OBJECTIVES

On- and Higher-level: Use *a* and *an* and read a class supplies list

Pre-level: Recognize *a* and *an* and read a class supplies list

LANGUAGE FOCUS

Grammar: Indefinite articles *(a pencil, an eraser)*

Vocabulary: *Adult school, binder, bring, English dictionary, eraser, notebook, open, pages, pen, supplies*

For vocabulary expansion, see this **Oxford Picture Dictionary** topic: A Classroom, pages 6–7

STRATEGY FOCUS

Interpret the meaning of a check mark in a list.

READINESS CONNECTION

In this lesson, students interpret and communicate information about school supplies.

PACING

To compress this lesson: Assign 2B as homework or conduct it as a whole-class activity.

To extend this lesson: Have students make a supply list. (See end of lesson.)

And/or have students complete **Workbook Introductory Level page 7** and **Multilevel Activities Introductory Level page 22.**

Lesson Notes

CORRELATIONS

CCRS: L.1.A Demonstrate command of the conventions of standard English grammar and usage when writing or speaking. i. Use determiners (e.g., articles, demonstratives).

SL.2.A Confirm understanding of a text read aloud or information presented orally or through other media by asking and answering questions about key details.

R.1.A Ask and answer questions about key details in a text.

R.7.A Use the illustrations and details in a text to describe its key ideas (e.g., maps, charts, photographs, political cartoons, etc.).

ELPS: 1. An ELL can construct meaning from oral presentations and literary and informational text through level-appropriate listening, reading, and viewing. 8. An ELL can determine the meaning of words and phrases in oral presentations and literary and informational text.

Warm-up and Review
10–15 minutes (books closed)

Ask volunteers to take turns writing the names of classroom items on the board. Help them with spelling. After students have run out of ideas, read each word aloud and have the class point to the item.

Introduction
5 minutes

1. Pronounce each of the words on the board again, using *a* or *an* as appropriate. Rewrite the words as a list with *a* or *an*. (Don't worry if you have no examples for *an*.) Say: *This is a list.*

2. State the objective: *Today we're going to learn how to use* a *and* an, *and we're going to read a list.*

1 Get ready to read

Presentation I
10–15 minutes

 1. Play the audio. Tell students to look at the pictures and listen to the words.

2. Check comprehension of the words. Ask students to point to examples of a binder, a notebook, an eraser, and an English dictionary in the classroom. Replay the audio and tell students to listen and repeat.

3. Write the words on the board. Underline *an* and connect it to the *e* in *eraser* and *English* to draw students' attention to the use of *an*. Practice the pronunciation of the words.

Guided Practice I
10–15 minutes

 1. Tell students to listen to number 1. Have them repeat *a notebook*.

2. Play the entire audio. Tell students to work individually to fill in the blanks with *an* or *a*. Stop after the first four and review the answers. Then play numbers 5–8 and have students complete the exercise.

3. Call on volunteers for the answers. Write the answers on the board. Practice pronouncing the article-noun combinations.

Answers	
1. a	5. a
2. an	6. a
3. a	7. an
4. an	8. a

TIP
After 1B, write *a, e, i, o, u* on the board and teach students the word *vowel*. Demonstrate that *an* is used with words that begin with a vowel sound.

Presentation II
5–10 minutes

 1. Direct students to look at the pictures. Say and have students repeat the words.

2. Go over each word as follows: For *adult*, draw or show a picture of an adult and a child and indicate which one is the adult. Write *18+* on the board. Ask the students if they are adults. Pantomime *bring*, and use classroom realia to demonstrate *supplies* and *pages*.

3. Check students' comprehension by pointing or acting out and asking *or* questions.

Guided Practice II
5 minutes

 1. Tell students to work individually to check the items they bring to school. Call on volunteers to read aloud the items they checked.

2. If you require students to bring all of these items, point out that everything should be checked.

TIP
After 1D, take the opportunity to demonstrate the importance of being prepared and organized. Use pantomime to demonstrate how students who come to class with their papers organized in a binder and all the necessary supplies can sit down and get straight to work. Pantomime a disorganized student, dropping papers, flipping madly through the notebook looking for things, sharpening pencils, or asking classmates for an eraser.

Throughout the semester, emphasize the importance of organization, and help students keep their papers and supplies in order.

2 Read a class supplies list

Guided Practice III
15–20 minutes

 1. Direct students to look at the list and count the checks in 2A. Ask if a check means *yes* or *no* [yes].

2. Ask students to read the list silently. Ask if there are any questions about the reading.

3. Check students' comprehension. Ask them to show thumbs up if the item is checked or thumbs down if it isn't.

 1. Ask students to look at the exercise and name the items in the pictures.

2. Have them work individually to circle *yes* or *no*.

3. Elicit the answers from the class and write them on the board.

Answers
1. yes
2. no
3. yes
4. no
5. yes
6. yes

MULTILEVEL STRATEGIES

Adapt 2B for your pre-level and higher-level students.

- **Pre-level** While other students are doing 2B, direct these students to write the correct word from the supplies list next to the picture. Then have them circle *yes* or *no*.

- **Higher-level** Ask these students to take out any other supplies they bring with them to class. Encourage them to ask you the names of the items.

Application
5–10 minutes

BRING IT TO LIFE

Draw students' attention to the picture in the *Bring It to Life* section. Tell them they will be making a list of class supplies at home. Allow them to ask you for names of items they would like to add to their lists.

TIP

In preparation for *Teamwork & Language Review*, have students review the unit vocabulary. Provide them with pictures you have collected or use the Picture Cards on pages 23–24 of *Multilevel Activities Introductory Level Unit 1*. Pair students and have them use the pictures as flashcards for recognition practice, dictation, or sentence writing.

EXTENSION ACTIVITY
Class Brainstorm

As a class, make a list of supplies that are important for your class and post it on the bulletin board.

TEAMWORK & LANGUAGE REVIEW

Lesson Overview

MULTILEVEL OBJECTIVES

On-, Pre-, and Higher-level: Expand upon and review unit language and content

LANGUAGE FOCUS

Grammar: Subject pronouns and the verb *be* (*It is a dictionary.*)

Vocabulary: Classroom items

For vocabulary expansion, see this **Oxford Picture Dictionary** topic: A Classroom, pages 6–7

STRATEGY FOCUS

Use teamwork to reinforce and expand vocabulary.

READINESS CONNECTION

In this review, students determine how to respond appropriately when they don't understand, and they work with a team to practice categorization, alphabetizing, writing, and problem solving.

PACING

To extend this review: Have students complete **Workbook Introductory Level page 8**, **Multilevel Activities Introductory Level Unit 1 pages 23–26**, and **Multilevel Grammar Exercises Introductory Level Unit 1**.

Lesson Notes

CORRELATIONS

CCRS: SL.1.A Participate in collaborative conversations with diverse partners in small and larger groups.

SL.6.A Speak audibly and express thoughts, feelings, and ideas clearly. Produce complete sentences when appropriate to task and situation.

R.7.A Use the illustrations and details in a text to describe its key ideas (e.g., maps, charts, photographs, political cartoons, etc.).

ELPS: 2. An ELL can participate in level-appropriate oral and written exchanges of information, ideas, and analyses, in various social and academic contexts, responding to peer, audience, or reader comments and questions. 10. An ELL can demonstrate command of the conventions of standard English to communicate in level-appropriate speech and writing.

Warm-up and Review
5–10 minutes (books closed)

1. Review the *Bring It to Life* assignment from Lesson 5.

2. Work together as a class to compile a "master list" of classroom supplies.

3. Call out the supply names and ask students to raise their hands if they have the items with them.

Introduction and Presentation
5 minutes

1. Group students and direct them to focus on the picture. Ask: *What do you see?*

2. State the objective: *Today we're going to review the words and grammar from Unit 1.*

Communicative Practice
15–20 minutes

A 1. Tell students to take turns naming one thing they see in the picture. Have three volunteers help you model turn-taking.

2. Tell students to put their pencils down and listen to each other so that they don't repeat ideas. Direct them to go around the group until they have run out of ideas.

B 1. Have students work in the same groups from A. Assign roles: secretary, reporter, editor, and manager. Write the roles on the board. As you explain each role, pantomime the duties you expect the person taking that role to perform. Explain that students work with their groups to write the words. Verify comprehension of the roles. (See the tip below.)

2. Set a time limit (five minutes) to complete the exercise. Circulate and answer any questions.

3. Call on the reporters from each group to say the numbers and words from their list. Write the words on the board. Go around the class until there are no more ideas.

4. Have the groups add new words from the board to their lists.

TIP
Whenever you do a teamwork activity, verify that students understand their roles. Pantomime the duties of each role again as you ask about it. Ask: *Who writes the words?* [secretary] *Who reads the words to the class?* [reporter] *Who checks the spelling in a dictionary or in the book?* [editor] *Who looks at the clock?* [manager] *Who says the words?* [everyone]

Possible Answers	
number	**word**
3	men
4	women
9	chairs
6	books
3	pencils
2	erasers
4	pens
1	binder
1	teacher
6	students
1	dictionary

MULTILEVEL STRATEGIES
For B, use mixed-level groups.
- **Pre-level** Assign these students the role of manager.
- **On-level** Assign these students the role of secretary or reporter.
- **Higher-level** Assign these students the role of editor.

C 1. Have the groups identify new words from the board and to look them up in a picture dictionary or a bilingual dictionary.

2. Tell students to add three new words to their chart. [New words might include: *marker, whiteboard, window, plant.*]

D 1. If you don't have a classroom alphabet up, write it on the board through *L*. Also copy the list of words from B on the board.

2. Underline the first letter of each word. Point out the letter in the alphabet. For *chair* and *clock*, underline the *h* and *l*. Point out their positions in the alphabet.

3. Tell students to look through the words in their chart and say which one goes above *book* [binder]. Ask them to identify the word that comes after *clock* [dictionary].

4. Have students work independently to write alphabetical lists in their notebooks.

E 1. Read number 1 aloud. Tell students to work independently to complete the sentences.

2. Call on volunteers to read the completed sentences aloud. Write the answers on the board.

Answers
1. It
2. They
3. is
4. a
5. are
6. is

F 1. Have students work independently to write two sentences.

2. Ask volunteers to write their sentences on the board. Correct them as a class.

> **MULTILEVEL STRATEGIES**
>
> For E and F, work with the pre-level students.
>
> • **Pre-level** Provide these students with the answers to E (out of order). Have them copy the answers into the correct sentences in their books. While other students complete E and F, read the sentences chorally with the pre-level group. Have them choose two of the sentences to copy onto the lines in F.
>
> • **Higher-level** When these students have finished F, have them write three additional sentences with *am*, *is*, and *are*.

PROBLEM SOLVING AT WORK
15–20 minutes

 1.  Direct students to look at the picture of the man. Point to his nametag. Tell them his name is Joel, and he has a problem.

2. Point to the other man. Write *boss* on the board. Mimic the garbled words from the boss.

3. Play the audio and have students listen and look at the pictures. Check comprehension. Ask: *Is Joel the boss?* [no]

4. Ask: *What's the problem?* Write *confused* on the board, and use gestures to convey the meaning. Play the audio again.

B 1. Tell students to look at the pictures. Read the captions and talk about them. For choice *a*, demonstrate how to pronounce *Excuse me?* as a question. For choice *b*, act out being apologetic.

2. Ask for a show of hands to see which solution the class likes best. Emphasize that either answer could be correct. Encourage students to express any other ideas they have. They may want to suggest *Please spell that*.

> **TIP**
>
> As a follow-up to *Problem Solving at Work*, say and have students repeat *Excuse me?* and *I'm sorry. I don't understand.* Make a garbled statement to several students and have them practice responding with one of the expressions.

Evaluation
20–25 minutes

To test students' understanding of the unit language and content, have them take the Unit 1 Test, available on the Teacher Resource Center.

> **TIP**
>
> Encourage students to reflect on what they have learned in this unit. Write these topics in a list on the board and elicit words, phrases, and sentences that students learned for each topic: *a) The alphabet; b) Classroom objects; c) Numbers; d) Subject pronouns and the verb be; e) Meeting new people; f) Class supplies.* Congratulate students on their progress.

UNIT 2
How Are You Feeling?

Unit Overview

This unit explores language to describe feelings, personal information, the verb *be*, addressing an envelope, and personal information forms.

KEY OBJECTIVES	
Lesson 1	Identify appropriate language to describe feelings and emotions
Lesson 2	Respond to questions about personal information; describe personal information
Lesson 3	Use negative statements with *be* to talk about people
Lesson 4	Respond to personal information questions; express regret
Lesson 5	Identify the information on an envelope; complete a personal information form
Teamwork & Language Review	Review unit language

UNIT FEATURES	
Employability Skills	• Listen actively • Cooperate with others • Communicate information • Understand teamwork • Work with others • Reflect on feelings • Differentiate between first and last names • Determine how to find a correct zip code

Resources	**Class Audio** CD1, Tracks 27–44
	Workbook Unit 2, pages 9–15
	Teacher Resource Center
	    Literacy Reproducible Activities Unit 2
	    Multilevel Activities Introductory Level Unit 2
	    Multilevel Grammar Exercises Introductory Level Unit 2
	    Unit 2 Test
	Oxford Picture Dictionary Feelings, Personal Information, The Post Office

LESSON 1 VOCABULARY

Lesson Overview	Lesson Notes
MULTILEVEL OBJECTIVES	
On-level: Identify feeling words **Pre-level:** Recognize feeling words **Higher-level:** Talk about feelings	
LANGUAGE FOCUS	
Grammar: *Be* + adjective *(I am happy.)* **Vocabulary:** Feelings For vocabulary expansion, see this **Oxford Picture Dictionary** topic: Feelings, pages 42–43	
STRATEGY FOCUS	
Use categorization to remember vocabulary.	
READINESS CONNECTION	
In this lesson, students reflect on feelings.	
PACING	
To compress this lesson: Conduct 2A as a whole-class activity. **To extend this lesson:** Play charades. (See end of lesson.) And/or have students complete **Workbook Introductory Level page 9** and **Multilevel Activities Introductory Level Unit 2 page 28.**	
CORRELATIONS	
CCRS: SL.2.A Confirm understanding of a text read aloud or information presented orally or through other media by asking and answering questions about key details and requesting clarification if something is not understood. RF.3.A Know and apply grade-level phonics and word analysis skills in decoding words. a. Demonstrate basic knowledge of one-to-one letter-sound correspondences by producing the primary sound or many of the most frequent sounds for each consonant. L.2.A Demonstrate command of the conventions of English capitalization, punctuation, and spelling when writing. g. Spell simple words phonetically, drawing on knowledge of sound-letter relationships.	**ELPS:** 1. An ELL can construct meaning from oral presentations and literary and informational text through level-appropriate listening, reading, and viewing.

Warm-up and Review
10–15 minutes (books closed)

Write *I, You, He, She,* and *They* on the board in one column and *am, is, are* in another column. Call on volunteers to say sentences using the words. Students may come up with sentences such as, *I am a student, You are a teacher, She is a woman.*

Introduction
5 minutes

1. Say: *I'm a teacher. You are good students. I am happy!*

2. State the objective: *Today we're going to learn feelings, like happy and sad.*

1 Learn feeling words

Presentation I
20–25 minutes

A Direct students to look at the pictures. Ask them if the pictures are of a man or woman [woman]. Encourage them to say any other words they know from the pictures.

B 🔊 1-27 1. Play the audio. Ask students to point to the correct picture as they listen. Circulate and monitor.

2. Check comprehension. Point to each picture and ask: *Is she excited? Is she sad?* Have students hold up one finger for *yes* and two for *no*.

C 🔊 1-27 1. Tell students to listen and repeat the words.

2. Write the words on the board one syllable at a time and help students sound out and pronounce each syllable.

3. Call out the numbers out of order and ask students to say the words.

Guided Practice I
15–20 minutes

D Direct students to take turns reading the words with a partner.

E 1. Model the activity with two volunteers. Direct one partner to point to the pictures or say the numbers. Have the other partner cover the words in 1C and identify the pictures from memory.

2. Have students practice in pairs.

> **MULTILEVEL STRATEGIES**
>
> For 1E, pair same-level students together.
>
> • **Pre-level** Tell these students to practice together by pointing to the pictures in 1B and saying the correct words.
>
> • **Higher-level** Tell these students to dictate the words to each other.

2 Talk about feelings

Guided Practice II
15–20 minutes

A 1. Direct students to look at the picture. Point to the people and ask *yes/no* questions: *Is he happy? Is she sick?* Call out the numbers and ask students to identify the feelings.

2. Copy number 1 on the board and have students spell *excited* aloud. Demonstrate how to write one letter on each line.

3. Tell students to work individually to complete the words.

4. Ask volunteers to spell the completed words aloud. Write the answers on the board. Read and have students repeat the words.

Answers	
1. e-x-c-i-t-e-d	5. h-a-p-p-y
2. s-a-d	6. t-h-i-r-s-t-y
3. f-i-n-e	7. h-u-n-g-r-y
4. t-i-r-e-d	8. s-i-c-k

B Give students time to copy the words into their notebooks. Monitor and check their writing.

Communicative Practice and Application
10–15 minutes

C 🔊 1-28 1. Play the audio. Have students read along silently.

2. Play the audio again. Tell students to listen and repeat. Ask: *Who is hungry?* [Al] *Who is tired?* [Zita and Inez]

3. Model the conversations with a volunteer. Tell students to act out the feeling as well as say it. Switch roles and model the conversations with another volunteer.

D 1. Model the conversations with volunteers. Then have two volunteers model each of the conversations. Emphasize that they should only use *too* when the feelings are the same.

2. Set a time limit (three minutes) and have partners practice their conversations in both roles. Encourage students to use all of the words. Circulate and provide feedback.

> **TIP**
>
> Conduct 2D as a mixer. Provide each student with a picture card of a feeling. (See Picture Cards 2.1–2.8 on page 33 of *Multilevel Activities Introductory Level Unit 2*.) Set a time limit (five minutes). Tell students to circulate around the room, using their pictures for the conversation in 2D. After they have practiced with one partner, have them exchange cards and move on to a new partner.

Application and Evaluation
10–15 minutes

TEST YOURSELF

1. Direct students to copy the chart into their notebooks. While they are doing that, copy it onto the board.

2. Point to the sad face and ask for another word that goes in that column (for example: *sad, hungry, thirsty, sick*). Write it on the board.

3. Ask students to work independently to complete their charts. Monitor and check their work.

> **MULTILEVEL STRATEGIES**
>
> Target the *Test Yourself* to the level of your students.
>
> • **Pre-level** Display or distribute to these students four pictures of the feelings listed in 1C. Have students open their books to page 19, identify the correct words to match the pictures, and copy them.
>
> • **Higher-level** Challenge these students to include words not presented in the unit.

> **EXTENSION ACTIVITY**
> **Charades**
> Pass out picture cards and ask volunteers to act out the feeling on the card. Have classmates guess the word. Applaud the performances.

LESSON 2 WRITING

Lesson Overview

MULTILEVEL OBJECTIVES
On- and Higher-level: Read and write about personal information
Pre-level: Recognize personal information

LANGUAGE FOCUS
Grammar: The verb *be* (*I am from Mexico.*)
Vocabulary: Country names, *birthplace, city, country, form, graph, personal/employee information, state*
For vocabulary expansion, see this **Oxford Picture Dictionary** topic: Personal Information, page 4

STRATEGY FOCUS
When filling out forms, use a comma between a last name followed by a first name.

READINESS CONNECTION
In this lesson, students differentiate between first and last names.

PACING
To compress this lesson: Have students do 3A for homework.
To extend this lesson: Have students present their countries on a map. (See end of lesson.)
And/or have students complete **Workbook Introductory Level page 10** and **Multilevel Activities Introductory Level Unit 2 page 29.**

Lesson Notes

CORRELATIONS

CCRS: R.7.A Use the illustrations and details in a text to describe its key ideas (e.g., maps, charts, photographs, political cartoons, etc.).

SL.1.A Participate in collaborative conversations with diverse partners in small and larger groups.

SL.2.A Confirm understanding of a text read aloud or information presented orally or through other media by asking and answering questions about key details.

L.6.A Use words and phrases acquired through conversations, reading and being read to, and responding to texts, including using frequently occurring conjunctions to signal simple relationships (e.g., *because*).

ELPS: 10. An ELL can demonstrate command of the conventions of standard English to communicate in level-appropriate speech and writing.

Warm-up and Review
10–15 minutes (books closed)

Put up a map of the U.S. Write *The United States* on the board and have students repeat it. Say and have students repeat the name of the city and state you live in. Point to them on the map. If you are from a different state or city, say *I am from* _____, point to the state or city, and use pantomime to show that you used to live there. Put up a world map. If you are from a different country, point to it and pronounce it for the students. Elicit the students' native countries, write them on the board, and have everyone repeat the country names.

Introduction
5 minutes

1. Make statements using the places you've written on the board: *I'm from the United States. Jorge is from Mexico. Ga Young is from Korea.*

2. State the objective: *Today we're going to read and write about personal information.*

1 Learn about countries

Presentation I
10–15 minutes

A 🔊 1-29 1. Direct students to look at the picture. Ask: *Where is the United States?*

2. Play the audio. Ask students to point to Marco and Jia. Ask: *Where is Marco from?* [Mexico] *Where is Jia from?* [China] *Where are you from?*

Guided Practice I
25–30 minutes

B Ask students to complete the activity independently. Monitor and check spelling.

Answers
1. Mexico
2. China
3. Answers will vary.

C 1. Provide students with a map, or help them locate their countries in the picture in 1A.

2. Model the activity with several volunteers. Direct students to walk around and talk to at least three partners.

> **TIP**
> If most of your students have smartphones, for 1C have them search for "world map with countries." They can then use the image on the phone for the activity and zoom in on countries as necessary.

D 1. Direct students to look at the graph. Read the names and the numbers along the axes. Show them how the number on each bar corresponds to a number on the y-axis.

2. Read number 1 aloud and show students how it corresponds to the information on the graph.

3. Direct students to complete the exercise independently. Then go over the answers as a class.

Answers
1. 21
2. 9
3. 3

E 1. Conduct this activity together as a class. Copy the blank chart on the board, but adjust the numbers on the y-axis to work with your class (for example, if you have a small class, use increments of 2 instead of 5). Starting with the country where most of your students are from, ask: *How many students are from _____?* Have students guide you in creating the bars.

2. When the class graph is complete, copy the sentence frame on the board. Call on a volunteer to use the frame to make a statement about the class.

3. Direct students to work with a partner to write sentences about the class. When they are finished, call on volunteers to read one of their sentences aloud.

> **TIP**
> If most of your students are from the same country, add state or city names to create the chart in 1E (e.g., Sonora, Mexico; Seoul, Korea).

2 Prepare to write: personal information

Presentation II
25–30 minutes

A Direct students to look at the form. Ask them to point to the country name.

B 🔊 1-30 1. Play the audio. Have students read along silently.

2. Check comprehension. Say the words out of order and have students call out the correct numbers. Then say the information on the form and have students call out the words, for example: *Texas* [state].

3. Replay the audio and ask students to repeat the words.

4. Talk about the places you wrote on the board during the warm-up. Elicit whether each place is a city, state, or country. Ask students to identify their birthplaces.

C 🔊 1-31 1. Play the audio. Have students read along silently.

2. Replay the audio and have students point to the form in 2A as they listen.

3. Check comprehension: Ask: *What's Camille's birthplace?* [Haiti] *What city is she in?* [Dallas] *What state is she in?* [Texas]

> **MULTILEVEL STRATEGIES**
>
> For 2C, seat students in mixed-level groups. After the whole-group practice, ask students to take turns reading the sentences aloud. Demonstrate turn-taking, with the first student reading number 1, the second number 2, and so on.
>
> • **Pre-level** Tell students who don't want to read aloud to listen to their classmates and follow along silently.

Guided Practice II
15–20 minutes

D 1. Read number 1 aloud. Ask students to work independently to complete the exercise.

2. Have students compare answers in pairs.

Answers	
1. state	4. country
2. city	5. birthplace
3. country	

E 🔊 1-32 Play the audio and have students check their answers.

F 🔊 1-33 1. Point to the photos. Ask: *Is Sameen a man or a woman?* [woman] *Is Iran a country or a city?* [country] *Is Illinois a city or a state?* [state] *Is Chicago a city or state?* [city]

2. Play the audio in segments. Direct students to work independently to choose the correct answers.

Answers	
1. a	3. b
2. b	4. a

G 1. Replay the audio and ask students to check their answers.

2. Call on students to read the completed sentences aloud.

3 Write about personal information

Communicative Practice
10–15 minutes

A 1. Introduce the new activity: *Now we are going to write about personal information.*

2. Copy the sentences (with blanks) on the board. Call on volunteers to complete the sentences aloud.

3. Tell students to work individually to complete the sentences with their own information. If a majority of your students are from the same country, ask them to use cities and countries.

B Ask students to read their sentences aloud to a partner. When they finish, ask them to read the sentences to a new partner.

> **MULTILEVEL STRATEGIES**
>
> Adapt 3A and 3B to the level of your students.
>
> • **Pre-level** While on- and higher-level students are completing 3A and 3B, work with these students in a group, or have them complete page 30 of the *Literacy Reproducible Activities Unit 2*.

AT WORK

Filling out a form

A 1. Direct students' attention to the *Writer's Note*. Ask: *What is her last name?* [Garcia] *What is her first name?* [Maria]

2. Draw a comma on the board and say the word *comma*. Then write your own name twice, first name first and then last name first. Point out that you only use a comma when the last name is first.

3. Ask two volunteers (preferably from different countries) to come to the board. Have them write their names the two different ways, guiding as necessary.

4. Direct students' attention to the form. Have them repeat the word *employee*. Say: *I am an employee of the school.* If you know where some students work, use them as an example: *Tomas is an employee of Al's Restaurant.* You can also use pictures of workplaces and point out the employees.

5. Have students complete the form independently. Monitor and check their work.

Evaluation
10 minutes

TEST YOURSELF

1. Copy the sentence frames on the board. Ask students for example answers.

2. Have students copy the frames into their notebooks and complete them.

3. Collect and correct students' work.

> **EXTENSION ACTIVITY**
>
> **Map Presentation**
>
> Call on volunteers to come to the front of the class, point out their country (or city) on the map, and say their sentences from 3A. Call on students who are listening to answer the question *Where is he/she from?*

LESSON 3 GRAMMAR

Lesson Overview

MULTILEVEL OBJECTIVES

On- and Higher-level: Use contractions and negative statements with *be*

Pre-level: Recognize contractions and negative statements with *be*

LANGUAGE FOCUS

Grammar: Contractions and negative statements with *be* (*I'm not tired.*)

Vocabulary: Feelings

For vocabulary expansion, see this **Oxford Picture Dictionary** topic: Feelings, pages 42–43

READINESS CONNECTION

In this lesson, students communicate with others about feelings.

PACING

To compress this lesson: Assign 2D as homework.

To extend this lesson: Do a picture activity. (See end of lesson.)

And/or have students complete **Workbook Introductory Level pages 11–12**, **Multilevel Activities Introductory Level Unit 2 page 30**, and **Multilevel Grammar Exercises Introductory Level Unit 2**.

Lesson Notes

CORRELATIONS

CCRS: L.1.A Demonstrate command of the conventions of standard English grammar and usage when writing or speaking. g. Use frequently occurring nouns and verbs.

SL.1.A Participate in collaborative conversations with diverse partners in small and larger groups.

SL.2.A Confirm understanding of a text read aloud or information presented orally or through other media by asking and answering questions about key details.

ELPS: 10. An ELL can demonstrate command of the conventions of standard English to communicate in level-appropriate speech and writing.

Warm-up and Review
10–15 minutes (books closed)

Review feeling words. Act out various emotions and ask volunteers to come to the board and write the words.

Introduction
5–10 minutes

1. Smile and say: *I am happy. I am not sad.* Look sad and say: *I am sad. I am not happy.*

2. State the objective: *Today we're going to learn* am not, is not, are not, *and contractions*.

1 Use negative statements with *be*

Presentation I
20–25 minutes

A 1. Direct students to look at the pictures. Ask: *Is he hungry?* [yes] *Is she tired?* [yes]

2. Read the captions aloud.

B Explain that negative means *no*. Ask students to underline the negative statements in 1A. Then have them repeat the negative sentences.

Answers
He is not sick.
She is not sick.

C 🔊 1-34 1. Play the audio. Ask students to read the chart and listen.

2. Demonstrate how to read the grammar chart as complete sentences. Read the chart through sentence by sentence. Then read it again, and have students repeat after you.

3. Assess students' understanding of the chart. Call on volunteers to say affirmative and negative sentences using the words they put on the board during the warm-up.

Guided Practice I
15–20 minutes

D 1. Direct students to work independently to complete the sentences.

2. Ask students to compare their answers with a partner. Then have volunteers read the completed sentences aloud.

Answers	
1. is not	4. is not
2. is not	5. are not
3. is not	6. are not

> **MULTILEVEL STRATEGIES**
>
> • **Higher-level** After these students complete 1D, have volunteers write two more negative/positive pairs of sentences with *be* on the board using *I* or *We* as the subject. Ask them to read aloud and act out the sentences for the class.

2 Use contractions with *be*

Presentation II
10–15 minutes

A 🔊 1-35 1. Direct students to look at the pictures. Help them identify Mexico, Colorado, and Illinois.

2. Play the audio one segment at a time and ask students to read along. Ask yes/no questions about each picture: *Is he from Mexico? Is she tired?*

3. Write *I am, She is, He is, They are, It is, You are*, and *We are* on the board. Show students how the two words are joined with an apostrophe in a contraction. Practice the pronunciation of the contractions.

B Direct students to underline the negative sentences. Go over the answers as a class. Point out that there are two ways to contract *is not* and *are not*.

Answers
1. He's not from Texas. He isn't from Arizona.
2. It's not a city. It isn't a country.
3. They're not in Texas. They aren't in New York.

C 🔊 1-36 1. Give students a minute to study the chart.

2. Play the audio and tell students to repeat.

Guided Practice II
10–15 minutes

D 1. Read sentence number 1 aloud. Show students that letter *c* is the same sentence as number 1 using a contraction. Tell students to work individually to match the sentences.

2. Write the numbers on the board and ask students to call out the letter of the answers.

Answers	
1. c	5. b
2. e	6. d
3. g	7. a
4. f	

E 1. Have students look at picture number 1. Read the first sentence aloud. Elicit the answer to the second sentence.

2. Ask students to work independently to complete the sentences with contractions and then compare their work with a partner. Go over the answers as a class.

Answers
1. 's, 's not/isn't
2. 's, 's not/isn't
3. 're not/aren't, 're

MULTILEVEL STRATEGIES
Adapt 2D and 2E to the level of your students.
• **Pre-level** Provide these students with the answers to the exercises and have them practice reading the sentences to each other, or have them complete page 31 of the *Literacy Reproducible Activities Unit 2*.
• **Higher-level** Challenge these students to write the negative contractions in a different way (using *isn't* and *aren't*).

3 Talk about feelings

Communicative Practice and Application
10–15 minutes

A 🔊 1-37 Have students find and point to Ana. Play the audio and ask them to repeat.

B Using the examples, model the activity with a volunteer. Emphasize the importance of turn-taking.

C 1. Read the three example sentences aloud. Ask students who they are about. [Ana is sad. Pia isn't sad. David is thirsty.]

2. Ask students to work with their partner. Student A writes a sentence and then passes the paper to Student B to write a different sentence until they run out of ideas.

3. Have four or five volunteers write one of their sentences on the board. Correct the sentences as a class. Elicit alternate versions of the sentences where appropriate (e.g., *He* instead of *David*, *he isn't* instead of *he's not*).

Evaluation
10–15 minutes

TEST YOURSELF

1. Direct pairs to look at the pictures on page 19, 2C. Ask them to work independently to write two sentences about each person.

2. Collect and correct their writing.

MULTILEVEL STRATEGIES
Target the *Test Yourself* to the level of your students.
• **Pre-level** Provide these students with sentence frames so that they only need to fill in the contraction:
1. Zita ___ tired. She ___ sad.
2. Lam ___ hungry. He ___ thirsty.
• **Higher-level** Ask these students to write four additional sentences about Inez and Al (on page 19, 2C).

EXTENSION ACTIVITY
Picture Writing
1. Seat students in mixed-level groups and pass out magazines to each group. Tell the groups to look for pictures that represent the feeling words they know. Alternatively, ask students to search for pictures online by typing the feeling words into an image search engine.
2. Ask them to write affirmative and negative statements about the pictures.
3. Have representatives from each group show a picture and read two sentences about it.

LESSON 4 EVERYDAY CONVERSATION

Lesson Overview

MULTILEVEL OBJECTIVES

On- and Higher-level: Ask and respond to questions about feelings

Pre-level: Respond to questions about feelings

LANGUAGE FOCUS

Grammar: Be + adjective (*I'm sick. I'm sorry.*)

Vocabulary: Feelings

For vocabulary expansion, see this **Oxford Picture Dictionary** topic: Feelings, pages 42–43

STRATEGY FOCUS

Practice phrases to respond appropriately to people's feelings.

READINESS CONNECTION

In this lesson, students listen actively for personal information questions.

PACING

To compress this lesson: Have students practice 3D with only one partner.

To extend this lesson: After completing *Test Yourself*, conduct a mixer activity. (See end of lesson.)

And/or have students complete **Workbook Introductory Level page 13** and **Multilevel Activities Introductory Level Unit 2 page 31**.

Lesson Notes

CORRELATIONS

CCRS: RF.2.A Demonstrate understanding of spoken words, syllables, and sounds (phonemes). c. Count, pronounce, blend, and segment syllables in spoken words.

SL.1.A Participate in collaborative conversations with diverse partners in small and larger groups.

SL.6.A Speak audibly and express thoughts, feelings, and ideas clearly. Produce complete sentences when appropriate to task and situation.

ELPS: 2. An ELL can participate in level-appropriate oral and written exchanges of information, ideas, and analyses, in various social and academic contexts, responding to peer, audience, or reader comments and questions.

Warm-up and Review
5 minutes (books closed)

Review contractions. Write the pronouns on the board in a column: *I, You, He, She, It, They, We*. In another column write several feeling words (*tired, hungry, thirsty*). Call on volunteers to write the appropriate contraction after the pronoun. Do the first one yourself as a model. Call on other volunteers to say sentences using the words from both columns.

Introduction
5 minutes

1. Say: *I'm sick. I'm tired. I'm happy. These are my feelings.*

2. State the objective: *Today we're going to learn to ask about feelings.*

1 Listen for personal information questions

Listening Extension
20–25 minutes

 1. Direct students to work independently to match the questions to the answers.

2. Read each question aloud and elicit the answer.

Answers
1. c
2. a
3. b

TIP

After 1A, teach students the words *question* and *answer*. Write several questions and answers on the board: *What's your name? My name is Rosa. Where are you from? I'm from Mexico. How are you feeling? I'm happy.* Point to each sentence and ask: *Question or answer?*

 🔊 1-38 1. Tell students to read the sentences. Ask: *Are these questions or answers?* [questions]

2. Play the entire audio once. Ask students to circle the question they hear.

3. Write the answers on the board. Have students repeat the questions.

Answers
1. a
2. a
3. b

 🔊 1-39 1. Tell students to read the sentences. Ask: *Are these questions or answers?* [answers] Explain that they will hear questions on the audio. Read number 1 aloud. Ask students which question from 1A they expect to hear [How are you today? or What's your name?].

2. Play the audio in segments. Ask for a show of hands to see if students answered *a* or *b*. Repeat the segment if necessary.

3. Write the answers on the board.

Answers
1. a
2. b
3. a
4. b

2 Practice your pronunciation

Pronunciation Extension
10–15 minutes

 🔊 1-40 1. Direct students to look at the chart. Pronounce the word *syllable* for them.

2. Play the audio. Read the words again, clapping or tapping out the syllables on the table.

 🔊 1-41 1. Play the entire audio once. Direct students to hold up one, two, or three fingers to show how many syllables they think the word has.

2. Replay the audio and ask students to check the correct column in the chart.

Answers	fine	thirsty	telephone	hungry	sad	twenty-three
1 syllable	✓				✓	
2 syllables		✓		✓		
3 syllables			✓			✓

 🔊 1-41 1. Replay the audio and ask students to check their answers.

2. Call on volunteers for the answers. Repeat the words and clap or tap out the syllables.

3. Have students repeat the words.

3 Make conversation: ask about feelings

Presentation
5–10 minutes

 1. Direct students to look at the pictures. Ask: *What's the man's name?* [Pedro] *What's the woman's name?* [Vanna]

2. Have students read the conversation silently. Elicit any questions.

36 Unit 2   Lesson 4   Everyday Conversation   Lesson Plans Intro

Guided Practice
5–10 minutes

B 🔊 **1-42** Play the audio. Have students read the conversation silently.

C 🔊 **1-42** 1. Play the audio again and have students repeat the conversation.

2. Do a choral reading of the conversation in 3B. Divide the class in half. Have one side be Pedro and one side be Vanna, and then have the sides switch roles.

Communicative Practice and Application
15–20 minutes

D 1. Model the conversation with a volunteer. Then switch roles and model it with another volunteer, using ideas from the *Need help?* box.

2. Elicit other ways to complete the conversation.

3. Set a time limit (five minutes). Ask students to practice the conversation with several partners. Encourage pantomime and improvisation.

4. Ask volunteer pairs to present their conversations to the class.

> **MULTILEVEL STRATEGIES**
>
> For 3D, seat pre-level students together.
>
> • **Pre-level** While other students are practicing the conversation, have these students complete page 32 in the *Literacy Reproducible Activities Unit 2*.

Evaluation
5 minutes

TEST YOURSELF

Set a time limit (three minutes). Have students walk around the class asking and responding to the question. Encourage them to respond to the question in different ways and to act out how they are feeling.

> **EXTENSION ACTIVITY**
>
> **Mixer**
>
> After *Test Yourself*, distribute cards and have students copy the three questions from 1A onto the cards. Set a time limit (five minutes). Have students walk around the room asking the questions on the card. After they have spoken to one partner, direct them to move on to a new partner.

LESSON 5 READING

Lesson Overview

MULTILEVEL OBJECTIVES

On- and Higher-level: Identify addresses and read an envelope

Pre-level: Recognize addresses and read an envelope

LANGUAGE FOCUS

Grammar: The verb *be (Susan is in Salem.)*

Vocabulary: *Address, city, envelope, form, mailing address, return address, state, zip code*

For vocabulary expansion, see these **Oxford Picture Dictionary** topics: Personal Information, page 4; The Post Office, pages 136–137

STRATEGY FOCUS

Identify abbreviations for U.S. states.

READINESS CONNECTION

In this lesson, students communicate information on envelopes and forms.

PACING

To compress this lesson: Assign 2B as homework or conduct it as a whole-class activity.

To extend this lesson: Have students address an envelope. (See end of lesson.)

And/or have students complete **Workbook Introductory Level page 14** and **Multilevel Activities Introductory Level Unit 2 page 32.**

Lesson Notes

CORRELATIONS

CCRS: R.1.A Ask and answer questions about key details in a text.

R.7.A Use the illustrations and details in a text to describe its key ideas (e.g., maps, charts, photographs, political cartoons, etc.).

L.6.A Use words and phrases acquired through conversations, reading and being read to, and responding to texts, including using frequently occurring conjunctions to signal simple relationships (e.g., *because*).

ELPS: 8. An ELL can determine the meaning of words and phrases in oral presentations and literary and informational text.

Warm-up and Review
10–15 minutes (books closed)

Draw a rectangle and write a name and a local address in the box. Ask students to identify the first, middle, and last names and the city and state. Write the word *address* on the board and show students that it refers to all of the information.

Introduction
5 minutes

1. Show students an envelope with a mailing address but no return address. Say: *We write the address here.*

2. State the objective: *Today we'll learn about addresses.*

1 Get ready to read

Presentation I
10–15 minutes

 1. Tell students to look at the envelope and listen to the words. Play the audio.

2. Check comprehension of the words. Ask students to identify the zip code in the address on the board. Ask students to say your city, your state, and the address of your school.

3. Replay the audio and tell students to listen and repeat.

Guided Practice I
10–15 minutes

 1. Direct students to work individually to match the items.

2. Call on volunteers for the answers and write them on the board.

Answers
1. c
2. b
3. a
4. d

TIP
After 1B, make large cards or sentence strips with the vocabulary plus the words *last name, middle name, first name.* Make another set with your first, middle, and last names, the school's address, the school's city, etc. Put all the cards on the board out of order and ask volunteers to come up, match them, and arrange them into two columns. Demonstrate the first one. After students have finished, take down the vocabulary cards and ask volunteers to arrange the information cards in proper address order.

Presentation and Guided Practice II
10–15 minutes

 1. Direct students to look at the pictures. Say and have students repeat the words.

2. Go over each word. Show an envelope and several examples of forms. Use pantomime to demonstrate the difference between *mailing address* and *return address.*

3. Read the information in the *Need help?* box and show students Georgia and North Carolina on a map. Elicit the postal abbreviation for your state and write it on the board.

4. Teach students how to write and pronounce an email address.

Communicative Practice and Application
10–15 minutes

 Read the direction line aloud. Point out the word *your.* Ask: *Do you write my address?* [no] *Do you write the school address?* [no]

TIP
As students are writing their addresses in 1D, walk around and assist them individually with the pronunciation of their street names. If students have not memorized their addresses, encourage them to do so. Give them class time to practice saying their addresses with a partner. Challenge them to come back to class the next day and tell you their address from memory.

2 Read a form and an envelope

Guided Practice III
15–20 minutes

 1. Direct students to look over the form and the envelope and identify the first and last names.

2. Ask students to read the two items silently. Ask if there are any questions about the reading.

3. Check students' comprehension. Ask: *What is the return address?* [Susan Kirkwood, 609 First Street, Atlanta, GA 74354] *What is the mailing address?* [River City Adult School, 3712 Maple Street, Salem, NC 60611]

TIP
Use this lesson as an opportunity to practice completing authentic forms. Cut off and copy the name and address portion of your school's registration form or another form your students may have to complete. Point out any differences from the practice form in 1D. After students complete the form, collect and correct their work.

B 1. Read number 1 aloud. Show students how to find the answer in both the form and the envelope. Tell students to work individually to complete the exercise.

2. Call on volunteers to read the completed sentences aloud. Write the answers on the board.

Answers
1. a
2. b
3. b
4. b
5. a

MULTILEVEL STRATEGIES

Adapt 2B for your pre-level students.

• **Pre-level** While other students are doing 2B, read the sentences aloud for these students and help them identify the answers on the form and the envelope.

Application
5–10 minutes

BRING IT TO LIFE

Read the directions. Show students a pre-printed envelope with a mailing and a return address (for example, a utility-bill envelope). Ask students which address to check and which to circle.

TIP

In preparation for *Teamwork & Language Review,* have students review the unit vocabulary. Provide them with pictures you have collected or use the Picture Cards on pages 33–34 of *Multilevel Activities Introductory Level Unit 2.* Pair students and have them use the pictures as flashcards for recognition practice, dictation, or sentence writing.

EXTENSION ACTIVITY

Address an Envelope

1. Write your name and the school address on the board.

2. Pass out envelopes and ask students to address the envelope to you and to use their own return address. Ask more advanced students to write a few sentences and put them in the envelope for you to correct. (For example: *My name is _____ . I am from _____ . I'm happy/sad/sick.*)

TEAMWORK & LANGUAGE REVIEW

Lesson Overview

MULTILEVEL OBJECTIVES

On-, Pre-, and Higher-level: Expand upon and review unit language and content

LANGUAGE FOCUS

Grammar: Contractions and negative statements with *be* (*They're not sick.*)

Vocabulary: Feelings

For vocabulary expansion, see this **Oxford Picture Dictionary** topic: Feelings, pages 42–43

STRATEGY FOCUS

Use teamwork to reinforce and expand vocabulary.

READINESS CONNECTION

In this review, students determine how to find a correct zip code.

PACING

To extend this review: Have students complete **Workbook Introductory Level page 15, Multilevel Activities Introductory Level Unit 2 pages 33–36,** and **Multilevel Grammar Exercises Introductory Level Unit 2**.

Lesson Notes

CORRELATIONS

CCRS: SL.1.A Participate in collaborative conversations with diverse partners in small and larger groups.

SL.6.A Speak audibly and express thoughts, feelings, and ideas clearly. Produce complete sentences when appropriate to task and situation.

R.7.A Use the illustrations and details in a text to describe its key ideas (e.g., maps, charts, photographs, political cartoons, etc.).

ELPS: 2. An ELL can participate in level-appropriate oral and written exchanges of information, ideas, and analyses, in various social and academic contexts, responding to peer, audience, or reader comments and questions.

Warm-up and Review
5–10 minutes (books closed)

1. Review the *Bring It to Life* assignment from Lesson 5.

2. Ask students to show the envelopes they brought. Ask other students to point out the mailing and return addresses.

3. Copy an address from one of the envelopes onto the board. Ask students to name the parts of the address (city, state, zip code).

Introduction and Presentation
5 minutes

1. Group students and direct them to focus on the picture. Ask: *What do you see?*

2. State the objective: *Today we're going to review the words and grammar from Unit 2.*

Communicative Practice
15–20 minutes

A 1. Tell students to take turns naming one thing they see in the picture. Have three volunteers help you model turn-taking.

2. Tell students to put their pencils down and listen to each other so that they don't repeat ideas. Direct them to go around the group until they have run out of ideas.

B 1. Have students work in the same groups from A. Assign roles: secretary, reporter, editor, and manager. Write the roles on the board. As you explain each role, pantomime the duties you expect the person taking that role to perform. Explain that students work with their groups to write the words. Verify the comprehension of roles.

2. Set a time limit (five minutes) to complete the chart. Circulate and answer any questions.

3. Call on the reporters from each group to say the words from their chart. Write the words on the board. Go around the class until there are no more ideas.

Possible Answers		
Things	**Feelings**	**Other**
map	happy	man
table	tired	woman
chair	hungry	
country	thirsty	
	sad	
	fine	

MULTILEVEL STRATEGIES

For B, use mixed-level groups.
- **Pre-level** Assign these students the role of manager.
- **On-level** Assign these students the role of secretary or reporter.
- **Higher-level** Assign these students the role of editor.

C 1. Have the groups identify new words from the board and to look them up in a picture dictionary or a bilingual dictionary.

2. Tell students to add three new words to their chart. [New words might include: *boy, girl, baby, food, plate*.]

D 1. Read number 1 aloud. Tell students to work independently to complete the sentences.

2. Call on volunteers to read the completed sentences aloud. Write the answers on the board.

Answers
1. They're, They're not
2. She's, She's not
3. He's not, He's
4. It's, It's not

E 1. Have students work independently to write two sentences.

2. Ask volunteers to write their sentences on the board. Correct them as a class.

MULTILEVEL STRATEGIES

Provide an extra challenge for on- and higher-level students while you work with pre-level students.

- **Pre-level** Go over D orally with these students. Allow them to copy the answers into their books. Read the sentences aloud while they follow along.
- **On- and Higher-level** For E, tell these students to write two affirmative and two negative sentences about two different things or people in the classroom. (For example: *It's not a desk. It's a clock. He's not hungry. He's thirsty.*)

PROBLEM SOLVING
15–20 minutes

A 1. Tell students the pictures in A tell a story about a man named Gary. He has a problem with an address.

2. Direct students to look at the picture on the left. Ask them to identify the name, city, and state in both the return and mailing addresses. Show them California and Massachusetts on a map.

3. Play the audio and have students listen and look at the pictures. Check comprehension: Ask: *Where is Gary?* [California] *Where is Emily?* [Massachusetts] *What is Emily's zip code?* [unknown]

B 1. Tell students to look at the pictures. Read the captions and talk about them. For choice *a,* say and have students repeat *post office.* Ask students where the local post office is. For choice *b,* say and have students repeat *computer.* Find out how many students have computers at home.

2. Ask for a show of hands to see which solution the class likes best. Emphasize that there is no correct answer. Encourage students to express any other ideas they have. They may want to suggest that Gary call Emily or that he send the letter with no zip code. Use pantomime and drawing to help students communicate their ideas.

Evaluation
20–25 minutes

To test students' understanding of the unit language and content, have them take the Unit 2 Test, available on the Teacher Resource Center.

> **TIP**
>
> Encourage students to reflect on what they have learned in this unit. Write these topics in a list on the board and elicit words, phrases, and sentences that students learned for each topic: *a) Feelings; b) Personal information; c) Negative statements and contractions; d) Asking about feelings; e) Reading an envelope.* Congratulate students on their progress.

UNIT 3: What Time Is It?

Unit Overview

This unit explores time, places in the community, and transportation within the context of talking about location and schedules.

KEY OBJECTIVES

Lesson 1	Interpret time with analog and digital clocks
Lesson 2	Identify places in the community; describe a work day
Lesson 3	Use *yes/no* questions and short answers with *be* to talk about time and location
Lesson 4	Ask for information about places in the community
Lesson 5	Identify types of transportation; interpret a schedule
Teamwork & Language Review	Review unit language

UNIT FEATURES

Academic Vocabulary	*schedule*
Employability Skills	• Listen actively • Communicate information • Cooperate with others • Communicate verbally • Interpret clock times • Interpret a bus schedule • Identify ways to solve a scheduling conflict

Resources	**Class Audio** CD1, Tracks 45–61
	Workbook Unit 3, pages 16–22
	Teacher Resource Center
	    Literacy Reproducible Activities Unit 3
	    Multilevel Activities Introductory Level Unit 3
	    Multilevel Grammar Exercises Introductory Level Unit 3
	    Unit 3 Test
	Oxford Picture Dictionary Time, City Streets, Public Transportation

LESSON 1 VOCABULARY

Lesson Overview

MULTILEVEL OBJECTIVES

On-level: Identify times of day
Pre-level: Recognize times of day
Higher-level: Talk about times of day

LANGUAGE FOCUS

Grammar: The verb *be* (*It's 10:00.*)

Vocabulary: *Afternoon, evening, midnight, morning, night, noon*

For vocabulary expansion, see this **Oxford Picture Dictionary** topic: Time, pages 18–19

STRATEGY FOCUS

Practice saying the time correctly.

READINESS CONNECTION

In this lesson, students interpret clock times.

PACING

To compress this lesson: Conduct 2A as a whole-class activity.

To extend this lesson: Play Bingo. (See end of lesson.)

And/or have students complete **Workbook Introductory Level page 16** and **Multilevel Activities Introductory Level Unit 3 page 38.**

Lesson Notes

CORRELATIONS

CCRS: L.6.A Use words and phrases acquired through conversations, reading and being read to, and responding to texts, including using frequently occurring conjunctions to signal simple relationships (e.g., *because*).

SL.2.A Confirm understanding of a text read aloud or information presented orally or through other media by asking and answering questions about key details and requesting clarification if something is not understood.

ELPS: 9. An ELL can create clear and coherent level-appropriate speech and text.

Warm-up and Review
10–15 minutes (books closed)

Review numbers. Write *10, 20, 30, 40, 50* on the board. Say and have students repeat the numbers. Help with pronunciation. Under *10*, write the numbers *11–19* and have students say the numbers. Do the same with *21–29*. Write numbers from *10–59* randomly on the board and have students call them out.

Introduction
5 minutes

1. Point to the clock and say the time. If you have a window, point outside and say the time of day (*morning, afternoon, evening*).

2. State the objective: *Today we're going to learn words for time.*

1 Learn to tell time

Presentation I
20–25 minutes

A Direct students to look at the pictures. Ask them to point to the clocks [images 5–10]. Note that image 8 is a watch and not technically referred to as a clock. Still, it is used to tell time. You may want to pre-teach the word *watch*.

B 🔊 1-45 1. Play the audio. Ask students to point to the correct picture as they listen. Circulate and monitor.

2. Check comprehension by asking *yes/no* questions. Have students use thumbs up (*yes*) or thumbs down (*no*) to respond. Point to each picture and ask, for example: *Is it morning? Is it 3:00?*

C 🔊 1-45 1. Tell students to listen and repeat the words.

2. Write the words on the board one syllable at a time and help students sound out and pronounce each syllable.

3. Call out the numbers out of order and ask students to say the words.

> **TIP**
> After 1C, help students understand an analog clock. Draw a clock on the board or make one ahead of time. (Cut a clock out of cardboard and punch a hole in the middle of it. Attach hour and minute hands with a metal fastener so that you can move them.) Demonstrate 1:00, 1:30, 2:00, 2:30, etc. When students are comfortable with recognizing and pronouncing *o'clock* and *thirty*, move on to 1:15 and 1:45.

Guided Practice I
10–15 minutes

D Direct students to take turns reading the words with a partner.

E 1. Model the activity with two volunteers. Direct one partner to point to the pictures or say the numbers. Have the other partner cover the words in 1C and identify the pictures from memory.

2. Have students practice in pairs.

> **MULTILEVEL STRATEGIES**
> For 1E, pair same-level students together.
> • **Pre-level** Tell these students to practice together by pointing to the pictures in 1B and saying the correct words.
> • **Higher-level** Tell these students to dictate the words to each other.

2 Talk about time

Guided Practice II
20–25 minutes

A 1. Direct students to look at the pictures. Call out times and ask students to identify the correct pictures.

2. Copy number 1 on the board and have students spell *morning* aloud. Demonstrate how to write one letter on each line.

3. Tell students to work individually to complete the words.

4. Ask volunteers to spell the completed words aloud. Write the answers on the board. Read and have students repeat the words.

Answers
1. m-o-r-n-i-n-g
2. n-o-o-n
3. a-f-t-e-r-n-o-o-n
4. e-v-e-n-i-n-g
5. n-i-g-h-t
6. m-i-d-n-i-g-h-t

B Give students time to copy the words into their notebooks. Monitor and check their writing.

C 🔊 1-46 1. Play the audio. Have students read along silently.

2. Play the audio again. Tell students to listen and repeat.

> **TIP**
> After 2C, provide more practice with the times of day by asking *or* questions: *Do you go to school in the morning or in the evening? Do you go to work in the afternoon or in the morning?* When students answer the questions, ask them *what time*.

Communicative Practice and Application
10–15 minutes

D 1. Model the conversation with a volunteer. Show students how to use the pictures in 1B and 2A. Switch roles and model the conversation with another volunteer.

2. Pair students. Have one pair model the conversation.

3. Set a time limit (five minutes) and have the partners practice the conversation in both roles. Encourage students to use all of the clock times on both pages. Circulate and monitor. Provide feedback.

Evaluation
10–15 minutes

TEST YOURSELF

1. Model the activity with a volunteer.

2. Have students work in pairs to take turns saying sentences. Monitor and provide feedback.

MULTILEVEL STRATEGIES

- **Pre-level** Display or distribute to these students three pictures of clocks or times of day listed in 1C. (See Picture Cards 3.1–3.10 on page 43 of *Multilevel Activities Introductory Level Unit 3*.) Have students open their books to page 32, identify the correct words to match the pictures, and copy them.
- **Higher-level** Give these students the sentence frame: *It's ___ in the morning/afternoon/evening.*

Tell them to work with a partner to say and then write sentences about the pictures in 2A.

EXTENSION ACTIVITY

Bingo

1. Have students fold a paper into nine squares. Tell them to write one word or time from 1C in each square (in any order). Give them paper clips to use as markers.

2. Call out the words and times out of order. Tell students to shout *Bingo!* when they have three words or times in a row. You can also use commercial time Bingo games, which are available at any teacher supply store and many stationery stores.

3. After you've done one round as a class, have students play in groups, with a higher-level student acting as the caller.

LESSON 2 WRITING

Lesson Overview

MULTILEVEL OBJECTIVES

On- and Higher-level: Read and write about places in the community

Pre-level: Recognize places in the community

LANGUAGE FOCUS

Grammar: *At* with time (*I go to work at 3:00.*)

Vocabulary: *Clinic, go, home, laundromat, library, park, post office, schedule, school, store, work*

For vocabulary expansion, see these **Oxford Picture Dictionary** topics: Time, pages 18–19; City Streets, pages 128–129

STRATEGY FOCUS

Write times and indicate time of day with *a.m.* or *p.m.*

READINESS CONNECTION

In this lesson, students communicate information about their daily schedules.

PACING

To compress this lesson: Assign the *Test Yourself* for homework.

To extend this lesson: Do a sentence-writing activity. (See end of lesson.)

And/or have students complete **Workbook Introductory Level page 17** and **Multilevel Activities Introductory Level Unit 3 page 39**.

Lesson Notes

CORRELATIONS

CCRS: R.1.A Ask and answer questions about key details in a text.

R.7.A Use the illustrations and details in a text to describe its key ideas (e.g., maps, charts, photographs, political cartoons, etc.).

SL.2.A Confirm understanding of a text read aloud or information presented orally or through other media by asking and answering questions about key details and requesting clarification if something is not understood.

ELPS: 10. An ELL can demonstrate command of the conventions of standard English to communicate in level-appropriate speech and writing.

Warm-up and Review
10–15 minutes (books closed)

Review time. Draw or post clock faces on the board and ask students to call out the times.

Introduction
5 minutes

1. Using the clocks on the board, tell students about your schedule. For example: *I go to work at 8:00. I go to the library in the afternoon. I go home at 6:00.*

2. State the objective: *Today we'll read and write about places in the community, but first we are going to listen for times with* a.m. *and* p.m.

1 Learn about times and places

Presentation I
25–30 minutes

A 1. Direct students to look at the pictures. Ask: *Is it morning or evening?* Read the captions aloud.

2. Check comprehension. Say times of day, for example: *7:00 in the morning, 4:00 in the afternoon, 10:00 at night.* Ask students to tell you if they are a.m. or p.m. times.

B 🔊 **1-47** 1. Play the audio. Have students work independently to circle the answers.

2. Go over the answers as a class.

Answers
1. morning
2. evening
3. evening
4. morning

C 🔊 **1-47** Replay the audio. Ask students to write the times they hear, including the a.m. or p.m. Ask volunteers to write the times on the board.

Answers
1. 7 a.m.
2. 7 p.m.
3. 9 p.m.
4. 10 a.m.

D 🔊 **1-48** 1. Play the audio. Tell students to listen and look at the pictures.

2. Check comprehension. Ask *yes/no* questions about the pictures: *Is he at the park or at the post office? Is it 3:00 in the morning or 3:00 in the afternoon?*

3. Say and have students repeat the place names.

Guided Practice I
5–10 minutes

E 1. Model the activity with a volunteer. Switch roles and model with another volunteer.

2. Have students work in pairs to talk about the pictures in 1D. Set a time limit (three minutes). Monitor and provide feedback.

2 Prepare to write: my day

Presentation II
25–30 minutes

A Direct students to look at the pictures. Say the numbers and tell students to call out the times. Ask: *Is Cindy a student?* [yes]

B 🔊 **1-49** 1. Play the audio. Have students read along silently.

2. Check comprehension. Direct students to cover the words and look at the pictures. Say the words out of order and have students call out the correct numbers. Then say the numbers and have students call out the words.

3. Replay the audio and ask students to repeat the words.

4. Ask students *yes/no* questions about their own schedules: *Do you go to work at 8:00? Do you go to the store in the morning?*

C 🔊 **1-50** 1. Read the instructions aloud. Ask students to point to Cindy in the pictures in 1A.

2. Play the audio. Have students read along silently.

3. Replay the audio and have students point to the pictures in 2A as they listen. If you have access to a projector, project the pictures in 2A and ask a volunteer to point to the correct area as you read the sentences.

4. Direct students' attention to the *Writer's Note*. Point out that there are different ways to write the same time. Tell them to write the time for noon two different ways [12:00 or 12 p.m.].

> **MULTILEVEL STRATEGIES**
>
> For 2C, seat students in mixed-level groups. After the whole-group practice, tell students to take turns reading the sentences aloud. Demonstrate turn-taking, with the first student reading number 1, the second number 2, and so on.
>
> • **Pre-level** Tell students who don't want to read aloud to listen to their classmates and follow along silently.

Guided Practice II
10–15 minutes

 D 1-51 1. Direct students to look at the picture. Say and have them repeat *Rick*. Read the instructions aloud.

2. Play number 1 and elicit the answer. Play the rest of the audio and ask students to circle the correct word.

Answers
1. b
2. a
3. a
4. b

E 1-51 1. Replay the entire audio so students can check their answers.

2. Ask students to read the completed sentences with a partner.

3 Write about your day

Communicative Practice
10–15 minutes

 A 1. Introduce the new activity: *Now you are going to write about your day.*

2. Call on volunteers to complete the sentences aloud.

3. Tell students to work individually to complete the sentences with their own information.

B Ask students to read their sentences aloud to a partner. When they finish, ask them to read the sentences to a new partner.

> **MULTILEVEL STRATEGIES**
>
> Adapt 3A and 3B to the level of your students.
>
> • **Pre-level** While on- and higher-level students are completing 3A and 3B, work with these students in a group, or have them complete page 36 of the *Literacy Reproducible Activities Unit 3*.

AT WORK

Read a schedule
10–15 minutes

 A 1. Point to the schedule. Say and have students repeat the word *schedule*. If possible, show them some examples of real schedules, for example, a bus schedule or the class schedule.

2. Read the names aloud. Ask: *Who works in the morning: Chris, Ria, or Diana?* [Ria and Diana]

 B 1. Read number 1 aloud. Show students how to follow Chris's name along the row to find his schedule. Elicit the answer [no].

2. Direct students to work independently to answer the questions. Ask them to compare answers with a partner.

3. Read each sentence aloud and have the class respond with thumbs up (*yes*) or thumbs down (*no*). Clarify any statements that elicit incorrect responses.

Answers
1. No
2. No
3. No
4. Yes

Evaluation
10 minutes

TEST YOURSELF

1. Ask students for example answers. Tell them to answer in complete sentences.

2. Have students work independently to write their answers to the questions.

3. Collect and correct students' work.

> **EXTENSION ACTIVITY**
>
> **Sentence Writing**
>
> Pass out pictures of the community places in 2B or use Picture Cards 3.11–3.17 on pages 43–44 of *Multilevel Activities Introductory Level Unit 3*. Tell students to choose a time and work in pairs to write statements about the cards: *It's 3:00. He's at home.*

LESSON 3 GRAMMAR

Lesson Overview	Lesson Notes
MULTILEVEL OBJECTIVES **On- and Higher-level:** Use *yes/no* questions and short answers with *be* **Pre-level:** Recognize *yes/no* questions and short answers with *be*	
LANGUAGE FOCUS **Grammar:** *Yes/No* questions and short answers with *be* (*Are you at the store? Yes, I am.*) **Vocabulary:** Community places For vocabulary expansion, see these **Oxford Picture Dictionary** topics: Time, pages 18–19; City Streets, pages 128–129	
STRATEGY FOCUS Practice different contractions to use in a negative response.	
READINESS CONNECTION In this lesson, students communicate verbally about time and location.	
PACING **To compress this lesson:** Assign 1E as homework. Have students practice 2B with only one partner. **To extend this lesson:** Conduct a board dictation. (See end of lesson.) And/or have students complete **Workbook Introductory Level pages 18–19, Multilevel Activities Introductory Level Unit 3 page 40,** and **Multilevel Grammar Exercises Introductory Level Unit 3**.	
CORRELATIONS	
CCRS: L.1.A Demonstrate command of conventions of standard English grammar and usage when writing or speaking. f. Use frequently occurring adjectives. SL.1.A Participate in collaborative conversations with diverse partners in small and larger groups.	**ELPS:** 10. An ELL can demonstrate command of the conventions of standard English to communicate in level-appropriate speech and writing.

Warm-up and Review
10–15 minutes (books closed)

Review community places. Put up pictures or symbols to represent *clinic, home, laundromat, library, park, post office, school, store,* and *work.* Elicit the vocabulary for each.

Introduction
5–10 minutes

1. Write a sentence with *be* under each picture: *I am at the store. He is at the library. You are at school.* etc. Say: *We know how to make sentences with* am, is, *and* are.

2. State the objective: *Today we're going to learn questions and answers with* am, is, *and* are.

1 Learn about *yes/no* questions with *be*

Presentation I
20–25 minutes

 1. Direct students to look at the pictures. Ask them to say what they see.

2. Read the captions aloud. Have students call out the answers.

 🔊 1-52 1. Play the audio. Ask students to read the chart and listen.

2. Demonstrate how to read the grammar chart as complete sentences. Read the chart through sentence by sentence. Then read it again, and have students repeat after you.

3. Direct students to re-read the questions in 1A and underline the verb *be*.

4. Assess students' understanding of the chart. Re-read the sentences you wrote on the board during the introduction and elicit how to change them into questions.

Guided Practice I
15–20 minutes

 1. Read number 1 aloud. Tell students to work individually to complete the questions.

2. Call on volunteers to read the completed questions aloud.

Answers	
1. Is	4. Are
2. Is	5. Are
3. Is	6. Is

D 1. Model the activity with a volunteer. Point to the picture in number 1 and ask: *Is she at school?* [yes]

2. Have students ask and answer the questions with a partner. Monitor and provide feedback.

E 1. Write *He is at school* and *Is he at school* on the board. Draw a period and a question mark and ask which one goes with which sentence. If necessary, do more examples. Then tell students to work individually to complete the statements and questions.

2. Call on volunteers for the answers. Write them on the board.

3. Model question versus statement intonation. Say and have students repeat the questions and statements 1E.

Answers	
1. .	5. .
2. ?	6. .
3. ?	7. ?
4. .	8. ?

TIP
After 1E, provide more practice with distinguishing questions from statements. Give a series of questions and statements and ask students to write a period or question mark. For example: *1. She is at the store 2. Is she at the library 3. They are at the clinic 4. Are they at work* Write the sentences on the board and have volunteers fill in the punctuation.

2 Use short answers with *be*

Presentation II
10–15 minutes

 🔊 1-53 1. Direct students to look at the picture. Ask where the people are. [Al is in the car. Nell is at the store.]

2. Play the audio. Ask students to repeat the questions and answers.

3. Ask questions and elicit the short answers from the class: *Are you at school?* [Yes, I am./Yes, we are.] *Are you at the clinic?* [No, I'm not./No, we aren't./No, we're not.] *Are you a teacher?* [No, I'm not./No, we aren't./No, we're not.] *Are you a student?* [Yes, I am./Yes, we are.]

Guided Practice II
10–15 minutes

 1. Model the first question and answer with a volunteer. Switch roles and model the second question with a different volunteer.

2. Set a time limit (five minutes). Ask students to take turns asking and answering the questions with several partners. Circulate and monitor. Provide feedback.

3. Call on volunteers to say the questions and answers for the class.

Call on students to make statements about their classmates. Encourage them to use names: *Maria is from Mexico*.

> **MULTILEVEL STRATEGIES**
>
> Adapt 2C to the level of your students.
>
> • **Pre-level** Work with these students to make statements about their classmates, or have them complete page 37 of the *Literacy Reproducible Activities Unit 3*.
>
> • **On- and Higher-level** Ask these students to write statements about their classmates on the board using names, for example, *Carlos and Tomas are from Nicaragua*. When you go over the sentences, call on another student to confirm the information by asking a *yes/no* question: *Are Carlos and Tomas from Guatemala?* [No, they're not./No, they aren't.]

3 Ask and answer questions with *be*

Presentation III
10–15 minutes

 1-54 1. Direct students' attention to the pictures. Ask them where the people are [at work/the office, at school, at the library].

2. Play the audio. Have students repeat the questions and answers.

3. Have students read the questions and answers in pairs. Call on pairs to read the conversations for the class.

4. Check comprehension. Indicating students in the room, ask: *Is she at school? Is he at home?* Call on individuals to provide short-answer responses.

Guided Practice III
10–15 minutes

B 1. Direct students to look at the pictures. Ask where the people are [at the store/supermarket, at the clinic].

2. Ask students to work independently to complete the questions and answers. Tell them to compare their answers with a partner.

3. Call on pairs to read the completed conversations for the class.

Answers
1. he is
2. he's not/he isn't
3. she's not/she isn't
4. she is

Communicative Practice
5–10 minutes

 1. Model the activity with a volunteer. Have students point to the pictures in 3A and 3B and ask and answer questions in pairs. Emphasize that they should make up new questions, not just ask the ones in the book.

2. Set a time limit (three minutes). Have students practice asking and answering questions in pairs. Call on pairs to say questions and answers for the class.

Evaluation
10–15 minutes

TEST YOURSELF

1. Direct pairs to look at the pictures on pages 34 and 35. Ask them to work in pairs to ask and answer questions about the people in the pictures.

2. Monitor and provide feedback.

> **MULTILEVEL STRATEGIES**
>
> Target the *Test Yourself* to the level of your students.
>
> • **Higher-level** Ask these students to write a question and answer for each of the pictures on page 25, 2E.

> **EXTENSION ACTIVITY**
>
> **Board Dictation**
>
> Review *yes/no* questions with *be*.
>
> 1. Put up several pictures of people at community places or of clocks.
>
> 2. Number the pictures and dictate a question to go with each picture: *Is she at the store? Is it 3:00?*, etc.
>
> 3. Have volunteers write the questions on the board. Ask other volunteers to say or write a short answer to each question.

LESSON 4 EVERYDAY CONVERSATION

Lesson Overview

MULTILEVEL OBJECTIVES

On- and Higher-level: Ask and respond to questions about time

Pre-level: Respond to questions about time

LANGUAGE FOCUS

Grammar: Questions with *be* (*What time is it? Is the store open?*)

Vocabulary: Community places, *closed*, *open*

For vocabulary expansion, see these **Oxford Picture Dictionary** topics: Time, pages 18–19; City Streets, pages 128–129

STRATEGY FOCUS

Practice responding to requests for information with *I don't know.*

READINESS CONNECTION

In this lesson, students listen actively for times and communicate verbally about time.

PACING

To compress this lesson: Have students practice 3D with only one partner.

To extend this lesson: After completing *Test Yourself*, conduct a line-up activity. (See end of lesson.)

And/or have students complete **Workbook Introductory Level page 20** and **Multilevel Activities Introductory Level Unit 3 page 41**.

Lesson Notes

CORRELATIONS

CCRS: SL.1.A Participate in collaborative conversations with diverse partners in small and larger groups.

SL.2.A Confirm understanding of a text read aloud or information presented orally or through other media by asking and answering questions about key details and requesting clarification if something is not understood.

RF.3.A Know and apply grade-level phonics and word analysis skills in decoding words. i. Read words with inflectional endings.

ELPS: 2. An ELL can participate in level-appropriate oral and written exchanges of information, ideas, and analyses, in various social and academic contexts, responding to peer, audience, or reader comments and questions.

Warm-up and Review
5 minutes (books closed)

Draw or post pictures of clocks on the board and ask *yes/no* questions: *Is it 5:00? Is it midnight?* Call on volunteers to respond with a short answer: *Yes, it is. No, it isn't.*

Introduction
5 minutes

1. Point to the clocks again and ask: *What time is it?*

2. State the objective: *Today we're going to ask about time.*

1 Listen for times

Listening Extension
20–25 minutes

A 🔊 1-55 1. Introduce the listening topic: *Now we're going to listen for times.* Write *a.m.* and *p.m.* on the board. Ask: *Is 7:00 in the morning a.m. or p.m.?* Ask about several times of day.

2. Direct students to look at the pictures. Ask them where the people are [school, work/clinic, library, store].

3. Play the entire audio once. Have students listen and point to the pictures.

B 🔊 1-55 1. Play the audio in segments. Tell students to circle *a* or *b*. After each number, ask for a show of hands to see how students answered. Repeat the segment if necessary.

2. Call on volunteers for the answers and write them on the board.

Answers
1. a
2. a
3. b
4. b

> **MULTILEVEL STRATEGIES**
>
> Replay 1B to allow pre-level students to catch up while you provide a challenge for higher-level students.
>
> • **Pre-level** Have these students listen again to circle the answers.
>
> • **On- and Higher-level** Ask these students to write a sentence about one of the places. Do the first one as an example: *The school is open.*

2 Practice your pronunciation

Pronunciation Extension
10–15 minutes

A 🔊 1-56 1. Say: *Now we're going to practice pronunciation of yes/no questions.* Direct students to read and listen to the questions. Point out how the arrows go up because the speaker's voice goes up.

2. Say several "statements" and "questions" with nonsense syllables and see if students can identify which is which.

B 🔊 1-57 Play the audio. Tell students to listen and repeat the questions.

C Have students practice reading the questions aloud with a partner. Circulate and monitor pronunciation.

3 Make conversation: ask about time

Presentation
5–10 minutes

A 1. Direct students to look at the pictures. Ask students to say what they see. Point out the *closed* sign. Elicit the meaning of *closed*. Ask about a local store that students will be familiar with: *When is [name of store] closed? When is it open?*

2. Direct students to read the conversation silently. Elicit any questions.

B 🔊 1-58 Play the audio. Have students read the conversation silently.

Guided Practice
5–10 minutes

C 🔊 1-58 1. Play the audio again and have students repeat the conversation.

2. Do a choral reading of the conversation in 3B. Divide the class in half. Have one side be Alfredo and one side be Pilar, and then have the sides switch roles.

Communicative Practice and Application
15–20 minutes

D 1. Model the conversation with a volunteer. Then switch roles and model it with another volunteer, using ideas from the *Need help?* box.

2. Elicit other ways to complete the conversation.

3. Set a time limit (five minutes). Ask students to practice the conversation with several partners. Encourage pantomime and improvisation.

4. Ask volunteer pairs to present their conversations to the class.

> **MULTILEVEL STRATEGIES**
>
> For 3D, seat pre-level students together.
>
> - **Pre-level** While other students are practicing the conversation, have these students complete page 38 in the *Literacy Reproducible Activities Unit 3*.
>
> - **Higher-level** Add another line to the conversation for these students. For example, have Student B say: *No, it's not. It's open in the morning.* Tell them to practice the conversation with several partners.

Evaluation
5 minutes

TEST YOURSELF

Set a time limit (three minutes). Have students walk around the class asking and responding to the questions.

> **EXTENSION ACTIVITY**
>
> **Line-up**
>
> Have students line up in two rows facing each other. Write times on picture cards of places (or use Picture Cards 3.11–3.17 on pages 43–44 of *Multilevel Activities Introductory Level Unit 3*) and pass them out to Row A. Direct Row A students to show their partners the card and ask: *What time is it?* and *Is the _____ open?* After the Row B students have answered the questions, have them all move forward one place and talk to a new Row A student. Halfway through, have the rows switch roles.

LESSON 5 READING

Lesson Overview

MULTILEVEL OBJECTIVES

On- and Higher-level: Identify kinds of transportation and read a bus schedule

Pre-level: Recognize kinds of transportation and read a bus schedule

LANGUAGE FOCUS

Grammar: Yes/No questions with *be* (*Is it 11:00?*)

Vocabulary: *Bus, car, hour, minute, plane, schedule, train*

For vocabulary expansion, see this **Oxford Picture Dictionary** topic: Public Transportation, page 156

STRATEGY FOCUS

Identify the symbol for *number*.

READINESS CONNECTION

In this lesson, students interpret a bus schedule.

PACING

To compress this lesson: Assign 2C as homework or conduct it as a whole-class activity.

To extend this lesson: Discuss train or bus schedules. (See end of lesson.)

And/or have students complete **Workbook Introductory Level page 21** and **Multilevel Activities Introductory Level Unit 3 page 42.**

Lesson Notes

CORRELATIONS

CCRS: SL.2.A Confirm understanding of a text read aloud or information presented orally or through other media by asking and answering questions about key details and requesting clarification if something is not understood.

L.6.A Use words and phrases acquired through conversations, reading and being read to, and responding to texts, including using frequently occurring conjunctions to signal simple relationships (e.g., *because*).

R.1.A Ask and answer questions about key details in a text.

R.7.A Use the illustrations and details in a text to describe its key ideas (e.g., maps, charts, photographs, political cartoons, etc.).

ELPS: 8. An ELL can determine the meaning of words and phrases in oral presentations and literary and informational text.

Warm-up and Review
10–15 minutes (books closed)

Draw a house and a school on the board and elicit the words. Draw a bus, a car, a train, and a person walking. Say the words and use pantomime to ask students how they come to school. Leave the drawings on the board.

Introduction
5 minutes

1. Using the illustrations on the board to help you convey the meaning, say: *Buses, cars, and trains are transportation.*

2. State the objective: *Today we're going to learn about kinds of transportation.*

1 Get ready to read

Presentation I
10–15 minutes

A 🔊 1-59 Tell students to look at the pictures and listen to the words. Play the audio.

2. Check comprehension of the words. Add an airplane to your pictures on the board, number those pictures, and ask: *Which number is car? Which number is bus?*, etc.

3. Replay the audio and tell students to listen and repeat.

Guided Practice I
10–15 minutes

B 🔊 1-60 1. Play number 1 and elicit the answer. Play the rest of the audio and have students work individually to circle the answers.

2. Call on volunteers for the answers. Write them on the board.

Answers
1. a
2. a
3. b
4. b

Presentation and Guided Practice II
10–15 minutes

C 1. Direct students to look at the pictures. Say and have students repeat the words and the question and answer.

2. Use your classroom clock or a clock with movable hands to reinforce the meaning of *hour* and *minute*.

3. Check comprehension by using your drawings from the warm-up. Draw a clock above the house (1:00) and another clock above the school (1:30), and draw a line between them to demonstrate that the clocks represent the travel time. Ask: *How long is the trip?* [half an hour] Change the clock times and repeat as necessary.

D Elicit the start and end time of your class and write them on the board. Ask students: *How long is our English class?* Ask several students: *How long is your trip to school?*

2 Read a bus schedule

Guided Practice III
15–20 minutes

A 1. Direct students to look at the bus schedule. Ask: *What is this?* Say and have students repeat *Newport, Springfield, Salem,* and *Sundale*. Ask what those words are [cities]. Read the numbers *23, 61, 94,* and *57* aloud. Ask what they are [bus numbers].

2. Ask students to read the bus schedule silently. Elicit any questions about the reading.

3. Check students' comprehension. Ask: *What time is Bus 23 in Newport?* [7:00 a.m.] *What time is Bus 23 in Sundale?* [10:30 a.m.] *What time is Bus 61 in Salem?* [10:50 a.m.] etc. If necessary, project the schedule or copy part of it on the board to show students how to read the grid.

B 1. Direct students to work individually to complete the exercise. Ask them to compare answers with a partner.

2. Call on volunteers for the answers and write them on the board.

Answers
1. 11:00 a.m.
2. 7:30 a.m.
3. 10:30 a.m.
4. 7:00 p.m.

C 1. Direct students to look at the picture of Carlos. Ask: *Where is Carlos?* [Newport]

2. Read number 1 aloud. Have students find Bus 23 on the schedule. Elicit the time that Bus 23 is in Newport [7 a.m.] and write it on the board. Elicit the time that Bus 23 is in Sundale [10:30 a.m.] and write that time. Ask: *How long is the trip?* and have the class count out 3½ hours.

3. Tell students to work individually to complete the exercise. Call on volunteers for the answers and write them on the board. Go over each question, showing how to find the starting and ending points on the schedule.

Answers
1. b
2. b
3. b
4. a

MULTILEVEL STRATEGIES

- **Pre-level** While other students are completing 2C, work with these students on grid reading. Show students how to line up a piece of paper at the bottom of a row and read the schedule across. Elicit times in order. *Bus 23 is in Newport at 7 a.m., no stop in Springfield, Salem at 10 a.m.*

TIP

For more practice with schedules after 2C, make a bus schedule like the one in 2A using local street or city names. Leave five or six of the times blank. Make a copy for each student, dictate times, and have students write them in the schedule. For example, *Bus 19 is in Norwalk at 4:00.* Correct the schedule together. Then write *How long* questions on the board and have students work with a partner to answer them.

Application
5–10 minutes

BRING IT TO LIFE

Read the *Bring it to Life* instructions aloud and direct students to look at the picture. Brainstorm search terms that students might use to find local bus or train schedules.

TIP

In preparation for *Teamwork & Language Review*, have students review the unit vocabulary. Provide them with pictures you have collected or use the Picture Cards on pages 43–44 of *Multilevel Activities Introductory Level Unit 3*. Pair students and have them use the pictures as flashcards for recognition practice, dictation, or sentence writing.

EXTENSION ACTIVITY

Discuss Schedules

Make copies of a real bus or train schedule for your area. Project them or distribute copies to students and help them with pronunciation of the street, city, or train stop names. Show them where to find the bus or train number. Write comprehension questions on the board and have students work together to find the answers.

TEAMWORK & LANGUAGE REVIEW

Lesson Overview

MULTILEVEL OBJECTIVES

On-, Pre-, and Higher-level: Expand upon and review unit language and content

LANGUAGE FOCUS

Grammar: Yes/No questions and short answers with *be* (*Is Deenah at the store? Yes, she is.*)

Vocabulary: Community places and time words

For vocabulary expansion, see these **Oxford Picture Dictionary** topics: Time, pages 18–19; City Streets, pages 128–129; Public Transportation, page 156

STRATEGY FOCUS

Use teamwork to reinforce and expand vocabulary.

READINESS CONNECTION

In this review, students cooperate with others and identify ways to solve a scheduling conflict.

PACING

To extend this review: Have students complete **Workbook Introductory Level page 22**, **Multilevel Activities Introductory Level Unit 3 pages 43–46**, and **Multilevel Grammar Exercises Introductory Level Unit 3**.

Lesson Notes

CORRELATIONS

CCRS: SL.2.A Confirm understanding of a text read aloud or information presented orally or through other media by asking and answering questions about key details and requesting clarification if something is not understood.

SL.4.A Describe people, places, things, and events with relevant details, expressing ideas and feelings clearly.

SL.6.A Speak audibly and express thoughts, feelings, and ideas clearly. Produce complete sentences when appropriate to task and situation.

R.1.A Ask and answer questions about key details in a text.

R.7.A Use the illustrations and details in a text to describe its key ideas (e.g., maps, charts, photographs, political cartoons, etc.).

ELPS: 2. An ELL can participate in level-appropriate oral and written exchanges of information, ideas, and analyses, in various social and academic contexts, responding to peer, audience, or reader comments and questions.

Warm-up and Review
5–10 minutes (books closed)

1. Review the *Bring It to Life* assignment from Lesson 5.

2. Call on volunteers to read two stop names and the arrival times. Write them on the board. Call on other students to answer the question: *How long is the trip?*

Introduction and Presentation
5 minutes

1. Group students and direct them to focus on the picture. Ask: *What do you see?*

2. State the objective: *Today we're going to review the words and grammar from Unit 3.*

Communicative Practice
15–20 minutes

A 1. Tell students to take turns naming one thing they see in the picture. Have three volunteers help you model turn-taking.

2. Tell students to put their pencils down and listen to each other so that they don't repeat ideas. Direct them to go around the group until they have run out of ideas.

B 1. Have students work in the same groups from A. Assign roles: secretary, reporter, editor, and manager. Write the roles on the board. As you explain each role, pantomime the duties you expect the person taking that role to perform. Explain that students work with their groups to write the words. Verify comprehension of roles.

2. Set a time limit (five minutes) to complete the chart. Circulate and answer any questions.

3. Call on the reporters from each group to say the words from their chart. Write the words on the board. Go around the class until there are no more ideas.

Possible Answers		
Places	**Things**	**Other**
store	book	man
clinic	bus	woman
library	car	students
school	clock	teacher
park		11:00
city		

C 1. Have the groups identify new words from the board and to look them up in a picture dictionary or a bilingual dictionary.

2. Tell students to add three new words to their chart. [New words might include: *driver, fire hydrant, passenger, sign.*]

MULTILEVEL STRATEGIES

For A-C, use mixed-level groups.

• **Pre-level** Assign these students the role of manager.

• **On-level** Assign these students the role of secretary or reporter.

• **Higher-level** Assign these students the role of editor.

D 1. Demonstrate alphabetical order on the board. Write four words students know, for example, *boy, chair, clock,* and *desk.* Underline the first letter(s) and show how they follow alphabetical order. Ask students where to put *clinic* and *dictionary* in your list.

2. Have students work as a group to determine the alphabetical order of their word lists. Tell them to write the words in their notebooks.

E 1. Read number 1 aloud. Tell students to work independently to complete the questions and answers.

2. Call on volunteers to read the completed sentences aloud. Write the answers on the board.

Answers	
1. she's not/she isn't	5. Is Natal/Is he
2. he is	6. Are they
3. it's not/it isn't	7. Is
4. they are	8. Is

F 1. Have students work independently to write two sentences.

2. Ask volunteers to write their sentences on the board. Correct them as a class.

PROBLEM SOLVING
15–20 minutes

A 🔊 **1-61** 1. Tell students the pictures in A tell a story about a man named Tony. He has a problem with time.

2. Direct students to look at the first picture. Ask: *Where is Tony going?* [the clinic]

3. Play the audio and have students listen and look at the pictures. Check comprehension. Ask: *What time is his clinic appointment?* [10 a.m.] *What time is his English class?* [9 a.m. to 12 p.m.] *Is this a problem?* [yes] Write the class time on the board. Ask: *How long is the English class?* [3 hours]

B 1. Tell students to look at the pictures. Read the captions and talk about them. For choice *a*, help students understand the meaning of *early*. Ask what time it is [9:45]. Point to the class time on the board and compare it. [Tony will have 45 minutes of class.] Check comprehension by asking questions about your class. For example: *Vin goes home at 11:00. Is that leaving class early?* Repeat the procedure for choice *b* and the word *late* so that students see Tony will also have 45 minutes of class if he comes late.

2. Ask for a show of hands to see which solution the class likes best. Emphasize that there can be more than one correct answer.

Evaluation
20–25 minutes

To test students' understanding of the unit language and content, have them take the Unit 3 Test, available on the Teacher Resource Center.

> **TIP**
> Encourage students to reflect on what they have learned in this unit. Write these topics in a list on the board and elicit words, phrases, and sentences that students learned for each topic: *a) Times of day; b) Places; c) Yes/No questions and answers with* be*; d) Asking about time; e) Transportation.* Congratulate students on their progress.

UNIT 4
What Day Is It?

Unit Overview

This unit explores calendar vocabulary, basic prepositions of time, question words, ways to say goodbye, and information on a job application.

KEY OBJECTIVES

Lesson 1	Identify the days of the week
Lesson 2	Identify the months of the year; describe an important date
Lesson 3	Use *on, at, when, where,* and *what time*
Lesson 4	Use appropriate language to say goodbye
Lesson 5	Interpret dates on a job application
Teamwork & Language Review	Review unit language

UNIT FEATURES

Academic Vocabulary	*registration*
Employability Skills	• Understand teamwork • Communicate information • Work with others • Communicate verbally • Speak so others can understand • Interpret a calendar • Determine what to do when late

Resources	**Class Audio** CD1, Tracks 62–81
	Workbook Unit 4, pages 23–29
	Teacher Resource Center
	    Literacy Reproducible Activities Unit 4
	    Multilevel Activities Introductory Level Unit 4
	    Multilevel Grammar Exercises Introductory Level Unit 4
	    Unit 4 Test
	Oxford Picture Dictionary The Calendar, Time, Numbers

LESSON 1 VOCABULARY

Lesson Overview

MULTILEVEL OBJECTIVES

On-level: Identify the days of the week
Pre-level: Recognize the days of the week
Higher-level: Talk about the days of the week

LANGUAGE FOCUS

Grammar: Questions with *be (What day is it?)*

Vocabulary: *Day, Friday, Monday, Saturday, Sunday, Thursday, today, tomorrow, Tuesday, Wednesday, week, weekend*

For vocabulary expansion, see this **Oxford Picture Dictionary** topic: The Calendar, pages 20–21

STRATEGY FOCUS

Interpret signs with days and times, including abbreviations for days.

READINESS CONNECTION

In this lesson, students communicate information about days of the week.

PACING

To compress this lesson: Conduct 2A as a whole-class activity.

To extend this lesson: Do a calendar dictation. (See end of lesson.)

And/or have students complete **Workbook Introductory Level page 23** and **Multilevel Activities Introductory Level Unit 4 page 48**.

Lesson Notes

CORRELATIONS

CCRS: L.2.A Demonstrate command of the conventions of English capitalization, punctuation, and spelling when writing. g. Spell simple words phonetically, drawing on knowledge of sound-letter relationships.

L.6.A Use words and phrases acquired through conversations, reading and being read to, and responding to texts, including using frequently occurring conjunctions to signal simple relationships (e.g., *because*).

SL.1.A Participate in collaborative conversations with diverse partners in small and larger groups.

R.7.A Use the illustrations and details in a text to describe its key ideas (e.g., maps, charts, photographs, political cartoons, etc.).

ELPS: 1. An ELL can construct meaning from oral presentations and literary and informational text through level-appropriate listening, reading, and viewing.

Warm-up and Review
10–15 minutes (books closed)

Review the question *What time is it?* Write the question on the board. Draw or post clocks with different times on them. Ask the class: *What time is it?* for each clock. Then call on volunteers to ask the question and other volunteers to answer it. Leave the question on the board.

Introduction
5 minutes

1. Hold up a calendar. Say the names of the days. Cross out *time* in the question on the board and write *day*.

2. State the objective: *Today we'll learn the days of the week.*

1 Learn the days of the week

Presentation
20–25 minutes

A Direct students to look at the calendar. Ask them to find the words *English Class* and say the time [9:00 to 12:00]. Then ask: *What time is the clinic appointment?* [3:00]

B 🔊 1-62 1. Play the audio. Ask students to point to the correct day as they listen. Circulate and monitor.

2. Check comprehension. Ask: *What number is Tuesday?* [3] *What number is weekend?* [12] etc.

C 🔊 1-62 1. Tell students to listen and repeat the words.

2. Write the words on the board one syllable at a time and help students sound out and pronounce each syllable.

3. Call out the numbers out of order and ask students to say the words.

Guided Practice I
15–20 minutes

D Direct students to take turns reading the words with a partner.

E 1. Model the activity with two volunteers. Direct one partner to point to the calendar or say the numbers. Have the other partner cover the words in 1C and identify the days from memory.

2. Have students practice in pairs.

> **MULTILEVEL STRATEGIES**
>
> For 1E, pair same-level students together.
>
> • **Pre-level** Tell these students to practice together by pointing to the calendar in 1B and saying the correct words.
>
> • **Higher-level** Tell these students to dictate the words to each other.

2 Talk about days of the week

Guided Practice II
15–20 minutes

A 1. Direct students to look at the picture. Ask: *Is the store open or closed?* [closed] Call out the numbers and ask students to identify the days in the picture.

2. Copy number 1 on the board and have students spell *weekend* aloud. Demonstrate how to write one letter on each line.

3. Tell students to work individually to complete the words.

4. Ask volunteers to spell the completed words aloud. Write the answers on the board. Read and have students repeat the words.

Answers	
1. w-e-e-k-e-n-d	6. F-r-i-d-a-y
2. M-o-n-d-a-y	7. S-a-t-u-r-d-a-y
3. T-u-e-s-d-a-y	8. S-u-n-d-a-y
4. W-e-d-n-e-s-d-a-y	9. w-e-e-k
5. T-h-u-r-s-d-a-y	

B Give students time to copy the words into their notebooks. Monitor and check their writing.

Communicative Practice and Application
10–15 minutes

C 🔊 1-63 1. Play the audio. Have students read along silently.

2. Play the audio again. Tell students to listen and repeat.

> **TIP**
>
> After 2C, provide extra practice with distinguishing *Tuesday* from *Thursday*. Write *1. Tuesday* and *2. Thursday* on the board. Say the words and have students hold up one finger for *Tuesday* and two for *Thursday*. After they can hear the difference, have them practice the pronunciation.

D 1. Pair students. Have one pair model the conversation.

2. Set a time limit (five minutes) and have partners practice the conversation in both roles. Encourage students to use all of the days. Circulate and monitor. Provide feedback.

> **TIP**
> After students have practiced with the days in 2D, focus on spelling. Have partners practice spelling the days to one another. Point out the abbreviations in 2A and have students practice writing the correct abbreviations as well as the complete words.

Application and Evaluation
10–15 minutes

TEST YOURSELF

1. Model the activity with a volunteer. Demonstrate that whichever day they point to is "today" for this activity.

2. Ask students to practice in pairs. Monitor and provide feedback.

> **EXTENSION ACTIVITY**
> **Calendar Dictation**
> 1. Have students open their books to page 47, 2D. Tell them to listen and write the times you say in the correct place in the calendar.
>
> 2. Dictate a series of times and days, for example, *9:30 a.m. on Wednesday, 2:00 p.m. on Friday*, and *1:30 p.m. on Saturday*.
>
> 3. Ask volunteers to repeat back the days and times.

LESSON 2 WRITING

Lesson Overview

MULTILEVEL OBJECTIVES

On- and Higher-level: Read and write about months and dates

Pre-level: Recognize the months and ordinal numbers

LANGUAGE FOCUS

Grammar: The verb *be* (*Next month is November.*)

Vocabulary: Months, *month*, *year*

For vocabulary expansion, see these **Oxford Picture Dictionary** topics: The Calendar, pages 20–21; Numbers, page 16

STRATEGY FOCUS

Use *in* with months and *on* with specific dates.

READINESS CONNECTION

In this lesson, students interpret a calendar.

PACING

To compress this lesson: Assign the *Test Yourself* for homework.

To extend this lesson: Use dice to help students associate months with numbers. (See end of lesson.)

And/or have students complete **Workbook Introductory Level page 24** and **Multilevel Activities Introductory Level Unit 4 page 49.**

Lesson Notes

CORRELATIONS

CCRS: R.1.A Ask and answer questions about key details in a text.

R.7.A Use the illustrations and details in a text to describe its key ideas (e.g., maps, charts, photographs, political cartoons, etc.).

SL.1.A Participate in collaborative conversations with diverse partners in small and larger groups.

SL.2.A Confirm understanding of a text read aloud or information presented orally or through other media by asking and answering questions about key details and requesting clarification if something is not understood.

ELPS: 1. An ELL can construct meaning from oral presentations and literary and informational text through level-appropriate listening, reading, and viewing. 10. An ELL can demonstrate command of the conventions of standard English to communicate in level-appropriate speech and writing.

Warm-up and Review
10–15 minutes (books closed)

Write the days on the board in scrambled form: 1. urSaatdy, 2. oaynMd, 3. Sduayn, 4. sTuedya, 5. uayrsThd, 6. ydWedanes, 7. yirdaF. Tell students not to copy the scrambled words. Give them a few minutes to work individually or with a partner to unscramble the words and write them correctly. Go over the answers, eliciting the day and then having the class spell it aloud as you rewrite it on the board. [1. Saturday, 2. Monday, 3. Sunday, 4. Tuesday, 5. Thursday, 6. Wednesday, 7. Friday]

Introduction
5 minutes

1. Hold up a current monthly calendar and elicit the days in order. Ask: *What day is it today?* Point to the month. Say: *The month is _____.*

2. State the objective: *Today we'll read and write about the months.*

1 Learn about the months

Presentation I
15–20 minutes

A Direct students to look at the picture. Ask them to point to the number 24 in any of the months on the calendar.

B 🔊 1-64 1. Play the audio. Have students read along silently.

2. Check comprehension. Direct students to look at the calendar. Say the months out of order and have students call out the correct numbers. Then say the numbers and have students call out the months.

3. Replay the audio and ask students to repeat the words.

Guided Practice I
15–20 minutes

C 1. Write *Jan.* and *January* on the board. Explain that *Jan.* is an abbreviation. Ask students to look through the activity and find the month that does not have an abbreviation [May].

2. Have students work independently to complete the activity.

3. Tell students to work with a partner to check their answers. Partner A reads the spelling of each month aloud, looking at the calendar. Partner B listens and checks his/her own spelling. Then the partners switch roles and repeat.

Answers	
1. January	7. July
2. February	8. August
3. March	9. September
4. April	10. October
5. May	11. November
6. June	12. December

2 Prepare to write: ordinal numbers

Presentation II
10–15 minutes

A 🔊 1-65 1. Direct students to look at the calendar. Ask them to identify the month [March].

2. Play the audio. Have students read along silently and point to the dates.

3. Check comprehension of the words. Say ordinal numbers out of order and ask students to point to the correct date on the calendar. Circulate and monitor.

Guided Practice II
15–20 minutes

B 1. Read number 1 aloud. Ask students to work independently to complete the exercise.

2. Have students compare their answers with a partner. Say the answers and have students repeat each ordinal in the activity.

Answers	
1. c	6. c
2. a	7. d
3. e	8. a
4. b	9. e
5. d	10. b

C 🔊 1-66 1. Play number 1 on the audio and have students call out the answer [2nd/second].

2. Play numbers 2–4 and have students work independently to complete the answers. Go over the answers as a class. Then repeat the procedure for number 5–8.

Answers	
1. 2nd	5. 8th
2. 4th	6. 25th
3. 3rd	7. 13th
4. 1st	8. 21st

D Replay the audio and have students repeat the dates. Repeat as necessary.

E 🔊 1-67 1. Point to picture of Olga in 1A on page 48. Ask: *When is Olga's birthday?* [November 24th]

2. Play the audio. Tell students to listen and read along silently.

3. Check comprehension. *What month is it?* [October] *What is next month?* [November]

F 🔊 1-68 1. Direct students to look at the picture. Say the name *Bill*. Read the instructions aloud.

2. Play number 1 and elicit the answer. Play the rest of the audio and ask students to circle the correct answer.

3. Replay the entire audio so students can check their work. Ask them to read the completed sentences with a partner.

Answers	
1. a	3. a
2. b	4. a

TIP

After 2F, prepare students for writing about their birthdays. Have them line up according to the months of their birthdays. Find out whose birthday is in January (if no one, move on to February), and have those people stand at one end of the room. Do the same with December, and have those students stand at the other end of the room. Direct everyone else to line up in order between January and December. To check the line, call out the months and tell students to raise their hands if they hear their birthday month. Once the line is in order, ask students in different parts of the line to say their birthday month.

3 Write about your birthday

Communicative Practice
10–15 minutes

 1. Introduce the new activity: *Now we are going to write about the months and your birthday.*

2. Direct students' attention to the *Writer's Note*. Read the note aloud. Check comprehension by writing months and dates on the board and having students call out *in* or *on*.

3. Call on volunteers to complete the sentences aloud.

4. Tell students to work individually to complete the sentences with their own information.

B Ask students to read their sentences aloud to a partner. When they finish, ask them to read the sentences to a new partner.

MULTILEVEL STRATEGIES

Adapt 3A and 3B to the level of your students.

• **Pre-level** While on- and higher-level students are completing 3A and 3B, work with these students in a group, or have them complete page 42 of the *Literacy Reproducible Activities Unit 4*.

AT WORK

Talk about day and night shifts
10–15 minutes

A 1. Point out the day-shift and night-shift icons. Elicit the colors associated with each one [green day shifts, blue night shifts]. Write two time frames on the board: 7 a.m.–7 p.m. and 7 p.m.–7 a.m. Ask: *When is the day shift?* [7 a.m.–7 p.m.] *When is the night shift?* [7 p.m.–7 a.m.]

2. Ask for a show of hands of students who work a day shift or a night shift. Call on individuals and ask them for the beginning and ending times of their shifts.

3. Verify that students understand the meaning of the different icons. Point to a date on the calendar with a day-shift icon. Ask: *Is Kevin working the day shift or the night shift?* [day shift] Point to a date with a night-shift icon. Repeat the question: *Is Kevin working the day shift or the night shift?* [night shift] Point to a date without an icon. Ask: *Is Kevin working on this day?* [no]

B 1-69 1. Play the audio. Tell students to listen without writing. Check students' understanding of the instructions by writing a circle, underline, check mark, and X on the board. Ask students when they need to use each.

2. Replay the audio, pausing after each instruction to give students time to mark the schedules.

3. Have students compare answers with a partner. Then go over the answers as a class.

Answers
Circle Kevin's day shifts in August: 7, 8, 11, 12, 14, 21, 22, 23, 27, 28, 29
Underline Kevin's night shifts in September: 1, 4, 8, 9, 10, 16, 17, 18, 25, 27, 28, 30
Check the days he's not working in August: 1, 2, 3, 5, 6, 10, 13, 15, 18, 19, 20, 24, 25, 26, 30
Put an "X" next to the days he's not working in September: 6, 7, 11, 15, 19, 21, 24, 26, 29

Evaluation
10 minutes

TEST YOURSELF

1. Direct students to talk to two partners and write their names and birthdays on the lines. Remind them to listen and write, not to pass their books.

2. Have students share the information with a new partner: *His name is Marco. His birthday is August 25th.*

> **EXTENSION ACTIVITY**
>
> **Dice Review**
>
> Use dice to help students associate months with numbers. Seat them in small groups and give each group one die. Tell them to take turns rolling and calling out the month that goes with each number (i.e., if they roll a 1, they call out "January"). After 2–3 minutes of this practice, give the groups a second die and do another round so that they get practice with July through December.

LESSON 3 GRAMMAR

Lesson Overview

MULTILEVEL OBJECTIVES

On- and Higher-level: Use *on* with days, *at* with times, and information questions

Pre-level: Recognize *on* with days, *at* with times, and information questions

LANGUAGE FOCUS

Grammar: *On* with days and *at* with times (*The party is on Tuesday at 7:00.*)

Vocabulary: Days of the week, *appointment*, *dentist*, *doctor*, *hairdresser*, *party*

For vocabulary expansion, see these **Oxford Picture Dictionary** topics: The Calendar, pages 20–21; Time, pages 18–19

STRATEGY FOCUS

Use the prepositions *on* and *at* correctly when answering questions about appointments.

READINESS CONNECTION

In this lesson, students work with others and communicate verbally.

PACING

To compress this lesson: Conduct 2D as a whole-class activity. Assign 3C for homework.

To extend this lesson: Do a calendar dictation. (See end of lesson.)

And/or have students complete **Workbook Introductory Level pages 25–26**, **Multilevel Activities Introductory Level Unit 4 page 50**, and **Multilevel Grammar Exercises Introductory Level Unit 4**.

Lesson Notes

CORRELATIONS

CCRS: L.1.A Demonstrate command of the conventions of standard English grammar and usage when writing or speaking. j. Use frequently occurring prepositions (e.g., *during*, *beyond*, *toward*).

R.1.A Ask and answer questions about key details in a text.

R.7.A Use the illustrations and details in a text to describe its key ideas (e.g., maps, charts, photographs, political cartoons, etc.).

SL.1.A Participate in collaborative conversations with diverse partners in small and larger groups.

SL.2.A Confirm understanding of a text read aloud or information presented orally or through other media by asking and answering questions about key details and requesting clarification if something is not understood.

ELPS: 10. An ELL can demonstrate command of the conventions of standard English to communicate in level-appropriate speech and writing.

Warm-up and Review
10–15 minutes (books closed)

Make cards with the months and the days on them, and another 10 cards with years. Write *Days* and *Months* and *Years* on the board as column heads. Pass the cards out around the class. Direct students to tape their cards under the correct heading and in order. Have the class repeat all of the words.

Introduction
5–10 minutes

1. Take all of the cards off the board except for the days. Say sentences using days and times: *I go to the library on Friday. I go to the store at 9:00.*

2. State the objective: *Today we'll learn on with days and at with times, and we'll practice asking questions.*

1 Learn about *on* and *at*

Presentation I
20–25 minutes

A 1. Direct students to look at the picture. Ask: *What month is the party?* [July]

2. Read the caption aloud.

B 🔊 1-70 1. Play the audio. Ask students to read the chart and listen.

2. Demonstrate how to read the grammar chart as complete sentences. Read the chart through sentence by sentence. Then read it again, and have students repeat after you.

3. Assess students' understanding of the chart. Write days and times on the board. Point to the words and ask: *on* or *at*?

Guided Practice I
15–20 minutes

C 🔊 1-71 1. Tell students they are going to listen for *on* and *at*. Play number 1 and ask which word they heard [on]. Play the entire audio and have students work individually to circle the answers.

2. Ask for a show of hands about each number to find out how students answered. Replay any problem sentences.

Answers	
1. on	5. at
2. at	6. on
3. at	7. at
4. on	8. on

D 1. Read number 1. Direct students to work individually to complete the sentences. Then ask them to read the sentences with a partner.

2. Call on volunteers to read the completed sentences aloud. Write the answers on the board.

Answers
1. on
2. at
3. on
4. on

MULTILEVEL STRATEGIES

For 1C and 1D, seat pre-level students together.

- **Pre-level** Provide these students with the answers to 1D. Have them copy the answers into their books and practice reading the sentences in 1D to each other.
- **On- and Higher-level** While the pre-level students are reading together, replay numbers 7 and 8 of 1C and have these students write the sentences they hear.

2 Ask information and *yes/no* questions

Presentation II
10–15 minutes

A 🔊 1-72 1. Direct students to look at the picture. Ask: *Is Gloria happy?* [yes]

2. Play the audio. Ask students to read along silently. Ask comprehension questions: *Is it Abena's birthday?* [no] *Is the party on Tuesday?* [yes]

3. Write *When, Where,* and *What time* on the board in a column. In another column, write *8:00, on Monday, at school.* Say the question words and ask students to choose the appropriate answer.

4. Have students read the conversation with a partner.

Guided Practice II
10–15 minutes

B 🔊 1-72 1. Replay the audio. Tell students to work with a partner to complete the questions.

2. Call on volunteer pairs to read the questions and answers aloud.

Answers
1. When
2. Where
3. What time
4. Are

C 1. Direct students to look at the invitation. Ask: *Is the party at the house?* [No, it's at Pizza Town.]

2. Read number 1 aloud. Show students how to find the answer on the invitation. Tell them to work individually to answer the questions.

3. Call on volunteers for the answers. Write them on the board.

Answers	
1. a	3. b
2. b	4. a

> **MULTILEVEL STRATEGIES**
>
> Adapt 2B and 2C for your pre-level students.
>
> • **Pre-level** Provide these students with the answers to the exercises and have them practice reading the sentences to each other, or have them complete page 43 of the *Literacy Reproducible Activities Unit 4*.

D 1. Direct students to work with a partner to read the questions and answers in 2C.

2. Call on volunteers to read their conversations to the class.

3 Ask and answer questions about dates and times

Communicative Practice and Application
20–25 minutes

A 🔊 **1-73** Direct students' attention to the pictures. Play the audio. Have them listen and repeat the words. Practice the pronunciation of each word, clapping out syllables and emphasizing the stressed syllable.

B 1. Point to the pictures and ask students to read out the words and times. Read the example conversation with a volunteer. Then model the substitution with a volunteer reading speaker B's part. Then have two volunteers model the conversation with a new substitution.

2. Have students practice the conversation in pairs.

C 1. Read the example sentence aloud. Elicit another example sentence from the class.

2. Have students work independently to write two sentences. Have several students write their sentences on the board.

> **MULTILEVEL STRATEGIES**
>
> Adapt 3B and 3C for your pre- and higher-level students.
>
> • **Pre-level** Have these students work with an on-level pair. Instruct the on-level students to practice the conversation together. After they have practiced a substitution, one on-level partner repeats the conversation with the pre-level student taking speaker B's part.
>
> • **Higher-level** While other students are finishing the 3B practice, ask these students to write additional sentences for 3C on the board. Correct them together as a class.

Evaluation
10–15 minutes

TEST YOURSELF

Direct students to take turns asking and answering the questions in complete sentences. Then have them switch partners and repeat two more times. Monitor and provide feedback.

> **MULTILEVEL STRATEGIES**
>
> Target the *Test Yourself* to the level of your students.
>
> • **Pre-level** Provide these students with sentence frames for answering the questions: *My birthday is ____. My classes are ____. My English class is ____.*

> **EXTENSION ACTIVITY**
>
> **Calendar Dictation**
>
> Provide more practice with days and times.
>
> 1. Give students a one-month calendar page. Write the words *party, clinic, library,* and *school* on the board. Tell students to listen to you and write the word and the time in the correct place on the calendar.
>
> 2. Say (for example): *The party is on Tuesday, June 3rd at 8:00. I go to the clinic on Wednesday, June 11th at 2:00. I go to the library on Fridays at 1:30. I go to school on Tuesday and Thursday at 9:00.* Stop after each sentence to allow students to write the word and time on the calendar. Circulate and monitor.
>
> 3. Copy the calendar on the board. Elicit and write the answers.

LESSON 4 EVERYDAY CONVERSATION

Lesson Overview

MULTILEVEL OBJECTIVES
On-, Pre- and Higher-level: Use appropriate language to say goodbye

LANGUAGE FOCUS
Grammar: Have (Have a nice weekend.)

Vocabulary: Days, first day of class, goodbye, holiday, last day of class, nice, registration, spring break

For vocabulary expansion, see these **Oxford Picture Dictionary** topics: The Calendar, pages 20–21; Time, pages 18–19

STRATEGY FOCUS
Use different expressions to say goodbye.

READINESS CONNECTION
In this lesson, students practice speaking so others can understand.

PACING
To compress this lesson: Skip the *Test Yourself*. Evaluate practice by monitoring 3D.

To extend this lesson: Discuss the school calendar. (See end of lesson.)

And/or have students complete **Workbook Introductory Level page 27** and **Multilevel Activities Introductory Level Unit 4 page 51**.

Lesson Notes

CORRELATIONS

CCRS: RF.2.A Demonstrate understanding of spoken words, syllables, and sounds (phonemes). g. Isolate and pronounce initial, medial vowel, and final sounds (phonemes) in spoken single-syllable words.

SL.1.A Participate in collaborative conversations with diverse partners in small and larger groups.

SL.2.A Confirm understanding of a text read aloud or information presented orally or through other media by asking and answering questions about key details and requesting clarification if something is not understood.

ELPS: 2. An ELL can participate in level-appropriate oral and written exchanges of information, ideas, and analyses, in various social and academic contexts, responding to peer, audience, or reader comments and questions.

Warm-up and Review
5 minutes (books closed)

Review times of day. Write *morning*, *afternoon*, *evening*, and *night* on the board. Pass out cards with times on them, for example, *6 a.m.*, *1 p.m.*, *5 p.m.*, *7 p.m.*, *11 p.m.* Ask students to place the cards in the correct column. Go over the results as a class, noting that some times could be placed in more than one column.

Introduction
5 minutes

1. Write your class ending time on the board and say: *Goodbye! Have a nice day!* (or *evening*) and walk out the door. See how students respond. Come back in.

2. State the objective: *Today we're going to read a school calendar and practice saying goodbye.*

1 Listen for important dates

Listening Extension
20–25 minutes

A 1. Ask students to read the calendar silently. Read the event words aloud, clarifying meaning as necessary. Read the *Need help?* box and ask students to name other holidays they know.

2. Play the audio and ask students to write the numbers/dates.

3. Replay the audio and ask students to check their work. Go over the answer as a class.

Answers
12/12th
18/18th
Mar. 31/31st
Jun. 20/20th

B 1. Read the first question and answer. Direct students to work independently to answer the questions.

2. Have students ask and answer the questions in pairs. Then go over the answers with the class.

Answers
1. January 10/10th
2. January 12/12th
3. March 27/27th
4. June 20/20th

TIP

After 1B, create a class work calendar for the month. Pass out blank monthly calendar pages (you can find them online) and have students fill in the month and numbers. Check the numbers by asking: *What day is the 23rd?*, etc. Dictate class information for students to write in the calendar, for example: *Friday the 8th—Unit 4 test. Monday the 5th—Unit 5.* Be sure that all of the words you want students to write are on the board for them to refer to.

2 Practice your pronunciation

Pronunciation Extension
10–15 minutes

A 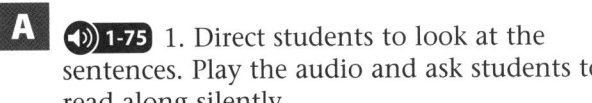 1. Direct students to look at the sentences. Play the audio and ask students to read along silently.

2. Show students your mouth position when you make the *t* sound and the *th* sound in *thanks*.

B Play the audio. Have students listen and repeat the words.

C 1. Play the audio. Direct students to work individually to complete the chart.

2. Circulate and monitor. If necessary, repeat the exercise.

3. Replay the audio. Ask students to repeat the words they hear.

Answers	1.	2.	3.	4.	5.	6.
t	✓		✓		✓	
th		✓		✓		✓

3 Make conversation: say goodbye

Presentation
5–10 minutes

A 1. Direct students to look at the pictures. Ask: *Where are they?* [work, school]

2. Have students read the conversations silently. Elicit any questions.

Guided Practice
5–10 minutes

B 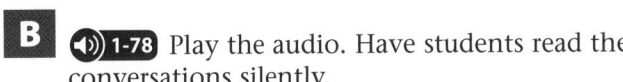 Play the audio. Have students read the conversations silently.

C 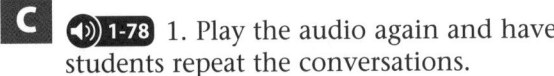 1. Play the audio again and have students repeat the conversations.

2. Do a choral reading of the conversations in 3B. Divide the class in half. Have one side be Arun and one side be Oscar, and then have the sides switch roles. Repeat with Mrs. Robledo and Tuan.

Communicative Practice and Application
15–20 minutes

 1. Model the conversation with a volunteer. Then switch roles and model it with another volunteer, using ideas from the *Need help?* box.

2. Elicit other ways to complete the conversation.

3. Set a time limit (five minutes). Ask students to practice the conversation with several partners. Encourage pantomime and improvisation.

4. Ask volunteer pairs to present their conversations to the class.

> **MULTILEVEL STRATEGIES**
>
> For 3D, seat pre-level students together.
> • **Pre-level** While other students are practicing the conversation, have these students complete page 44 in the *Literacy Reproducible Activities Unit 4*.

Evaluation
5 minutes

TEST YOURSELF

1. Elicit ways to say hello [Hi, Hello, Good morning, etc.] and write them on the board.

2. Set a time limit (three minutes). Have students walk around greeting each other and then saying goodbye. Encourage them to use different ways of greeting and saying goodbye.

> **EXTENSION ACTIVITY**
>
> **Discuss the Calendar**
>
> After *Test Yourself*, project or distribute copies of the school calendar. Using words they know, ask students to identify dates. For example: *When's the first day of registration? When's the first day of spring break? What date is the first holiday?*

LESSON 5 READING

Lesson Overview

MULTILEVEL OBJECTIVES

On- and Higher-level: Identify dates and read information on a job application

Pre-level: Recognize dates and read information on a job application

LANGUAGE FOCUS

Grammar: Dates with *from-to* (*from August 2009 to January 2014*)

Vocabulary: *Bakery, garage, hotel, restaurant*

For vocabulary expansion, see these **Oxford Picture Dictionary** topics: The Calendar, page 20–21; Numbers, page 16

STRATEGY FOCUS

Practice writing dates in the correct format on forms.

READINESS CONNECTION

In this lesson, students communicate information on job applications.

PACING

To compress this lesson: Assign 2B as homework or conduct it as a whole-class activity.

To extend this lesson: Do a numbers dictation. (See end of lesson.)

And/or have students complete **Workbook Introductory Level page 28** and **Multilevel Activities Introductory Level Unit 4 page 52.**

Lesson Notes

CORRELATIONS

CCRS: R.1.A Ask and answer questions about key details in the text.

R.7.A Use the illustrations and details in a text to describe its key ideas (e.g., maps, charts, photographs, political cartoons, etc.).

SL.2.A Confirm understanding of a text read aloud or information presented orally or through other media by asking and answering questions about key details and requesting clarification if something is not understood.

L.6.A Use words and phrases acquired through conversations, reading and being read to, and responding to texts, including using frequently occurring conjunctions to signal simple relationships (e.g., *because*).

ELPS: 8. An ELL can determine the meaning of words and phrases in oral presentations and literary and informational text.

Warm-up and Review
10–15 minutes (books closed)

Put up a one-month calendar. Say and have students repeat the numbers 1 to 31.

Introduction
5 minutes

1. Point to the first day of the month and say the date as numbers (for example, *ten-one-two thousand eighteen*) and then say it as a date: *October first, two thousand eighteen.*

2. State the objective: *Today we'll learn how to say dates and read a job application.*

1 Get ready to read

Presentation I
10–15 minutes

A 1-79 1. Say: *First, we're going to listen for years.*

2. Write the current year on the board and help students pronounce it. Do the same with 1990 or another possible birth year for your students.

3. Play the audio. Have students listen and repeat the years. Call on volunteers to say the years for the class.

B 1. Read the dates aloud, first as dates and then as numbers (*six-four-two thousand eighteen*).

2. Draw students' attention to the *Need help?* box and point out that in the United States, the month always comes first.

Guided Practice I
15–20 minutes

C 1-80 1. Play the audio in segments. After number 1, stop the audio and have students read the sample answer. Continue the audio, stopping after each date. Ask for a show of hands to see how students answered. Repeat the segment if necessary.

2. Call on volunteers to read the answers aloud. Write them on the board.

Answers	
1. b	5. b
2. a	6. a
3. b	7. b
4. b	8. a

D Have students practice pronouncing the dates in pairs. Tell them to say the month, not the number.

Presentation and Guided Practice II
10–15 minutes

E Direct students to look at the pictures. Say and have students repeat the words. Elicit the name of a well-known restaurant and hotel in your area.

F 1. Say and have students repeat the questions. Tell them to ask the students nearby.

2. Ask if anyone answered *yes* to one of the questions.

2 Read a job application

Guided Practice III
15–20 minutes

A 1. Direct students to look over the job application and identify the years.

2. Ask students to read the application silently. Ask if there are any questions about the reading.

3. Check students' comprehension. Ask: *What is MM?* [month] *What is YYYY?* [year] *Which job is in 2017?* [Best Hotel] Point out the order of the dates (most recent first).

B 1. Read number 1 aloud. Show students how to find the answer in the job application.

2. Direct students to work individually to complete the sentences.

3. Call on volunteers to read the completed sentences aloud.

Answers
1. August 2009, September 2012
2. November 2013, November 2014
3. September 2014, December 2014
4. June 2015, December 2017

C 1. Direct students to read the example. Elicit the dates [from February 1, 2017 to October 1, 2017]. Point out that the year is the same and the length of time is 8 months.

2. Give students a couple of minutes to figure out the length of time for the next two jobs. Have them share their answers with a partner. Encourage them to use the prepositions: *From October 30, 2015 to October 30, 2017 is two years.* Call on individuals to say the answers.

Answers
CB's Bakery: 8 months
Best Store: 2 years
Mike's Garage: 2 years, 3 months

MULTILEVEL STRATEGIES
Adapt 2C for your pre-level students.
• **Pre-level** While other students are completing 2C, help these students practice reading the dates on the job application.

Application

5–10 minutes

BRING IT TO LIFE

Give students several URLs for finding a job application. Tell them (or, if possible, show them how) to print only one page.

> **TIP**
>
> In preparation for *Teamwork & Language Review,* have students review the unit vocabulary. Provide them with pictures you have collected or use the Picture Cards on pages 53–54 of *Multilevel Activities Introductory Level Unit 4.* Pair students and have them use the pictures as flashcards for recognition practice, dictation, or sentence writing.

EXTENSION ACTIVITY

Numbers Dictation

1. Say the months (out of order) and have students write the corresponding number.

2. Call on volunteers to give the answers with the number and month.

TEAMWORK & LANGUAGE REVIEW

Lesson Overview

MULTILEVEL OBJECTIVES

On-, Pre-, and Higher-level: Expand upon and review unit language and content

LANGUAGE FOCUS

Grammar: *On* with days and *at* with times (*The party is on Friday at 8:00.*); information questions (*Where is the party?*)

Vocabulary: Months, days, calendar events

For vocabulary expansion, see these **Oxford Picture Dictionary** topics: The Calendar, pages 20–21; Time, pages 18–19

STRATEGY FOCUS

Use teamwork to reinforce and expand vocabulary.

READINESS CONNECTION

In this review, students practice teamwork and problem-solving skills by determining what to do when they're late.

PACING

To extend this review: Have students complete **Workbook Introductory Level page 29**, **Multilevel Activities Introductory Level Unit 4 pages 53–56**, and **Multilevel Grammar Exercises Introductory Level Unit 4**.

Lesson Notes

CORRELATIONS

CCRS: R.1.A Ask and answer questions about key details in the text.

R.7.A Use the illustrations and details in a text to describe its key ideas (e.g., maps, charts, photographs, political cartoons, etc.).

SL.1.A Participate in collaborative conversations with diverse partners in small and larger groups.

SL.4.A Describe people, places, things, and events with relevant details, expressing ideas and feelings clearly.

SL.6.A Speak audibly and express thoughts, feelings, and ideas clearly. Produce complete sentences when appropriate to task and situation.

L.1.A Demonstrate command of the conventions of standard English grammar usage when writing and speaking. k. Understand and use question words (interrogatives) (e.g., *who, what, where, when, why, how*).

ELPS: 2. An ELL can participate in level-appropriate oral and written exchanges of information, ideas, and analyses, in various social and academic contexts, responding to peer, audience, or reader comments and questions.

Warm-up and Review
5–10 minutes (books closed)

1. Review the *Bring It to Life* assignment from Lesson 5.

2. Ask students to show the job applications they brought. Ask other students to point out the employment history section of the applications.

Introduction and Presentation
5 minutes

1. Group students and direct them to focus on the calendar. Ask: *What do you see?*

2. State the objective: *Today we're going to review question words, times with* at, *and dates with* on.

Communicative Practice
15–20 minutes

A Call on students to say familiar words from the calendar.

B 1. Have students work in groups. Assign roles: secretary, reporter, editor, and manager. Write the roles on the board. As you explain each role, pantomime the duties you expect the person taking that role to perform. Explain that students work with their groups to complete the exercise, taking turns around the group. Verify comprehension of roles.

2. Set a time limit (five minutes) to complete the activity. Circulate and answer any questions.

3. Call on pairs from each group to share a question and answer. Write the answers on the board.

Answers	
1. February 19th	5. When is
2. 6:30 p.m.	6. What time is
3. Best Bakery	7. Where is
4. Yes, it is.	8. When is

MULTILEVEL STRATEGIES

For B, use mixed-level groups.

- **Pre-level** Assign these students the role of manager.
- **On-level** Assign these students the role of secretary or reporter.
- **Higher-level** Assign these students the role of editor.

C 1. Have students work with the same groups from 1B. Model the activity with one group.

2. Tell students to continue asking and answering questions around the group until they run out of ideas.

D 1. Read number 1 aloud. Tell students to work independently to complete the sentences.

2. Call on volunteers to read the completed sentences aloud. Write the answers on the board.

Answers
1. on February 2nd at 2 p.m.
2. on February 11th at 6:30 p.m.
3. on February 14th from 9 a.m. to 5 p.m.
4. on February 19th at 8 p.m.

E 1. Have students work independently to write two sentences.

2. Ask volunteers to write their sentences on the board. Correct them as a class.

PROBLEM SOLVING AT SCHOOL
15–20 minutes

A 🔊 1-81 1. Tell students the picture in A tells a story about a woman named Sharon. She has a problem with time.

2. Direct students to look at the pictures. Ask: *Where is she?* [at home] *When is registration day?* [Tuesday, September 3]

3. Play the audio and have students listen and look at the pictures. Check comprehension. Ask: *What time is it?* [10 a.m.] *What time is registration?* [from 8 a.m. to 10 a.m.]

B 1. Tell students to look at the pictures. Read the captions and pantomime the actions in the pictures.

2. Ask for a show of hands to see which solution the class likes best. Emphasize that there can be more than one correct answer.

Evaluation
20–25 minutes

To test students' understanding of the unit language and content, have them take the Unit 4 Test, available on the Teacher Resource Center.

TIP

Encourage students to reflect on what they have learned in this unit. Write these topics in a list on the board and elicit words, phrases, and sentences that students learned for each topic: *a) Days; b) Months; c) On and at; information questions; d) Saying goodbye; e) Ordinal numbers*. Congratulate students on their progress.

UNIT 5
How Much Is It?

Unit Overview

This unit explores shopping, money, prices, and methods of payments.

KEY OBJECTIVES	
Lesson 1	Identify coins and currency
Lesson 2	Identify common articles of clothing; interpret price tags; describe shopping experiences
Lesson 3	Use demonstrative pronouns to talk about prices
Lesson 4	Discuss prices
Lesson 5	Identify methods of payment
Teamwork & Language Review	Review unit language

UNIT FEATURES	
Academic Vocabulary	*credit card, percent*
Employability Skills	• Use math to solve problems and communicate • Understand teamwork • Communicate information • Work with others • Communicate verbally • Interpret price tags • Decide what to do when short on cash

Resources	**Class Audio** CD2, Tracks 02–20
	Workbook Unit 5, pages 30–36
	Teacher Resource Center
	    Literacy Reproducible Activities Unit 5
	    Multilevel Activities Introductory Level Unit 5
	    Multilevel Grammar Exercises Introductory Level Unit 5
	    Unit 5 Test
	Oxford Picture Dictionary Money, Everyday Clothes, A Classroom, Shopping, A Bathroom

LESSON 1 VOCABULARY

Lesson Overview	Lesson Notes
MULTILEVEL OBJECTIVES	
On-level: Identify words for money **Pre-level:** Recognize words for money **Higher-level:** Talk about money	
LANGUAGE FOCUS	
Grammar: The verb *be* (*It's $5.*) **Vocabulary:** *Bills, cents, coins, dime, dollar, nickel, penny, quarter* For vocabulary expansion, see this **Oxford Picture Dictionary** topic: Money, page 26	
STRATEGY FOCUS	
Recognize different ways of writing prices.	
READINESS CONNECTION	
In this lesson, students communicate verbally about money.	
PACING	
To compress this lesson: Conduct 2A as a whole-class activity. **To extend this lesson:** Practice with fake money. (See end of lesson.) And/or have students complete **Workbook Introductory Level page 30** and **Multilevel Activities Introductory Level Unit 5 page 58.**	
CORRELATIONS	
CCRS: SL.2.A Confirm understanding of a text read aloud or information presented orally or through other media by asking and answering questions about key details and requesting clarification if something is not understood. L.6.A Use words and phrases acquired through conversations, reading and being read to, and responding to texts, including using frequently occurring conjunctions to signal simple relationships (e.g., *because*).	**ELPS:** 9. An ELL can create clear and coherent level-appropriate speech and text.

Warm-up and Review
10–15 minutes (books closed)

Review high numbers. Write *10, 20, 30*, etc., up to *100* on the board. Count by tens and have students repeat. Then write high numbers (*68, 75, 99*) and elicit them from volunteers. Have the class repeat.

Introduction
5 minutes

1. Show students various amounts of money and name the quantities. *Sixty-five cents. Ten dollars.*

2. State the objective: *Today we'll learn words for money.*

1 Learn words for money

Presentation
20–25 minutes

A Direct students to look at the pictures. Ask them to count the money [$36.00, $1.41].

B 🔊 2-02 1. Play the audio. Ask students to point to the correct picture as they listen. Circulate and monitor.

2. Check comprehension by asking *yes/no* questions. Have students use thumbs up (*yes*) or thumbs down (*no*) to respond. Point to each picture and ask, for example: *Is it a nickel? Is it 10 cents?*

C 🔊 2-02 1. Tell students to listen and repeat the words.

2. Write *quarter* on the board and help students pronounce the first syllable and then the word.

3. Call out the numbers out of order and ask students to say the words.

4. Point out how the prices are written. Write *75* on the board. Elicit how to write $75.00. Then elicit both ways to write 75 cents [$0.75 and 75¢].

Guided Practice I
10–15 minutes

D Direct students to take turns reading the words with a partner.

E 1. Model the activity with two volunteers. Direct one partner to point to the pictures or say the numbers. Have the other partner cover the words in 1C and identify the pictures from memory.

2. Have students practice in pairs.

> **MULTILEVEL STRATEGIES**
>
> For 1E, pair same-level students together.
> - **Pre-level** Tell these students to practice together by pointing to the pictures in 1B and saying the correct words.
> - **Higher-level** Tell these students to dictate the words to each other.

> **TIP**
>
> After 1E, direct students to take out their coins and say what they have. *One penny, three dimes, two quarters.* Find out who is carrying the most of each coin.

2 Talk about money

Guided Practice II
20–25 minutes

A 1. Direct students to look at the picture. Call out denominations and ask students to identify the correct number.

2. Copy number 1 on the board and have students spell *penny* aloud. Demonstrate how to write one letter on each line.

3. Tell students to work individually to complete the words.

4. Ask volunteers to spell the completed words aloud. Write the answers on the board. Read and have students repeat the words.

Answers	
1. p-e-n-n-y	5. c-o-i-n-s
2. d-i-m-e	6. n-i-c-k-e-l
3. b-i-l-l-s	7. q-u-a-r-t-e-r
4. d-o-l-l-a-r	8. c-e-n-t-s

B Give students time to copy the words into their notebooks. Monitor and check their writing.

C 🔊 2-03 1. Read number 1 *a* and *b* aloud. Play the audio and ask students which price they heard.

2. Play the rest of the audio in segments. Tell students to listen and circle *a* or *b*. After each number, ask for a show of hands to find out how students answered. If necessary, repeat the segment.

3. Call on volunteers for the answers and write them on the board.

Answers	
1. b	4. b
2. a	5. a
3. a	6. a

D 🔊 2-04 1. Play the audio. Have students read along silently.

2. Play the audio again. Tell students to listen and repeat.

> **TIP**
> After 2D, provide more practice listening for prices. Put up pictures of classroom items (book, paper, pencil, pen, notebook, binder, eraser, clock) with prices on them. Pass out *yes/no* cards and make statements about the pictures. *The book is $5. The clock is $17.* Have students hold up the cards.

Communicative Practice and Application
10–15 minutes

 1. Model the conversations with a volunteer. Show students how to use the pictures in 2A. Switch roles and model the conversations with another volunteer.

2. Pair students. Have one pair model the conversation.

3. Set a time limit (five minutes) and have the partners practice the conversation in both roles. Encourage students to use all of the words. Circulate and monitor. Provide feedback.

Evaluation
10–15 minutes

TEST YOURSELF

1. Model the activity with a volunteer.

2. Have students work in pairs to take turns asking and answering the questions. Monitor and provide feedback.

> **MULTILEVEL STRATEGIES**
>
> Target the *Test Yourself* to the level of your students.
>
> • **Pre-level** Display or distribute to these students four pictures of money listed in 1C. Have students open their books to page 60, identify the correct words to match the pictures, and copy them.
>
> • **Higher-level** After they ask and answer the questions, direct these students to write as many of the words as they can remember.

> **EXTENSION ACTIVITY**
>
> **Count Money**
>
> Pass out fake money to pairs of students. Call out different amounts and have students count those amounts out. Alternate amounts with kinds of coins, for example: 1. two dollars and 75 cents, 2. two nickels and a dime, etc. Circulate and monitor.

Lesson Plans Intro

LESSON 2 WRITING

Lesson Overview	Lesson Notes
MULTILEVEL OBJECTIVES	
On- and Higher-level: Read and write about shopping **Pre-level:** Recognize shopping words	
LANGUAGE FOCUS	
Grammar: The verb *be (The prices are low.)* **Vocabulary:** *Cheap, clothes, expensive, friendly, high, jacket, low, pants, price, shirt, shoes, socks, sweater* For vocabulary expansion, see these **Oxford Picture Dictionary** topics: Everyday Clothes, pages 86–87; Shopping, page 27	
STRATEGY FOCUS	
Use capital letters for names of places.	
READINESS CONNECTION	
In this lesson, students interpret price tags and communicate information related to shopping.	
PACING	
To compress this lesson: Assign the *Test Yourself* for homework. **To extend this lesson:** Practice with clothing pictures. (See end of lesson.) And/or have students complete **Workbook Introductory Level page 31** and **Multilevel Activities Introductory Level Unit 5 page 59.**	
CORRELATIONS	
CCRS: L.6.A Use words and phrases acquired through conversations, reading and being read to, and responding to texts, including using frequently occurring conjunctions to signal simple relationships (e.g., *because*). SL.2.A Confirm understanding of a text read aloud or information presented orally or through other media by asking and answering questions about key details and requesting clarification if something is not understood.	**ELPS:** 1. An ELL can construct meaning from oral presentations and literary and informational text through level-appropriate listening, reading, and viewing. 9. An ELL can create clear and coherent level-appropriate speech and text.

Warm-up and Review
10–15 minutes (books closed)

Draw or write the following on large cards: a dollar sign, a cent sign, a decimal, two zeros, a single zero, and several numbers. Arrange them to show various prices, and then say and have students repeat the prices. Call out prices and have volunteers arrange the cards in the correct order.

Introduction
5 minutes

1. Show students a large department store ad and talk about some of the prices. *These pants are $42. They're not cheap! This shirt is $199. It's expensive!*

2. State the objective: *Today we're going to read and write about shopping.*

1 Learn about shopping

Presentation I
15–20 minutes

A Direct students to look at the picture. Ask students to point to the numbers. Say and have students repeat *$165.99*. Ask: *Where is Daniela?* [at Clothes Mart]

B 🔊 2-05 1. Play the audio. Have students read along silently.

2. Check comprehension. Direct students to cover the words and look at the picture. Say the words out of order and have students call out the correct numbers. Then say the numbers and have students call out the words.

3. Replay the audio and ask students to repeat the words.

4. Point to students' clothing (jacket, shirt, sweater, pants, socks, and shoes) and elicit the words. Point to the items on the board from the warm-up and ask: *Is it/Are they cheap or expensive?*

Guided Practice I
5–10 minutes

C 1. Read number 1 aloud. Direct students to look at number 2 and then find $32 in the picture. Elicit the answer.

2. Have students work independently to complete the activity. Ask them to read their completed sentences to a partner.

Answers	
1. clothes	5. cheap
2. sweater	6. pants
3. socks	7. shirts
4. price	8. shoes, expensive

2 Prepare to write: shopping

Presentation II
25–30 minutes

A 🔊 2-06 1. Direct students to look at the pictures. Ask: *How much are the sweaters at the two stores?* [$15 and $90]

2. Play the audio. Have students read along silently.

3. Check comprehension. Ask students to point to the clerk in the pictures. Use facial expressions and gestures, and have them call out *friendly* or *not friendly*. Point to the high-heeled shoes in the picture in 1A. Ask: *Is this price low or high?* [high]

4. Finally, ask students where they want to shop. Have students hold up one finger for the first shop and two fingers for the second shop.

B 🔊 2-07 1. Play the audio. Have students read along silently.

2. Check comprehension. Direct students to cover the words and look at the pictures. Say: *Point to the friendly clerks. Point to the clerks who aren't friendly. Is $150 a high price or a low price for a shirt?* [high] *Is $15 a high price or low price for a sweater?* [low]

3. Replay the audio and ask students to repeat the words.

C 🔊 2-08 1. Play the audio. Have students read along silently.

2. Check comprehension. Ask: *Where does Daniela shop?* [at Clothes Mart] *Why does Daniela like Clothes Mart?* [The clerks are friendly. The clothes are good. The prices are low.]

3. Direct students' attention to the *Writer's Note*. Elicit some names of popular stores in your area. Write the names on the board and underline the capital letters.

> **MULTILEVEL STRATEGIES**
>
> For 2C, seat students in mixed-level groups. After the whole-group practice, ask students to take turns reading the sentences aloud. Demonstrate turn-taking, with the first student reading number 1, the second number 2, and so on.
>
> • **Pre-level** Tell students who don't want to read aloud to listen to their classmates and follow along silently.

Guided Practice II
10–15 minutes

D 🔊 2-09 1. Direct students to look at the picture. Say and have them repeat *Ken*. Read the instructions aloud.

2. Play number 1 and elicit the answer. Play the rest of the audio and ask students to circle the correct word.

3. Replay the entire audio so students can check their work. Call on volunteers to read the completed sentences aloud.

Answers
1. b
2. a
3. b
4. b

3 Write about shopping

Communicative Practice
10–15 minutes

A 1. Introduce the new activity: *Now you are going to write about shopping.*

2. Call on volunteers to complete the sentences aloud.

3. Tell students to work individually to complete the sentences with their own information. Remind them to capitalize the name of the store.

B Ask students to read their sentences aloud to a partner. When they finish, ask them to read the sentences to a new partner.

> **MULTILEVEL STRATEGIES**
>
> Adapt 3A and 3B to the level of your students.
>
> • **Pre-level** While on- and higher-level students are completing 3A and 3B, work with these students in a group, or have them complete page 48 of the *Literacy Reproducible Activities Unit 5*.

▶ AT WORK

Calculate sale prices

10–15 minutes

A 1. Direct students to look at the picture. Ask them to say the names of the items and the prices. Say and have students repeat the word *lamp*.

2. Read the words *Everything 50% off.* Show students that *everything* refers to all of the items in the picture.

3. Demonstrate *50% off* using fake money. For example, start with two $10 bills. Then take one away to show 50%. Point out the *Need help?* note to reiterate that fifty percent equals one half.

4. Write some sample problems on the board: *$100 × 0.5 = $50. $60 × 0.5 = $30.*

B 1. Read number 1 aloud. Direct students to work individually to do the math.

2. Go over the answers as a class. Ask volunteers to show the problem using fake money.

Answers
1. 0.25, 0.25
2. 0.50, 0.50
3. 1.25, 1.25
4. 15.00, 15.00

Evaluation
10 minutes

TEST YOURSELF

1. Copy the sentence frames on the board. Ask students for example answers.

2. Have students copy the frames into their notebooks and complete them.

3. Collect and correct students' work.

> **EXTENSION ACTIVITY**
>
> **Clothing Pictures**
>
> Put up pictures of clothing items with prices. Ask students to make statements about the items: *The socks are cheap. They're 50¢. The shirt is expensive. It's $85.*

LESSON 3 GRAMMAR

Lesson Overview	Lesson Notes
MULTILEVEL OBJECTIVES	
On- and Higher-level: Use *this*, *that*, *these*, and *those* **Pre-level:** Recognize *this*, *that*, *these*, and *those*	
LANGUAGE FOCUS	
Grammar: *This*, *that*, *these*, and *those* (*Those shoes are expensive.*) **Vocabulary:** Clothes, classroom items, bathroom items For vocabulary expansion, see these **Oxford Picture Dictionary** topics: Everyday Clothes, pages 86–87; A Classroom, pages 6–7; A Bathroom, page 57	
STRATEGY FOCUS	
To ask and answer questions about prices, you can use the demonstratives *this*, *that*, *these*, and *those* to refer to specific items.	
READINESS CONNECTION	
In this lesson, students communicate verbally about prices.	
PACING	
To compress this lesson: Conduct 1D as a whole-class activity. Assign the *Test Yourself* for homework. **To extend this lesson:** Practice with classroom items. (See end of lesson.) And/or have students complete **Workbook Introductory Level pages 32–33**, **Multilevel Activities Introductory Level Unit 5 page 60**, and **Multilevel Grammar Exercises Introductory Level Unit 5**.	
CORRELATIONS	
CCRS: L.1.A Demonstrate command of the conventions of standard English grammar and usage when writing or speaking. i. Use determiners (e.g., articles, demonstratives). SL.3.A Ask and answer questions in order to seek help, get information, or clarify something that is not understood.	**ELPS:** 10. An ELL can demonstrate command of the conventions of standard English to communicate in level-appropriate speech and writing.

Warm-up and Review
10–15 minutes (books closed)

Put up or draw pictures of a shirt, a sweater, socks, shoes, a book, an eraser, a box of pencils, and a chair. Elicit the names of the items. Then say prices for the items and ask volunteers to come up and write the prices on the correct items.

Introduction
5–10 minutes

1. Make *this*, *that*, *these*, and *those* statements about the pictures, touching the nearby ones and pointing to farther ones to emphasize the meaning.

2. State the objective: *Today we're going to learn* this, that, these, *and* those. Take down the plural items and say: *We're going to start with* this *and* that.

1 Use *This* and *That*

Presentation I
20–25 minutes

A Direct students to look at the pictures. Ask: *Where is the man?* [at a store] Ask them how many shirts they see [five: the one the man is wearing, the yellow one in his hand, the green one in his hand, the blue one on the wall, and the white one on the wall].

B 🔊 2-10 1. Play the audio. Tell students to listen and repeat the sentences.

2. Use gestures to demonstrate the difference between *this* and *that*.

C 1. Ask students to demonstrate the meaning of *that* by pointing.

2. Check comprehension. Hold a book and say: *This book or that book?* Point to a book far away and say: *This book or that book?*

> **TIP**
> After 1C, work on the recognition and pronunciation of the *th* sound in *this* and *that*. Show or draw students a diagram illustrating the mouth position. Write *1. d* and *2. th* on the board. Say words beginning with each of the sounds and ask students to hold up one or two fingers to indicate which sound they heard. Possible words: *dish, this, day, they, dare, there, Dan, than.*

Guided Practice I
15–20 minutes

D 1. Direct students to look at the pictures. Elicit what they see.

2. Tell students to work individually to complete the sentences and then read the sentences with a partner.

3. Call on volunteers to read the completed sentences aloud. Write the answers on the board.

Answers
1. a
2. b
3. a
4. b

2 Use *These* and *Those*

Presentation II
10–15 minutes

A 🔊 2-11 1. Direct students to look at the pictures. Ask: *Are the pants cheap or expensive?* [cheap (on the left), expensive (on the right)] *Is the woman in the purple shirt happy?* [no (on the left), yes (on the right)]

2. Play the audio. Tell students to listen and repeat the sentences.

3. Point at items in the room or pictures and make statements to demonstrate the difference between *these* and *those*. Write: *These pencils, those pencils; these books, those books; these chairs, those chairs* on the board. Ask volunteers to point at nearby and far items and say the appropriate phrase.

Guided Practice II
10–15 minutes

B 1. Read sentence number 1 aloud. Have students look at picture *b*. Elicit what they see. [Responses might include the following: green pants, price tag, salesperson/clerk, bags, shoes, black belt.]

2. Tell students to work individually to match the pictures with the sentences. Call on volunteers for the answers. Write them on the board.

3. Post or draw pictures of plural items (socks, shoes, pencils, books) and ask volunteers to make statements about the pictures.

Answers
1. b
2. a
3. e
4. f
5. c
6. d

C 1. Add pictures of singular items to the plural ones you have already posted. Point at the pictures and make statements with *this, that, these,* and *those* to illustrate the difference.

2. Direct students to read number 1. Elicit the reason for the answer. [There is only one pencil.] Tell students to work individually to complete the sentences.

3. Call on volunteers to read the completed sentences aloud. Write the answers on the board.

Answers
1. a
2. b
3. a
4. b
5. b
6. a

MULTILEVEL STRATEGIES

Adapt 2B and 2C for your pre-level students.

• **Pre-level** Provide these students with the answers to the exercises and have them practice reading the sentences to each other, or have them complete page 49 of the *Literacy Reproducible Activities Unit 5*.

D 1. Have students work with a partner to read the sentences in 2B and 2C. When they finish, ask them to look around the room and make statements about the things they see using *this, that, these,* and *those*.

2. Call on volunteers to share their sentences with the class.

3 Talk about prices

Presentation III
10–15 minutes

A 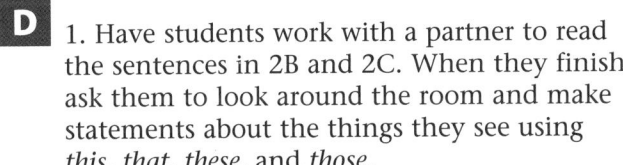 1. Direct students' attention to the pictures. Ask them if the items are expensive or cheap.

2. Play the audio. Have students repeat the words.

3. Check comprehension. Ask about the item prices out of order: *How much are the combs?* [$5.95]

Communicative Practice
15–20 minutes

B 1. Model the activity with a volunteer using the example and then making a substitution.

2. Have students practice asking and answering the questions in pairs. Emphasize that they should point at the pictures in their own books to emphasize *this* and *these*.

3. Call on pairs to say questions and answers for the class.

C 1. Model the activity with a volunteer. Demonstrate that students should point to the pictures in their partner's book to emphasize *that* and *those*.

2. Have students practice asking and answering the questions in pairs. Call on pairs to say questions and answers for the class.

D 1. Read the example sentence. Elicit a plural sentence from the class.

2. Have students work independently to write sentences about the pictures in 3A. Ask volunteers to write one of their sentences on the board.

Evaluation
10–15 minutes

TEST YOURSELF

1. Direct students to look at the pictures on page 62, 1A. Ask them to work independently to write sentences.

2. Collect and correct their work.

MULTILEVEL STRATEGIES

Target the *Test Yourself* to the level of your students.

• **Pre-level** Provide these students with sentence frames:

_____ *book is expensive.*

_____ *shoes are cheap.*

Ask students to complete the frames with *this, that, these,* or *those*.

• **Higher-level** In addition to the three sentences, ask these students to write a singular and plural question and answer for the picture on page 62.

EXTENSION ACTIVITY

Classroom Item Practice

Provide more practice after 2D. Give each student a classroom item or a piece of clothing (pictures or real items). Have the group stand in a circle and hold their pictures/items up so that everyone can see them. (If you have a large class, set them up in two or three circles and move from one to the other to monitor.) Direct students to make a statement about the item they are holding, using *this* or *these,* and an item someone else is holding, using *that* or *those*. Have them go around the circle once, with everyone making two statements.

LESSON 4 EVERYDAY CONVERSATION

Lesson Overview

MULTILEVEL OBJECTIVES

On- and Higher-level: Ask and respond to questions about prices

Pre-level: Respond to questions about prices

LANGUAGE FOCUS

Grammar: The verb *be* (It's $35.)

Vocabulary: Clothing, classroom items

For vocabulary expansion, see these **Oxford Picture Dictionary** topics: Money, page 26; Everyday Clothes, pages 86–87; Shopping, page 27

STRATEGY FOCUS

After asking about the price of one item, you can ask for the price of a second item using the phrase *How about…?*

READINESS CONNECTION

In this lesson, students work with others and communicate verbally about prices.

PACING

To compress this lesson: Conduct 1A–C as whole-class activities.

To extend this lesson: Set up a classroom store. (See end of lesson.)

And/or have students complete **Workbook Introductory Level page 34** and **Multilevel Activities Introductory Level page 61.**

Lesson Notes

CORRELATIONS

CCRS: RF.2.A Demonstrate understanding of spoken words, syllables, and sounds (phonemes). g. Isolate and pronounce initial, medial vowel, and final sounds (phonemes) in spoken single-syllable words.

SL.1.A Participate in collaborative conversations with diverse partners in small and larger groups.

SL.2.A Confirm understanding of a text read aloud or information presented orally or through other media by asking and answering questions about key details and requesting clarification if something is not understood.

ELPS: 2. An ELL can participate in level-appropriate oral and written exchanges of information, ideas, and analyses, in various social and academic contexts, responding to peer, audience, or reader comments and questions.

Warm-up and Review
5 minutes (books closed)

Review *is* and *are*. Write a series of sentences with blanks on the board: *The _____ is 35¢. The _____ are $45*, etc. Pass out cards with clothing and classroom item words written on them (the same number of cards as sentences). Ask students to consult with a partner and then place the card in a sentence where they think it makes sense. Read the sentences together and discuss whether the sentence is grammatically correct and logical.

Introduction
5 minutes

1. Ask students their opinions of the prices on the board: *Is it cheap or expensive?*

2. State the objective: *Today we'll learn to talk about prices. To begin, we're going to listen for change amounts.*

1 Listen for amounts

Listening Extension
20–25 minutes

A Direct students to look at the pictures in 1B. Ask them to name the coins and say some of the amounts in the pictures [1. a. $0.45, b. $0.35; 2. a. $0.07, b. $0.06; 3. a. $0.25, b. $0.07; 4. a. $0.21, b. $0.25; 5. a. $1.10, b. $1.05; 6. a. $6.00, b. $7.00].

B 🔊 **2-13** 1. Play the entire audio once. Ask students to circle *a* or *b*.

2. Play the audio again in segments. Ask for a show of hands to see how students answered. Repeat the segment if necessary.

3. Call on volunteers for the answers. Write them on the board.

Answers
1. b
2. a
3. a
4. a
5. a
6. b

MULTILEVEL STRATEGIES

Replay 2B to allow pre-level students to catch up while you provide a challenge for higher-level students.

- **Pre-level** Have these students listen again to circle the answers.
- **On- and Higher-level** Ask these students to listen and write the amounts they hear. Challenge them to write the words as well as the numerals.

2 Practice your pronunciation

Pronunciation Extension
10–15 minutes

A 🔊 **2-14** 1. Say: *Now we're going to practice the pronunciation of* s *and* sh *sounds.* Play the audio. Direct students to read and listen to the words.

2. Say some of the words in the box and ask students to hold up one finger for *s* and two fingers for *sh*. Repeat as necessary.

B 🔊 **2-15** Play the audio. Ask students to listen and check the sounds they hear. Go over the answers as a class.

Answers	1.	2.	3.	4.	5.
s	✓		✓		✓
sh		✓		✓	

C 🔊 **2-15** Replay the audio and ask students to repeat the words.

3 Make conversation: talk about prices

Presentation
5–10 minutes

A 1. Direct students to look at the pictures. Ask: *Is the shirt expensive?* [yes] *Are the shoes expensive?* [no]

2. Direct students to read the conversation silently. Elicit any questions.

B 🔊 **2-16** Play the audio. Have students read the conversation silently.

Guided Practice
5–10 minutes

C 🔊 **2-16** 1. Play the audio again and have students repeat the conversation.

2. Do a choral reading of the conversation in 3B. Divide the class in half. Have one side be George and one side be Kumi, and then have the sides switch roles.

Communicative Practice and Application
15–20 minutes

D 1. Model the conversation with a volunteer. Then switch roles and model it with another volunteer, using ideas from the *Need help?* box.

2. Elicit other ways to complete the conversation.

3. Set a time limit (five minutes). Ask students to practice the conversation with several partners. Encourage pantomime and improvisation.

4. Ask volunteer pairs to present their conversations to the class.

> **MULTILEVEL STRATEGIES**
>
> For 3D, adapt the practice to the level of your students.
>
> • **Pre-level** While other students are practicing the conversation, have these students complete page 50 in the *Literacy Reproducible Activities Unit 5*.
>
> • **Higher-level** Encourage these students to practice with several partners.

Evaluation
5 minutes

TEST YOURSELF

Set a time limit (three minutes). Have students walk around the class asking and responding to the questions.

> **EXTENSION ACTIVITY**
>
> **Classroom Store**
>
> 1. Set up a store at the front of the room. Put prices on items.
>
> 2. Appoint a few students to be clerks and have others stand in line to be customers.
>
> 3. Instruct the "customers" to stand in line and take turns inquiring about the prices of the items.
>
> 4. After the clerks have talked to a few customers, appoint other students to be the clerks.

LESSON 5 READING

Lesson Overview

MULTILEVEL OBJECTIVES
On- and Higher-level: Identify and read about ways to pay
Pre-level: Recognize ways to pay

LANGUAGE FOCUS
Grammar: The verb *be* (*My gas bill is expensive.*)
Vocabulary: *Bill, cash, check, credit card, debit card, electric, gas, money order, pay*
For vocabulary expansion, see this **Oxford Picture Dictionary** topic: Money, page 26

STRATEGY FOCUS
Interpret a pie chart.

READINESS CONNECTION
In this lesson, students use math to solve problems and communicate.

PACING
To compress this lesson: Assign 2C as homework or conduct it as a whole-class activity.
To extend this lesson: Make a pie chart. (See end of lesson.)
And/or have students complete **Workbook Introductory Level page 35** and **Multilevel Activities Introductory Level Unit 5 page 62.**

Lesson Notes

CORRELATIONS

CCRS: L.6.A Use words and phrases acquired through conversations, reading and being read to, and responding to texts, including using frequently occurring conjunctions to signal simple relationships (e.g., *because*).
R.1.A Ask and answer questions about key details in the text.
R.7.A Use the illustrations and details in a text to describe its key ideas (e.g., maps, charts, photographs, political cartoons, etc.).

ELPS: 8. An ELL can determine the meaning of words and phrases in oral presentations and literary and informational text.

Warm-up and Review
10–15 minutes (books closed)

Review bills and coins. Display pictures of various bills and coins. Elicit their names. Draw or show pictures of a refrigerator, a sofa, a car, and a utility bill. Ask students if most people use coins and bills to pay for these things [no].

Introduction
5 minutes

1. Say: *Bills and coins are called cash.* Elicit other ways to pay.

2. State the objective: *Today we'll learn about other ways to pay.*

1 Get ready to read

Presentation
10–15 minutes

 2-17 1. Tell students to look at the pictures and listen to the words. Play the audio.

2. Check comprehension of the words. Show real examples of a check, a credit card, a debit card, and (if possible) a pre-paid card. Ask students to identify them.

3. Replay the audio and tell students to listen and repeat.

Guided Practice I
10–15 minutes

 2-18 1. Direct students to look at the pictures and say the words. Play the audio. Tell students to work individually to circle *a* or *b*.

2. Call on volunteers for the answers. Write them on the board.

3. Have students practice the words with a partner. Direct them to take turns pointing to the pictures in 1B and saying the words. Review by pointing to the pictures and asking *or* questions: *Cash or credit? Credit or debit? Check or pre-paid card?*

Answers
1. b
2. b
3. a
4. a
5. b
6. b

 1. Use gestures to remind students of the meaning of *high* and *low*.

2. Have students work independently to complete the sentences. Ask them to read their completed sentences with a partner. Call on volunteers to read a sentence aloud.

2 Read about ways to pay

Guided Practice II
15–20 minutes

 1. Direct students' attention to the *Reading Note*. If possible, show them a picture of a real pie. Have them repeat the percentages.

2. Have them look at the pie chart in the reading. Ask: *How many people pay with checks?* [15%]

3. Give students a couple of minutes to read the sentences and look at the pie chart.

B **2-19** Play the audio and have students read along silently.

C 1. Read number 1. Show students how to find the word *stores* in the reading. Tell them to read the sentence and then elicit the answer to the question.

2. Repeat this procedure for each item. For number 2, have them find the word *bills* in the text. For 3 and 4, show them how to find the answers in the pie chart.

Answers
1. a
2. b
3. b
4. a

MULTILEVEL STRATEGIES
• **Pre-level** While other students are completing 2C, work with these students on reading the pie chart. Ask questions about the percentages: *How many people use pre-paid cards?* [7%]

Application
5–10 minutes

BRING IT TO LIFE

Direct students to look at the picture of the electric bill with one word circled. Read the directions aloud.

> **TIP**
>
> In preparation for *Teamwork & Language Review,* have students review the unit vocabulary. Provide them with pictures you have collected or use the Picture Cards on pages 63–64 of *Multilevel Activities Introductory Level Unit 5.* Pair students and have them use the pictures as flashcards for recognition practice, dictation, or sentence writing.

EXTENSION ACTIVITY

Pie Chart

1. Provide more practice with pie charts by creating one on the board using information about the students. Choose a method for dividing the class into three groups, but be careful to avoid anything students might feel is private information. For example, divide the class according to how many students are wearing a sweater, a jacket, or neither, or divide them by how many are wearing black pants, blue pants, or something else.

2. Write the number of students on the board. Draw a circle on the board and say: *This is the whole class. This is 100% of the class.*

3. Ask students to stand and move to different parts of the room according to which group they are in. Have each group report its number and write those numbers on the board. Draw a wildly inaccurate division of the circle (for example, evenly divided in thirds) and ask students if it's right. Explain that you need the numbers to make the pie chart look right.

4. Show students how to find the percentage by dividing the number in the group by the total number of students. (Have a student with a smartphone find the percentages for you.) Then have the class guide you in dividing the circle to make a pie chart.

TEAMWORK & LANGUAGE REVIEW

Lesson Overview

MULTILEVEL OBJECTIVES

On-, Pre-, and Higher-level: Expand upon and review unit language and content

LANGUAGE FOCUS

Grammar: *This, that, these,* and *those (This shirt is expensive.)*

Vocabulary: Clothing and classroom items

For vocabulary expansion, see these **Oxford Picture Dictionary** topics: Money, page 26; Everyday Clothes, pages 86–87; Shopping, page 27

STRATEGY FOCUS

Use teamwork to reinforce and expand vocabulary.

READINESS CONNECTION

In this review, students practice teamwork and decide what to do when they are short on cash.

PACING

To extend this review: Have students complete **Workbook Introductory Level page 36**, **Multilevel Activities Introductory Level Unit 5 pages 63–66**, and **Multilevel Grammar Exercises Introductory Level Unit 5**.

CORRELATIONS

CCRS: R.7.A Use the illustrations and details in a text to describe its key ideas (e.g., maps, charts, photographs, political cartoons, etc.).

SL.1.A Participate in collaborative conversations with diverse partners in small and larger groups.

SL.4.A Describe people, places, things, and events with relevant details, expressing ideas and feelings clearly.

SL.6.A Speak audibly and express thoughts, feelings, and ideas clearly. Produce complete sentences when appropriate to task and situation.

ELPS: 2. An ELL can participate in level-appropriate oral and written exchanges of information, ideas, and analyses, in various social and academic contexts, responding to peer, audience, or reader comments and questions.

Lesson Notes

Warm-up and Review
5–10 minutes (books closed)

1. Review the *Bring It to Life* assignment from Lesson 5.

2. Ask students what bill they looked at. Ask them if they mind sharing the amount of the bill. Invite them to show the bill to the class if they brought it.

3. Call on other students and ask: *Is that cheap or expensive?*

Introduction and Presentation
5 minutes

1. Ask: *How about clothes? Are clothes cheap or expensive?*

2. State the objective: *Today we're going to review the words and grammar from Unit 5.*

Communicative Practice
15–20 minutes

A 1. Tell students to take turns naming one thing they see in the picture. Have three volunteers help you model turn-taking.

2. Tell students to put their pencils down and listen to each other so that they don't repeat ideas. Direct them to go around the group until they have run out of ideas.

B 1. Have students work in the same groups from A. Assign roles: secretary, reporter, editor, and manager. Write the roles on the board. As you explain each role, pantomime the duties you expect the person taking that role to perform. Explain that students work with their groups to write the words. Verify comprehension of the roles.

2. Set a time limit (five minutes) to complete the chart. Circulate and answer any questions.

3. Call on the reporters from each group to say the words from their chart. Write the words on the board. Go around the class until there are no more ideas.

Possible Answers		
Clothes	**People**	**Other**
shirt	man	brush
sweater	woman	comb
shoes	clerk	table
jacket	customer	credit card
socks		cash
		price
		sale

C 1. Have the groups identify new words from the board and to look them up in a picture dictionary or a bilingual dictionary.

2. Tell students to add three new words to their chart. [New words might include: *sign, price tag, counter, hanger.*]

> **MULTILEVEL STRATEGIES**
>
> For A–C, use mixed-level groups.
>
> • **Pre-level** Assign these students the role of manager.
>
> • **On-level** Assign these students the role of secretary or reporter.
>
> • **Higher-level** Assign these students the role of editor.

D Model the activity. Have students talk about the picture with a partner. Circulate and provide feedback.

E 1. Read number 1 aloud. Tell students to work independently to complete the questions and answers.

2. Call on volunteers to read the completed sentences aloud. Write the answers on the board.

Answers
1. much
2. prices
3. expensive
4. on sale
5. is
6. friendly

F 1. Have students work independently to write two sentences.

2. Ask volunteers to write their sentences on the board. Correct them as a class.

PROBLEM SOLVING
15–20 minutes

A 🔊 2-20 1. Tell students the pictures in A tell a story about a man named Ivan. He has a problem with money.

2. Direct students to look at the picture. Ask: *Where is Ivan?* [store] *What is he buying?* [shoes]

3. Play the audio and have students listen and look at the pictures. Check comprehension. Ask: *How much are the shoes?* [$20.15] *How much money does Ivan have?* [$20.05]

B 1. Tell students to look at the pictures. Read the captions and talk about them. For choice *a*, pantomime asking your students for a dime. For choice *b*, pantomime putting the shoes on the counter and walking sadly out the door. For choice *c*, point out that the cheaper shoes are not as nice as the shoes Ivan wants.

2. Ask for a show of hands to see which solution the class likes best. Emphasize that there can be more than one correct answer. Encourage students to express any other ideas they have. They may want to suggest asking the clerk to hold the shoes, going to an ATM, or using a credit card. Use pantomime and drawing to help students communicate their ideas.

Evaluation
20–25 minutes

To test students' understanding of the unit language and content, have them take the Unit 5 Test, available on the Teacher Resource Center.

TIP
Encourage students to reflect on what they have learned in this unit. Write these topics in a list on the board and elicit words, phrases, and sentences that students learned for each topic: *a) Money; b) Shopping and clothes; c) This, that, these, and those; d) Talking about prices; e) Ways to pay.* Congratulate students on their progress.

UNIT 6 That's My Son

Unit Overview

This unit explores family and marital relationships, the simple present tense, basic ways to describe people, and the U.S. educational system.

KEY OBJECTIVES

Lesson 1	Identify friends and family members
Lesson 2	Describe family members, friends, and marital status
Lesson 3	Use possessive adjectives and the simple present to discuss family
Lesson 4	Discuss friends and family members
Lesson 5	Identify school requirements; interpret a note from a teacher
Teamwork & Language Review	Review unit language

UNIT FEATURES

Academic Vocabulary	*emergency contact*, *marital status*
Employability Skills	• Use math to solve problems and communicate • Understand teamwork • Communicate information • Cooperate with others • Communicate verbally • Interpret a chart • Decide how a parent should respond to a child who receives a failing grade

Resources	**Class Audio** CD2, Tracks 21–36
	Workbook Unit 6, pages 37–43
	Teacher Resource Center
	    Literacy Reproducible Activities Unit 6
	    Multilevel Activities Introductory Level Unit 6
	    Multilevel Grammar Exercises Introductory Level Unit 6
	    Unit 6 Test
	Oxford Picture Dictionary Families, Schools and Subjects, Measurements

LESSON 1 VOCABULARY

Lesson Overview

MULTILEVEL OBJECTIVES

On-level: Identify family members
Pre-level: Recognize family members
Higher-level: Talk about family members

LANGUAGE FOCUS

Grammar: *This/that (Is this the father?)*
Vocabulary: *Baby, boy, father, friend, girl, husband, mother, parents, wife*

For vocabulary expansion, see this **Oxford Picture Dictionary** topic: Families, pages 34–35

STRATEGY FOCUS

To help remember vocabulary, differentiate and categorize family member words by gender.

READINESS CONNECTION

In this lesson, students communicate verbally about family members.

PACING

To compress this lesson: Conduct 2A as a whole-class activity.

To extend this lesson: List family names. (See end of lesson.)

And/or have students complete **Workbook Introductory Level page 37** and **Multilevel Activities Introductory Level Unit 6 page 68.**

Lesson Notes

CORRELATIONS

CCRS: SL.1.A Participate in collaborative conversations with diverse partners in small and larger groups.

SL.2.A Confirm understanding of a text read aloud or information presented orally or through other media by asking and answering questions about key details and requesting clarification if something is not understood.

L.6.A Use words and phrases acquired through conversations, reading and being read to, and responding to texts, including using frequently occurring conjunctions to signal simple relationships (e.g., *because*).

ELPS: 9. An ELL can create clear and coherent level-appropriate speech and text.

Warm-up and Review
10–15 minutes (books closed)

Review the pronunciation of *man/men* and *woman/women*. Draw stick figures on the board of a man, two men, a woman, and two women. Label them 1–4. Ask: *What number is men? What number is woman?* Do the same for *women* and *man*. Call on volunteers to say the words and have the class say the number.

Introduction
5 minutes

1. Show the students pictures of people in your family and tell them about the pictures: *This man is my husband. This woman is my mother.*

2. State the objective: *Today we'll learn words for family and friends.*

1 Learn about friends and family

Presentation
20–25 minutes

A Direct students to look at the pictures. Tell them to count the men and women. [There are five males and four females but two men and two women.]

B 🔊 2-21 1. Play the audio. Tell students to point to the correct picture as they listen. Circulate and monitor.

2. Check comprehension. Point to each picture and ask: *Is this the mother? Is this the boy?* Have students hold their thumbs up (*yes*) or thumbs down (*no*) in order to get a nonverbal response.

C 🔊 2-21 1. Tell students to listen and repeat the words.

2. Write the words on the board one syllable at a time and help students sound out and pronounce each syllable.

3. Call out the numbers out of order and ask students to say the words.

Guided Practice I
15–20 minutes

D Direct students to take turns reading the words with a partner.

E 1. Model the activity with two volunteers. Direct one partner to point to the pictures or say the numbers. Have the other partner cover the words in 1C and identify the pictures from memory.

2. Have students practice in pairs.

> **MULTILEVEL STRATEGIES**
>
> For 1E, pair same-level students together.
>
> • **Pre-level** Tell these students to practice together by pointing to the pictures in 1B and saying the correct words.
>
> • **Higher-level** Tell these students to dictate the words to each other.

2 Talk about families

Guided Practice II
15–20 minutes

A 1. Direct students to look at the picture. Call out the numbers and ask students to identify the family members in the picture.

2. Copy number 1 on the board and have students spell *wife* aloud. Demonstrate how to write one letter on each line.

3. Tell students to work individually to complete the words.

4. Ask volunteers to spell the completed words aloud. Write the answers on the board. Read and have students repeat the words.

Answers	
1. w-i-f-e	6. b-a-b-y
2. h-u-s-b-a-n-d	7. b-o-y
3. f-a-t-h-e-r	8. g-i-r-l
4. p-a-r-e-n-t-s	9. f-r-i-e-n-d
5. m-o-t-h-e-r	

B Give students time to copy the words into their notebooks. Monitor and check their writing.

C 🔊 2-22 1. Play the audio. Have students read along silently.

2. Play the audio again. Tell students to listen and repeat.

Communicative Practice and Application
10–15 minutes

D 1. Pair students. Have one pair model the conversation.

2. Set a time limit (five minutes) and have partners practice the conversation in both roles. Encourage students to use all of the words for family and friends. Circulate and monitor. Provide feedback.

> **TIP**
>
> After 2D, encourage students to bring in pictures of friends or family members for them to talk about during the rest of the unit.

Application and Evaluation
10–15 minutes

TEST YOURSELF

1. Direct students to copy the chart into their notebooks using the man and woman symbols as the headings in the chart. Model this on the board.

2. Ask students to work independently to complete their charts. Monitor and provide feedback.

> **MULTILEVEL STRATEGIES**
>
> Target the *Test Yourself* to the level of your students.
>
> • **Pre-level** Display or distribute to these students four pictures of people and family members listed in 1C. Have students open their books to page 74, identify the correct words to match the pictures, and copy them.
>
> • **Higher-level** Direct these students to add any other family words they know to each column. Have them check their work in the **Oxford Picture Dictionary**, pages 34–35, or another picture dictionary.

> **EXTENSION ACTIVITY**
>
> **Family Names**
>
> Write the words from 1C on the board with a blank next to each one. Put in some names from your family that fit those words and tell your students about them. *Sasha is a baby. Boris is a friend. Ivan and Rita are my parents.* Ask students to make similar lists with names of their own family members. Then have them make sentences about their family members to tell to a partner.

LESSON 2 WRITING

Lesson Overview

MULTILEVEL OBJECTIVES
On- and Higher-level: Read and write about families
Pre-level: Recognize family words

LANGUAGE FOCUS
Grammar: The verb *be* (*She is 10 years old.*)
Vocabulary: *Brother, child, children, daughter, divorced, emergency contact, married, relationship, single, sister, son*
For vocabulary expansion, see this **Oxford Picture Dictionary** topic: Families, pages 34–35

STRATEGY FOCUS
Use capital letters and periods in sentences to make your writing clear.

READINESS CONNECTION
In this lesson, students communicate information about their families and cooperate with others.

PACING
To compress this lesson: Assign the *Test Yourself* for homework.
To extend this lesson: Conduct a group writing about family relationships. (See end of lesson.)
And/or have students complete **Workbook Introductory Level page 38** and **Multilevel Activities Introductory Level Unit 6 page 69**.

Lesson Notes

CORRELATIONS

CCRS: R.7.A Use the illustrations and details in a text to describe its key ideas (e.g., maps, charts, photographs, political cartoons, etc.).

SL.1.A Participate in collaborative conversations with diverse partners in small and larger groups.

SL.2.A Confirm understanding of a text read aloud or information presented orally or through other media by asking and answering questions about key details and requesting clarification if something is not understood.

L.6.A Use words and phrases acquired through conversations, reading and being read to, and responding to texts, including using frequently occurring conjunctions to signal simple relationships (e.g., *because*).

ELPS: 10. An ELL can demonstrate command of the conventions of standard English to communicate in level-appropriate speech and writing.

Warm-up and Review
10–15 minutes (books closed)

Review family members. Draw or show pictures and elicit the words *boy, girl, man, woman, father, mother, husband,* and *wife*. Elicit the spelling of the words and write them on the board.

Introduction
5 minutes

1. Talk about the drawings on the board: *This is the girl. This is her father. This is the man. This is his wife.*

2. State the objective: *Today we're going to read and write about families. But first, we're going to listen for marital status.*

1 Learn about marital status

Presentation I
15–20 minutes

A 🔊 **2-23** 1. Direct students to look at the pictures. Play the *Marital Status* section of the audio. Have them listen and repeat the sentences.

2. Point out the names in the *Titles* section. Ask whether they are using first names or last names after the titles [last names]. Play the rest of the audio and have students listen and read along silently.

B 1. Pronounce *Mr.* (*mister*). Show students how to look at the sentences in 1A to determine if the title belongs to someone married, single, or either.

2. Have students work independently to complete the activity. Go over the answers as a class.

3. Say and have students repeat each title. Clap out the syllables for *Mrs.* and *Mr.*

Answers
1. a, b
2. a
3. a, b
4. b

Guided Practice I
20–25 minutes

C 🔊 **2-24** 1. Play number 1. Ask students which title they hear. Play the rest of the audio and have students circle what they hear.

2. Replay the audio one at a time and have students check their answers. Ask about each title: *Is it for a man or a woman? Does it mean married or single?* Have them repeat the titles again.

Answers
1. a
2. b
3. b
4. a

D 1. Ask students where they use a title and a last name [for example: a job interview, a business meeting, a meeting with a child's teacher]. Model the conversation with a volunteer. Model formal introduction behavior, for example, making eye contact and giving a firm handshake. Remind students to use their last names with their titles.

2. Have students walk around the room, "formally" introducing themselves to each other.

2 Prepare to write: family information

Presentation II
10–15 minutes

A Direct students to look at the pictures. Tell students to point to the girls. Then have them point to the boys. Ask: *Is Sandra a woman or a girl?* [woman]

B 🔊 **2-25** 1. Play the audio. Have students read along silently.

2. Check comprehension. Direct students to cover the words and look at the pictures. Say the words out of order and have students call out the correct numbers. Then say the numbers and have students call out the words.

3. Replay the audio and ask students to repeat the words.

4. Refer back to the pictures on the board from the warm-up and elicit the new family words. *He is the _____. She is his _____.*

C 🔊 **2-26** 1. Read the instructions aloud. Ask students to point to Sandra in the picture in 2A.

2. Play the audio. Have students read along silently.

3. Replay the audio and have students point to the picture in 2A as they listen. If you have access to a projector, ask a volunteer to point to the correct area as you read the sentences.

4. Direct students' attention to the *Writer's Note*. Point out the periods and capital letters in the sentences.

> **MULTILEVEL STRATEGIES**
>
> For 2C, seat students in mixed-level groups. After the whole-group practice, ask students to take turns reading the sentences aloud. Demonstrate turn-taking, with the first student reading number 1, the second number 2, and so on.
> • **Pre-level** Tell students who don't want to read aloud to listen to their classmates and follow along silently.

Guided Practice II
15–20 minutes

 1. Read number 1 aloud. Ask students to work independently to complete the exercise.

2. Have students compare their answers with a partner. Say the answers and have students repeat each sentence.

Answers
1. children
2. daughter
3. son
4. sister

 2-27 1. Point to the picture of Mr. Awad. Ask: *What is he looking at?* [a family photo/a picture of his children]

2. Play the audio. Tell students to listen and read along silently.

3. Check comprehension. Ask: *Who is in the picture?* [Mr. Awad's children] *Is Fadi a boy or a girl?* [boy] *How old is he?* [15]

4. Play number 1 and elicit the answer. Play the rest of the audio and ask students to work independently to complete the sentences.

5. Replay the entire audio so students can check their work. Ask them to read the completed sentences with a partner.

Answers
1. children
2. son
3. 15/fifteen
4. daughter
5. 20/twenty

3 Write about your family or friends

Communicative Practice
10–15 minutes

 1. Introduce the new activity: *Now we are going to write about our family or friends.*

2. Call on volunteers to complete the sentences aloud. Encourage them to show or draw a picture of the people they are talking about.

3. Tell students to copy the sentence frames in their notebooks and to work individually to complete the sentences with their own ideas. Ask them to show or draw a picture with their work.

4. Tell students to review their sentences for periods and capital letters.

B Ask students to read their sentences aloud to a partner. When they finish, ask them to read the story to a new partner.

> **MULTILEVEL STRATEGIES**
>
> Adapt 3A and 3B to the level of your students.
> • **Pre-level** While on- and higher-level students are completing 3A and 3B, work with these students in a group, or have them complete page 54 of the *Literacy Reproducible Activities Unit 6*.

▶ AT WORK

Complete an employee information form
10–15 minutes

 1. Direct students to look at the employee information forms. Ask them to find and repeat the words *Emergency Contact Information*. Explain the idea using gestures: *If I have an emergency, the school calls my husband.*

2. Tell students to read the first form. Ask: *Who is the employee?* [Eric Wang] *If Eric has an emergency at work, who do they call?* [Jill Wang] *Is that Jill's phone number or Eric's phone number?* [Jill's] Point out the word *relationship*. Ask: *What is Jill's relationship to Eric?* [She's his wife.]

3. Allow students time to read the other two forms silently. Then repeat the questioning procedure for each one.

B Ask a few students: *Who is your emergency contact? What's his/her name?* Have them work independently to complete the form. Monitor and provide feedback.

Evaluation
10 minutes

TEST YOURSELF

1. Copy the sentence frames on the board. Ask students for example answers.

2. Have students copy the frames into their notebooks and complete them.

3. Collect and correct students' work.

> **EXTENSION ACTIVITY**
>
> **Group Writing**
>
> 1. Show students a large picture of a family with people's names labeled. Elicit relationships and write sentences on the board:
>
> > *Jim and Diana are husband and wife. Diana and Petra are mother and daughter. Jim and Petra are ____ and ____.*
>
> 2. Have students work in small groups to complete or write more sentences about the picture.
>
> 3. Have groups present their pictures and sentences to the class.

LESSON 3 GRAMMAR

Lesson Overview

MULTILEVEL OBJECTIVES

On- and Higher-level: Use possessive adjectives and the simple present

Pre-level: Recognize possessive adjectives and the simple present

LANGUAGE FOCUS

Grammar: Possessive adjectives *(Her name is Silvia.)*; simple present *(She lives in Kansas.)*

Vocabulary: Family words, the verb *live*

For vocabulary expansion, see this **Oxford Picture Dictionary** topic: Families, pages 34–35

STRATEGY FOCUS

Associate abbreviations with the names of U.S. states.

READINESS CONNECTION

In this lesson, students interpret a chart and communicate verbally about names and places.

PACING

To compress this lesson: Have students practice 2E with only one partner. Assign 3C for homework.

To extend this lesson: Have group conversations. (See end of lesson.)

And/or have students complete **Workbook Introductory Level pages 39–40**, **Multilevel Activities Introductory Level Unit 6 page 70**, and **Multilevel Grammar Exercises Introductory Level Unit 6.**

Lesson Notes

CORRELATIONS

CCRS: L.1.A Demonstrate command of the conventions of standard English grammar and usage when writing or speaking. d. Use personal, possessive, and indefinite pronouns (e.g., *I, me, my, they, them, their, anyone, everything*). e. Use verbs to convey a sense of past, present, and future (e.g., *Yesterday I walked home; Today I walk home; Tomorrow I will walk home.*).

SL.1.A Participate in collaborative conversations with diverse partners in small and larger groups.

ELPS: 10. An ELL can demonstrate command of the conventions of standard English to communicate in level-appropriate speech and writing.

Warm-up and Review
10–15 minutes (books closed)

Review subject pronouns. Point to yourself and write *I* on the board. Use pantomime to elicit the other subject pronouns and write them on the board. Call on volunteers to say a sentence with each pronoun.

Introduction
5–10 minutes

1. Show students a picture of a friend or family member and make statements using *I* and *my*. For example: *I am a mother. This is my daughter. She lives in Texas.*

2. State the objective: *Today we'll practice with* my, your, his, her, our, *and* their, *and the present tense.*

1 Use possessive adjectives

Presentation I
20–25 minutes

A 1. Direct students to look at the pictures. Ask them to point to the woman's sister.

2. Play the audio and have students read along silently.

3. Use the possessive adjectives to talk about your students: *Her name is (Lotai). His name is (Juan). Their names are (Jonathan and Sothea).*

4. Draw students' attention to the list of subject pronouns on the board from the warm-up. Elicit the possessive adjective to go with each pronoun and write them in a second column.

B 1. Have students look at the pronouns in 1A again. Elicit which ones are plural [their, our]. Point out that *you* can also be plural.

2. Write *My name is ____, Her name is ____, His name is ____, Their names are ____ and ____,* and *Our names are ____ and ____* on the board. Call on volunteers to complete the sentences aloud using their own and their classmates' names.

Guided Practice I
15–20 minutes

C 1. Read number 1 aloud. Show students how the possessive should be based on the pronoun in the first sentence. Tell students to work individually to choose the correct answers.

2. Call on volunteers to read the completed sentences aloud. Write the answers on the board.

Answers
1. b
2. b
3. b
4. a
5. b
6. a

D Ask students to take turns reading the sentences aloud with a partner.

> **MULTILEVEL STRATEGIES**
>
> For 1C and 1D, seat pre-level students together.
>
> • **Pre-level** While other students are completing the exercise, work with these students. Read each sentence aloud and elicit the answer. Have students circle the answer before you move on to the next sentence.

2 Learn about the simple present

Presentation II
10–15 minutes

A 1. Direct students to look at the pictures and read the sentences. Ask if they know any of the places.

2. Read the captions aloud. Show California, New York, Texas, and Florida on a map.

B 2-29 1. Play the audio. Ask students to read the chart and listen.

2. Demonstrate how to read the grammar chart as complete sentences. Read the chart through sentence by sentence. Then read it again, and have students repeat after you.

3. Direct students to re-read the sentences in 2A and underline the *s* in *lives* in numbers 1–3.

4. Assess students' understanding of the chart. Draw stick figures with a state or country name next to each one. Say: *He lives in Illinois. She ____ in Canada. They ____ in Mexico.* Elicit completions.

Guided Practice II
10–15 minutes

C 1. Direct students to look at the map. Elicit the names of the states and help with pronunciation [WA=Washington, OR=Oregon, CA=California, NV=Nevada]. Read number 1 aloud. Tell students to work individually to complete the rest of the sentences.

2. Call on volunteers to read the completed sentences aloud.

3. Ask students to take turns reading the sentences in 2C aloud with a partner. Emphasize the importance of pronouncing the *s* ending. Tell them to listen for their partners' pronunciation of the *s*.

Answers
1. a
2. b
3. b
4. a

D 1. Read number 1 aloud. Tell students to work individually to complete the rest of the sentences.

2. Call on volunteers to write the answers on the board. Read the sentences aloud as a class.

Answers
1. lives
2. live
3. live
4. lives
5. live
6. live

E 1. Direct students to work with a partner to talk about their own family. Have them switch partners two or three times and repeat.

2. Call on volunteers to share their information with the class.

> **MULTILEVEL STRATEGIES**
>
> Adapt 2D and 2E to the level of your students.
>
> • **Pre-level** Provide these students with the answers to 2D and have them practice reading the sentences to each other, or have them complete page 55 of the *Literacy Reproducible Activities Unit 6*.
>
> • **Higher-level** When talking about family members or friends in 2E, have these students share their names as well.

3 Talk about names and places

Communicative Practice and Application
20–25 minutes

A 🔊 2-30 1. Direct students' attention to the pictures. Read the state names and help students identify them on a map.

2. Play the audio and have students repeat. Ask them to identify Mick, Maria, and Kai in the picture.

B 1. Model the conversations with volunteers, showing them how to replace the shaded words with information from the picture.

2. Have students practice the conversation in pairs.

C 1. Read the example sentences aloud. Elicit another example sentence from the class.

2. Have students work independently to write two sentences. Have several students write their sentences on the board.

> **MULTILEVEL STRATEGIES**
>
> Adapt 3B and 3C to the level of your students.
>
> • **Pre-level** Have these students work with an on-level pair. Instruct the on-level students to make statements about the people in 3A. Instruct the pre-level students to repeat their partners' sentences and point to the correct pictures in 3A. For 3C, have these students copy two of their partners' sentences.
>
> • **On- and Higher-level** Ask these students to write some of their 3C sentences on the board. Correct them together as a class.

Evaluation
10–15 minutes

TEST YOURSELF

Direct students to take turns telling a partner about some of their friends and family who live in different places. Then have them switch partners and repeat two more times. Monitor and provide feedback.

> **MULTILEVEL STRATEGIES**
>
> Target the *Test Yourself* to the level of your students.
>
> • **Pre-level** Provide these students with sentence frames for speaking: *My friend lives in ____. Her name is ____. My ____ lives in ____. His name is ____.*

> **EXTENSION ACTIVITY**
>
> **Group Conversation**
>
> Have students talk about relationships. Have students draw groups of stick figures to represent their family and/or friends. Tell them to write the people's names but not the relationships. Seat them in groups and direct them to talk about their pictures. *He is my ____. His name is ____. He lives in ____.*

LESSON 4 EVERYDAY CONVERSATION

Lesson Overview

MULTILEVEL OBJECTIVES
On- and Higher-level: Talk about family and friends
Pre-level: Respond to questions about family and friends

LANGUAGE FOCUS
Grammar: Possessive adjectives *(Her name is Patricia.)*
Vocabulary: Family words
For vocabulary expansion, see these **Oxford Picture Dictionary** topics: Families, pages 34–35; Measurements, page 17

STRATEGY FOCUS
Use a ruler for measurement.

READINESS CONNECTION
In this lesson, students use math to solve problems and communicate.

PACING
To compress this lesson: Skip the *Test Yourself*. Evaluate practice by monitoring 3D.
To extend this lesson: Write about pictures. (See end of lesson.)
And/or have students complete **Workbook Introductory Level page 41** and **Multilevel Activities Introductory Level Unit 6 page 71.**

CORRELATIONS
CCRS: SL.1.A Participate in collaborative conversations with diverse partners in small and larger groups.
SL.2.A Confirm understanding of a text read aloud or information presented orally or through other media by asking and answering questions about key details and requesting clarification if something is not understood.
RF.2.A Demonstrate understanding of spoken words, syllables, and sounds (phonemes). e. Orally produce single-syllable words by blending sounds (phonemes), including consonant sounds.

ELPS: 2. An ELL can participate in level-appropriate oral and written exchanges of information, ideas, and analyses, in various social and academic contexts, responding to peer, audience, or reader comments and questions.

Lesson Notes

Warm-up and Review
5 minutes (books closed)

Review family words. Put pictures of people of different ages on the board. Tell students the people are a family. Elicit the relationships and arrange the pictures accordingly. Ask volunteers to write the family words on the board next to the pictures.

Introduction
5 minutes

1. Point to the pictures. Say: *That's the mother. That's the father.*, etc.

2. State the objective: *Today we'll talk about our families. To begin, we are going to learn how to describe people's height.*

1 Listen for height

Listening Extension
15–20 minutes

A 1. Direct students to look at the ruler. Say and have students repeat *inches* and *foot*. Show students the inch demarcations on a real ruler. Draw their attention to the *Need help?* box and pronounce *foot* and *feet*.

2. Say: *One foot is 12 inches. How many feet is 24 inches?* Write the problem on the board: *24 ÷ 12 = 2*. Ask how many feet are in 26 inches [2, with 2 inches remaining].

B 🔊 2-31 1. Play the audio. Tell students to work individually to complete the answers.

2. Read the questions aloud and ask students to read the answers chorally.

3. Check comprehension. Ask several students: *How tall are you?*

> **TIP**
> Students may know their height in centimeters but not in feet/inches. Show them how they can type the information into a search engine to get the equivalent.

Answers
1. 5, 2
2. 4, 8

2 Practice your pronunciation

Pronunciation Extension
10–15 minutes

A 🔊 2-32 1. Direct students to look at the questions. Play the audio and ask students to read along silently.

2. Show students your mouth position when you make the vowel sounds in *who* and *how*.

B 🔊 2-33 1. Play the audio. Direct students to work individually to complete the chart.

2. Circulate and monitor. If necessary, repeat the exercise.

Answers	1.	2.	3.	4.	5.	6.
Who		✓	✓		✓	
How	✓			✓		✓

C 🔊 2-33 Replay the audio. Ask students to repeat the questions they hear.

3 Make conversation: talk about families and friends

Presentation
5–10 minutes

A 1. Direct students to look at the pictures. Ask if Chang Sun and Nancy are friends or family [friends].

2. Have students read the conversation silently. Elicit any questions.

Guided Practice
5–10 minutes

B 🔊 2-34 1. Play the audio. Have students read the conversation silently.

2. Point out that Chang Sun asks *How old is she?* because they are talking about a child. Explain that we don't usually ask adults how old they are—it's considered a personal question. Also point out the use of *too* in the conversation. Explain that Chang Sun uses *too* because Nancy's daughter and his father both live in Houston.

C 🔊 2-34 1. Play the audio again and have students repeat the conversation.

2. Do a choral reading of the conversation in 3B. Divide the class in half. Have one side be Nancy and one side be Chang Sun, and then have the sides switch roles.

Communicative Practice and Application
15–20 minutes

D 1. Model the conversation with a volunteer. Then switch roles and model it with another volunteer.

2. Elicit other ways to complete the conversation.

3. Set a time limit (five minutes). Ask students to practice the conversation with several partners. Encourage pantomime and improvisation.

4. Ask volunteer pairs to present their conversations to the class.

> **MULTILEVEL STRATEGIES**
>
> For 3D, seat pre-level students together.
>
> • **Pre-level** While other students are practicing the conversation, have these students complete page 56 in the *Literacy Reproducible Activities Unit 6*.

Evaluation
5 minutes

TEST YOURSELF

1. Direct students to look at page 77. Have two volunteers model the activity.

2. Set a time limit (three minutes). Have students practice with a partner. Ask students who finish early to switch partners and repeat.

> **EXTENSION ACTIVITY**
>
> **Write About Pictures**
>
> Provide sentence frames and have students write about someone in a photo.
>
> *This is my _____. His/Her name is _____. He/She lives in _____. He/She is _____ years old.*
>
> Photocopy or scan students' pictures and post them together with their stories.

LESSON 5 READING

Lesson Overview

MULTILEVEL OBJECTIVES

On- and Higher-level: Interpret information about the U.S. school system and read a note from a teacher

Pre-level: Read information about the U.S. school system and a note from a teacher

LANGUAGE FOCUS

Grammar: Simple present *(She comes to school every day.)*

Vocabulary: *Come, do homework, elementary school, every day, grade, high school, junior high school, kindergarten, middle school, on time*

For vocabulary expansion, see this **Oxford Picture Dictionary** topic: Schools and Subjects, pages 200–201

STRATEGY FOCUS

Identify a company or school name in a letterhead.

READINESS CONNECTION

In this lesson, students interpret a chart with information about students' ages, grades, and schools.

PACING

To compress this lesson: Assign 2C as homework or conduct it as a whole-class activity.

To extend this lesson: Have students write a note. (See end of lesson.)

And/or have students complete **Workbook Introductory Level page 42** and **Multilevel Activities Introductory Level Unit 6 page 72.**

Lesson Notes

CORRELATIONS

CCRS: R.1.A Ask and answer questions about key details in the text.

R.7.A Use the illustrations and details in a text to describe its key ideas (e.g., maps, charts, photographs, political cartoons, etc.).

L.6.A Use words and phrases acquired through conversations, reading and being read to, and responding to texts, including using frequently occurring conjunctions to signal simple relationships (e.g., *because*).

ELPS: 8. An ELL can determine the meaning of words and phrases in oral presentations and literary and informational text.

Warm-up and Review
10–15 minutes (books closed)

Show pictures of children of different ages. Ask students to guess the ages of the children and write their guesses next to the pictures as statements: *He is 10 years old.*

Introduction
5 minutes

1. Tell students what kind of school the children might be in: *He is 10 years old. He's in elementary school. She's 16 years old. She's in high school.*

2. State the objective: *Today we'll learn about types of schools, and we'll read a note from a teacher.*

1 Get ready to read

Presentation I
10–15 minutes

A 1. Tell students to look at the chart.

2. Check comprehension of the chart. Ask students to give a grade or a kind of school for all of the children discussed in the warm-up.

3. Show students how to read the information in the chart. Connect some of the pictures on the board to the information on the chart: *She's seven years old. She's in first or second grade. She's in elementary school.*

> **TIP**
>
> After 1A, discuss the chart as it relates to your local school system. Find out if students know what grades are included in the local elementary schools and whether your school system has middle schools or junior highs.

Guided Practice I
15–20 minutes

B 1. Read sentence number 1 aloud. Direct students to find where *eight years old* falls on the chart. Tell students to work individually to complete the rest of the sentences.

2. Call on volunteers for the answers. Write them on the board.

Answers
1. b
2. b
3. a
4. b

Presentation and Guided Practice II
10–15 minutes

C 1. Direct students to look at the pictures. Say and have students repeat the words.

2. Go over each word. Contrast *come* with *go* by walking in and out the door. Ask students to pantomime actions that they do every day (eat, sleep, etc.). Elicit what *on time* means in your class. Talk about whether your students do homework.

D Ask students to check the sentences about themselves. Call on volunteers to read their sentences aloud.

2 Read a note

Guided Practice III
15–20 minutes

A 1. Ask students to look at the note and find the teacher's name, the student's name, and the grade level [Selma Romero, Lila, fourth grade]. Ask if this is an elementary or a high-school teacher [elementary].

2. Ask students to read the note silently. Ask if there are any questions about the reading.

3. Check students' comprehension. Ask: *Is Lila a good student?* [yes] *Does she come on time?* [yes] *Does she do her homework?* [yes]

B 🔊 2-35 Play the audio. Have students read along silently.

C 1. Read number 1 aloud. Show students how to find the answer in the note.

2. Direct students to work individually to complete the sentences.

3. Call on volunteers to read the completed sentences aloud.

Answers
1. b
2. b
3. a
4. b

> **MULTILEVEL STRATEGIES**
>
> Adapt 2C for your pre-level students.
>
> • **Pre-level** While other students are completing 2C, read 2A aloud for these students. Then read the sentences in 2C aloud and elicit the answers. Have students copy the answers off the board.

> **TIP**
>
> After 2C, find out if there are any parents of school-aged children in your class who have questions and concerns about their children's education. Ask students for the names of the schools that their children, grandchildren, or siblings attend. Write the school names and the grades of the children on the board. Find out if your students know about any special programs at their children's schools (parent education or tutoring, for example). Encourage students whose children attend the same school to share information about programs and teachers. Show students a grade report and teach them the meaning of the grades.

Application
5–10 minutes

BRING IT TO LIFE

Read the directions aloud. Give the students search terms or, if they all live in the same district, the URL for the school district website.

> **TIP**
>
> In preparation for *Teamwork & Language Review*, have students review the unit vocabulary. Provide them with pictures you have collected or use the Picture Cards on pages 73–74 of *Multilevel Activities Introductory Level Unit 6*. Pair students and have them use the pictures as flashcards for recognition practice, dictation, or sentence writing.

EXTENSION ACTIVITY

Write a Note

Have students write a note about a child they know. Write sentence frames on the board:

My _____ is in _____ grade. He/She is a good student. He/She comes to class every day. He/She comes to class on time.

Ask them to read their notes to a partner.

TEAMWORK & LANGUAGE REVIEW

Lesson Overview

MULTILEVEL OBJECTIVES

On-, Pre-, and Higher-level: Expand upon and review unit language and content

LANGUAGE FOCUS

Grammar: Simple present *(He comes to class on time.)*; possessive adjectives *(His name is Tomas.)*

Vocabulary: Family

For vocabulary expansion, see this **Oxford Picture Dictionary** topic: Families, pages 34–35

STRATEGY FOCUS

Use teamwork to reinforce and expand vocabulary.

READINESS CONNECTION

In this review, students practice teamwork and communicate verbally to decide how a parent should respond to a child who receives a failing grade.

PACING

To extend this review: Have students complete **Workbook Introductory Level page 43**, **Multilevel Activities Introductory Level Unit 6 pages 73–76**, and **Multilevel Grammar Exercises Introductory Level Unit 6**.

Lesson Notes

CORRELATIONS

CCRS: L.6.A Use words and phrases acquired through conversations, reading and being read to, and responding to texts, including using frequently occurring conjunctions to signal simple relationships (e.g., *because*).

R.7.A Use the illustrations and details in a text to describe its key ideas (e.g., maps, charts, photographs, political cartoons, etc.).

SL.1.A Participate in collaborative conversations with diverse partners in small and larger groups.

SL.4.A Describe people, places, things, and events with relevant details, expressing ideas and feelings clearly.

SL.6.A Speak audibly and express thoughts, feelings, and ideas clearly. Produce complete sentences when appropriate to task and situation.

ELPS: 2. An ELL can participate in level-appropriate oral and written exchanges of information, ideas, and analyses, in various social and academic contexts, responding to peer, audience, or reader comments and questions.

Warm-up and Review
5–10 minutes (books closed)

1. Review the *Bring It to Life* assignment from Lesson 5.

2. Elicit the names and the types of schools and write them on the board. Ask students who did not bring school names to say what grades go with each school.

Introduction and Presentation
5 minutes

1. Point to one of the schools on the board and make up sentences about a child: *My friend has a son. His name is Tommy. He's 10 years old. He lives in this city. He goes to Wilson Elementary School.*

2. State the objective: *Today we're going to review the words and grammar from Unit 6.*

Communicative Practice
15–20 minutes

A 1. Tell students to take turns naming one thing they see in the picture. Have three volunteers help you model turn-taking.

2. Tell students to put their pencils down and listen to each other so that they don't repeat ideas. Direct them to go around the group until they have run out of ideas.

B 1. Have students work in the same groups from A. Assign roles: secretary, reporter, editor, and manager. Write the roles on the board. As you explain each role, pantomime the duties you expect the person taking that role to perform. Explain that students work with their groups to write the words. Verify comprehension of roles.

2. Set a time limit (five minutes) to complete the chart. Circulate and answer any questions.

3. Call on the reporters from each group to say the words from their chart. Write the words on the board. Go around the class until there are no more ideas.

Possible Answers		
Family		**Other**
Male	**Female**	baby
father	mother	friend
son	daughter	address
brother	sister	zip code
boy	girl	married
husband	wife	homework
		parents
		children

C 1. Have the groups identify new words from the board and to look them up in a picture dictionary or a bilingual dictionary.

2. Tell students to add three new words to their chart. [New words might include: *sofa*, *table*, *letter*, and *picture frame*.]

MULTILEVEL STRATEGIES

For A–C, use mixed-level groups.

• **Pre-level** Assign these students the role of manager.

• **On-level** Assign these students the role of secretary or reporter.

• **Higher-level** Assign these students the role of editor.

D 1. Read number 1 aloud. Point to the baby in the picture. Tell students to work independently to complete the sentences.

2. Call on volunteers to read the completed sentences aloud. Write the answers on the board.

Answers	
1. baby, His	3. son/boy, His
2. daughter/girl, Her	4. father, friend

E 1. Have students work independently to write two sentences.

2. Ask volunteers to write their sentences on the board. Correct them as a class.

PROBLEM SOLVING AT HOME
15–20 minutes

A  1. Tell students the pictures in A tell a story about a woman named Rosa. She has a problem with her son. Ask students to guess how old the son is. Ask what game the son is playing. Write *baseball* on the board.

2. Play the audio. Check comprehension. Ask: *What grade is Rosa's son in?* [4th] *Is he a good student?* [no] *Is he a good baseball player?* [yes]

B 1. Tell students to look at the pictures. Read the captions and talk about them.

2. Ask for a show of hands to see which solution the class likes best. Emphasize that there can be more than one correct answer. Encourage students to express any other ideas they have.

Evaluation
20–25 minutes

To test students' understanding of the unit language and content, have them take the Unit 6 Test, available on the Teacher Resource Center.

TIP

Encourage students to reflect on what they have learned in this unit. Write these topics in a list on the board and elicit words, phrases, and sentences that students learned for each topic: a) Talk about family; b) Use titles; c) Use *my, your, his, her, our, their*; d) Use the present tense; e) The U.S. school system. Congratulate students on their progress.

UNIT 7 Do You Need Apples?

Unit Overview

This unit explores food preferences, food shopping and prices, and healthy eating habits.

KEY OBJECTIVES	
Lesson 1	Identify fruit and vegetables
Lesson 2	Describe food preferences
Lesson 3	Use the simple present to express likes, dislikes, and needs
Lesson 4	State needs; identify prices
Lesson 5	Identify containers; read a shopping list
Teamwork & Language Review	Review unit language

UNIT FEATURES	
Employability Skills	• Work with others • Understand teamwork • Communicate information • Speak so others can understand • Communicate verbally • Interpret a shopping list • Interpret food ads • Determine how to improve poor eating habits

Resources	**Class Audio** CD2, Tracks 37–53
	Workbook Unit 7, pages 44–50
	Teacher Resource Center
	    Literacy Reproducible Activities Unit 7
	    Multilevel Activities Introductory Level Unit 7
	    Multilevel Grammar Exercises Introductory Level Unit 7
	    Unit 7 Test
	Oxford Picture Dictionary Fruit, Vegetables, Meat and Poultry, Back from the Market, A Grocery Store, Containers and Packaging

LESSON 1 VOCABULARY

Lesson Overview

MULTILEVEL OBJECTIVES

On-level: Identify fruit and vegetables
Pre-level: Recognize fruit and vegetables
Higher-level: Talk about fruit and vegetables

LANGUAGE FOCUS

Grammar: Where + be questions *(Where are the apples?)*
Vocabulary: *Apples, bananas, broccoli, cabbage, corn, fruit, grapes, oranges, vegetables*

For vocabulary expansion, see these **Oxford Picture Dictionary** topics: Fruit, page 68; Vegetables, page 69

STRATEGY FOCUS

Use *right here* to answer questions about the location of something that's very close to you.

READINESS CONNECTION

In this lesson, students communicate verbally about where to find fruit and vegetables.

PACING

To compress this lesson: Conduct 2A as a whole-class activity.
To extend this lesson: Practice with plastic fruit. (See end of lesson.)
And/or have students complete **Workbook Introductory Level page 44** and **Multilevel Activities Introductory Level Unit 7 page 78.**

Lesson Notes

CORRELATIONS

CCRS: L.6.A Use words and phrases acquired through conversations, reading and being read to, and responding to texts, including using frequently occurring conjunctions to signal simple relationships (e.g., *because*).

SL.1.A Participate in collaborative conversations with diverse partners in small and larger groups.

ELPS: 1. An ELL can construct meaning from oral presentations and literary and informational text through level-appropriate listening, reading, and viewing.

Warm-up and Review
10–15 minutes (books closed)

Find out what fruit or vegetables your students already know the names for. Bring in plastic fruit and vegetables and elicit the names. Ask which ones are expensive and which are cheap.

Introduction
5 minutes

1. Say the names of the fruit and vegetables you brought with you.

2. State the objective: *Today we'll learn about fruit and vegetables.*

1 Learn about fruit and vegetables

Presentation
20–25 minutes

A Direct students to look at the pictures. Ask them to say the prices.

B 🔊 2-37 1. Play the audio. Ask students to point to the correct picture as they listen. Circulate and monitor.

2. Check comprehension by asking *yes/no* questions. Point to each picture and ask, for example: *Are these bananas? Is this cabbage?* Have students use thumbs up (*yes*) or thumbs down (*no*) to respond.

C 🔊 2-37 1. Tell students to listen and repeat the words.

2. Write *vegetable* on the board and help students pronounce it. Clap out the syllables to show that we pronounce it with three syllables.

3. Call out the numbers out of order and ask students to say the words.

Guided Practice I
10–15 minutes

D Direct students to take turns reading the words with a partner.

E 1. Model the activity with two volunteers. Direct one partner to point to the pictures or say the numbers. Have the other partner cover the words in 1C and identify the pictures from memory.

2. Have students practice in pairs.

MULTILEVEL STRATEGIES

For 1E, pair same-level students together.

- **Pre-level** Tell these students to practice together by pointing to the pictures in 1B and saying the correct words.
- **Higher-level** Tell these students to dictate the words to each other.
---

2 Talk about fruit and vegetables

Guided Practice II
20–25 minutes

A 1. Direct students to look at the picture. Call out words and ask students to identify the correct number.

2. Copy number 1 on the board and have students spell *bananas* aloud. Demonstrate how to write one letter on each line.

3. Tell students to work individually to complete the words.

4. Ask volunteers to spell the completed words aloud. Write the answers on the board. Read and have students repeat the words.

Answers	
1. b-a-n-a-n-a-s	6. c-o-r-n
2. g-r-a-p-e-s	7. b-r-o-c-c-o-l-i
3. o-r-a-n-g-e-s	8. c-a-b-b-a-g-e
4. a-p-p-l-e-s	9. v-e-g-e-t-a-b-l-e-s
5. f-r-u-i-t	

B Give students time to copy the words into their notebooks. Monitor and check their writing.

C 🔊 2-38 1. Play the audio. Have students read along silently.

2. Play the audio again. Tell students to listen and repeat.

Communicative Practice and Application
10–15 minutes

D 1. Model the conversations with a volunteer. Show students how to use the pictures in 2A. Switch roles and model the conversations with another volunteer.

2. Pair students. Have one pair model the conversation.

3. Set a time limit (five minutes) and have the partners practice the conversation in both roles. Encourage students to use all of the words. Circulate and monitor. Provide feedback.

> **TIP**
>
> For more practice after 2D, pass out pictures of fruit and vegetables (or use Picture Cards 7.1–7.9 on page 83 of *Multilevel Activities Introductory Level Unit 7*). Dictate prices and have students write them on the pictures. *The apples are 65¢, The cabbage is $1.25,* etc. After you finish, call on volunteers for the prices. *How much are the apples? How much is the corn?*

Evaluation
10–15 minutes

TEST YOURSELF

1. Have students copy the chart in their notebooks.

2. Have students work independently to complete the chart. Monitor and provide feedback.

> **MULTILEVEL STRATEGIES**
>
> Target the *Test Yourself* to the level of your students.
>
> • **Pre-level** Have these students work with their books open.
>
> • **Higher-level** Have these students close their books. Challenge them to include words not presented in the unit. Have them check their answers in a picture dictionary.

> **EXTENSION ACTIVITY**
>
> **Plastic Fruit Game**
>
> 1. Have students stand in a circle around the room. Pass out plastic fruit and vegetables to a few students.
>
> 2. Call out the name of one of the fruits. The student holding that fruit needs to repeat the name of the fruit and throw it to someone else in the circle who isn't holding a fruit or vegetable. The recipient needs to say the name as he or she catches it. Call out the words in rapid succession so that students throw quickly.
>
> 3. If you have multiple circles, demonstrate the game and then appoint a higher-level student as the caller for the circle.

LESSON 2 WRITING

Lesson Overview

MULTILEVEL OBJECTIVES
On- and Higher-level: Read and write about food
Pre-level: Recognize words for food

LANGUAGE FOCUS
Grammar: Present tense (*I like cheese.*)
Vocabulary: *Beef, bread, cheese, chicken, eggs, lamb, meat, milk, pork, rice*

For vocabulary expansion, see these **Oxford Picture Dictionary** topics: Meat and Poultry, page 70; Back from the Market, pages 66–67

STRATEGY FOCUS
To improve your writing, proofread it for specific errors.

READINESS CONNECTION
In this lesson, students communicate information about food preferences.

PACING
To compress this lesson: Assign *At Work* A for homework.
To extend this lesson: Conduct a picture card activity. (See end of lesson.)

And/or have students complete **Workbook Introductory Level page 45** and **Multilevel Activities Introductory Level Unit 7 page 79.**

Lesson Notes

CORRELATIONS

CCRS: L.6.A Use words and phrases acquired through conversations, reading and being read to, and responding to texts, including using frequently occurring conjunctions to signal simple relationships (e.g., *because*).

SL.1.A Participate in collaborative conversations with diverse partners in small and larger groups.

SL.2.A Confirm understanding of a text read aloud or information presented orally or through other media by asking and answering questions about key details and requesting clarification if something is not understood.

SL.6.A Speak audibly and express thoughts, feelings, and ideas clearly. Produce complete sentences when appropriate to task and situation.

R.1.A Ask and answer questions about key details in the text.

R.7.A Use the illustrations and details in a text to describe its key ideas (e.g., maps, charts, photographs, political cartoons, etc.).

ELPS: 1. An ELL can construct meaning from oral presentations and literary and informational text through level-appropriate listening, reading, and viewing. 9. An ELL can create clear and coherent level-appropriate speech and text.

Warm-up and Review
10–15 minutes (books closed)

Review fruit and vegetables. Write *fruit* and *vegetables* on the board. Ask volunteers to come to the board and write examples of each. Correct the words together and have the class repeat them.

Introduction
5 minutes

1. Tell students about which fruit and vegetables you like: *I like ____. I don't like ____.*

2. State the objective: *Today we're going to write about foods that we like and don't like.*

1 Learn about more food groups

Presentation I
15–20 minutes

 2-39 1. Play the audio. Have students look at the pictures and read the words silently.

2. Check comprehension. Say the words out of order and have students call out the correct numbers.

3. Replay the audio and ask students to repeat the words.

4. Say the numbers and have students call out the words.

Guided Practice I
5–10 minutes

 1. Write *Meat* on the board as a column heading. Say: *Pork is a meat. What is another meat?* Elicit *beef, chicken,* and *lamb* and write the words under *Meat*. Direct students to follow your example in their books. Repeat with the rest of the food groups.

2. Ask students to compare their completed food-group charts with a partner. Tell them to look at their partner's spelling and to take turns saying the words.

Possible Answers				
Meat	**Dairy**	**Grains**	**Fruit**	**Vegetables**
pork	milk	bread	apples	cabbage
lamb	cheese	rice	bananas	broccoli
beef			grapes	corn

 2-40 1. Play number 1 and elicit the answer. Then play the rest of the audio and have students work independently to circle the correct answers.

2. Replay the audio one item at a time. Elicit the answer for each item and repeat if necessary.

Answers	
1. b	4. a
2. b	5. b
3. a	6. a

2 Prepare to write: food I like

Presentation II
25–30 minutes

A Direct students to look at the pictures. Ask them to say the foods they see [bread, milk, eggs, cheese, broccoli, beef, lamb, chicken, pork, rice]. Point to the woman in the different pictures. Ask: *Is Barbara happy?* [yes, no, yes]

B 2-41 1. Play the audio. Have students read along silently.

2. Replay the audio and ask students to repeat the sentences. Have students point to the pictures in 2A as they listen. If you have access to an overhead projector, make a transparency of the pictures in 2A and ask a volunteer to point to the correct area as you read the sentences.

3. Check comprehension. Make *true/false* statements and ask students to respond with thumbs up (*true*) or thumbs down (*false*). For example: *Barbara likes cheese* [thumbs up]. *Barbara likes pork* [thumbs down]. *Barbara's husband likes chicken* [thumbs down]. Encourage students to correct the false statements.

> **MULTILEVEL STRATEGIES**
>
> For 2B, seat students in mixed-level groups. After the whole-group practice, ask students to take turns reading the sentences aloud. Demonstrate turn-taking, with the first student reading number 1, the second number 2, and so on.
>
> • **Pre-level** Tell students who don't want to read aloud to listen to their classmates and follow along silently.

C 1. Model the activity with a volunteer, showing students how to substitute the highlighted words. Then ask two volunteers to model the conversation.

2. Have students practice with a partner. Then have them switch partners and practice again. Repeat two or three times.

Guided Practice II
10–15 minutes

 D))) **2-42** 1. Direct students to look at the picture. Say and have them repeat *Don*. Read the instructions aloud.

2. Play number 1 and elicit the answer. Play the rest of the audio and ask students to circle the correct word.

3. Replay the entire audio so students can check their work. Go over the answers as a class.

Answers	
1. a	3. a
2. b	4. b

3 Write about food you like

Communicative Practice
10–15 minutes

A 1. Introduce the new activity: *Now you are going to write about food you like.*

2. Call on volunteers to complete the sentences aloud.

3. Tell students to work individually to complete the sentences with their own information.

4. Direct students' attention to the *Writer's Note*. Have them check their work. Then tell them to check a partner's work for capital letters, periods, and spelling.

 B Ask students to read their sentences aloud to a partner. When they finish, ask them to read the sentences to a new partner.

> **MULTILEVEL STRATEGIES**
>
> Adapt 3A and 3B to the level of your students.
>
> • **Pre-level** While on- and higher-level students are completing 3A and 3B, work with these students in a group, or have them complete page 60 of the *Literacy Reproducible Activities Unit 7*.

AT WORK

Read supermarket job ads
10–15 minutes

 A 1. Direct students to look at the job ads. Say and have them repeat the job titles. Ask if they know anyone with one of these jobs.

2. Write *Tues.–Thurs.* and *Tues., Thurs.* on the board. Demonstrate the importance of the punctuation. Show students that *Tues.–Thurs.* includes Wednesday, while *Tues., Thurs.* does not. Tell them to look at the job ad and say the days that each person works.

3. Go over the examples in the chart. Show students how to find the information in the job ads. Have students work independently to complete the chart.

4. Go over the answers as a class.

Answers	work on Saturdays	work in the evening	work on Wednesday	work in the morning
bagger	✓	✓		
manager	✓	✓	✓	
cashier			✓	✓

 **B** Elicit students' answers to the question.

> **TIP**
>
> Research the average wage for each of these occupations in your area. Write the wages on the board and help students calculate the monthly salary for each of the jobs in the ad.

Evaluation
10 minutes

TEST YOURSELF

1. Copy the sentence frames on the board. Ask students for example answers.

2. Have students copy the frames into their notebooks and complete them.

3. Collect and correct students' work.

> **EXTENSION ACTIVITY**
>
> **Picture Cards**
>
> Use Picture Cards 7.1–7.16 on pages 83–84 of *Multilevel Activities Introductory Level Unit 7* or other pictures of food. Have students work with a partner and make an *I like* or *I don't like* statement about each card.

LESSON 3 GRAMMAR

Lesson Overview

MULTILEVEL OBJECTIVES

On- and Higher-level: Use simple present negative statements and *yes/no* questions

Pre-level: Recognize simple present negative statements and *yes/no* questions

LANGUAGE FOCUS

Grammar: Simple present negative statements (*I don't like cabbage.*); simple present *yes/no* questions and answers (*Do you need rice? Yes, I do.*)

Vocabulary: Food

For vocabulary expansion, see these **Oxford Picture Dictionary** topics: Fruit, page 68; Vegetables, page 69; Meat and Poultry, page 70; Back from the Market, pages 66–67

STRATEGY FOCUS

Pay attention to people's facial expressions and gestures to understand what they like and don't like.

READINESS CONNECTION

In this lesson, students communicate verbally about what people need and like.

PACING

To compress this lesson: Assign 3E and the *Test Yourself* for homework.

To extend this lesson: Practice with picture cards. (See end of lesson.)

And/or have students complete **Workbook Introductory Level pages 46–47, Multilevel Activities Introductory Level Unit 7 page 80,** and **Multilevel Grammar Exercises Introductory Level Unit 7.**

Lesson Notes

CORRELATIONS

CCRS: L.1.A Demonstrate command of the conventions of standard English grammar and usage when writing or speaking. e. Use verbs to convey a sense of past, present, and future (e.g., *Yesterday I walked home; Today I walk home; Tomorrow I will walk home.*). I. Produce and expand complete simple and compound declarative, interrogative, imperative, and exclamatory sentences in response to prompts.

SL.1.A Participate in collaborative conversations with diverse partners in small and larger groups.

SL.2.A Confirm understanding of a text read aloud or information presented orally or through other media by asking and answering questions about key details and requesting clarification if something is not understood.

ELPS: 10. An ELL can demonstrate command of the conventions of standard English to communicate in level-appropriate speech and writing.

Warm-up and Review
10–15 minutes (books closed)

Review food words. Write scrambled words in categories on the board: Meat: *rpko, ebef, knciceh,* and *malb*. Fruit: *aesplp, aansban, raonsge,* and *esrgap*. Ask students to work together to unscramble the words. Do the first one as an example. Elicit the answers and write the words correctly. [Meat: pork, beef, chicken, lamb; Fruit: apples, bananas, oranges, grapes]

Introduction
5–10 minutes

1. Make statements about which foods on the board you like and don't like. Elicit similar statements from students. Restate them in the third person: *Laura doesn't like chicken. Marc likes apples.*

2. State the objective: *Today we're going to learn negative statements and questions with the simple present.*

1 Use negative statements with the simple present

Presentation I
20–25 minutes

A 1. Direct students to look at the pictures. Ask them to name the foods they see [rice, vegetables, meat/pork, bananas, cabbage, chicken].

2. Read the captions aloud.

B 🔊 2-43 1. Play the audio. Tell students to read the chart and listen.

2. Demonstrate how to read the grammar chart as complete sentences. Read the chart through sentence by sentence. Then read it again, and have students repeat after you.

3. Direct students to re-read the sentences in 1A and underline the verbs. Read the underlined words aloud.

4. Assess students' understanding of the chart. Call on a volunteer to make *I like/I don't like* statements. Restate the information in the third person, sometimes correctly, sometimes incorrectly: *Maria likes/doesn't like apples.* Have the class respond with thumbs up (*true*) or thumbs down (*false*).

Guided Practice I
15–20 minutes

C 1. Direct students to look at the pictures. Elicit what they see.

2. Tell students to work individually to complete the sentences and then read the sentences with a partner.

3. Call on volunteers to read the completed sentences aloud. Write the answers on the board.

Answers
1. doesn't like
2. doesn't like
3. doesn't like
4. don't like

2 Learn about *yes/no* questions with the simple present

Presentation II
10–15 minutes

A 🔊 2-44 1. Direct students to look at the pictures. Ask them to identify the food in the pictures.

2. Introduce the new topic: *Now we're going to learn yes/no questions and answers.*

3. Play the first conversation and ask students to read along silently. Replay the conversation and have students repeat it. Do the same with the rest of the conversations.

Guided Practice II
10–15 minutes

B 1. Direct students to look at the picture and read the items on the shopping list. Ask: *Does he need grapes?* [Yes, he does.]

2. Tell students to work individually to complete the questions and answers, using the information on the shopping list.

3. Have students read their completed questions and answers with a partner. Call on pairs to read the questions and answers for the class.

Answers
1. Does, does
2. Does, doesn't

C Point out the shopping list in the picture. Then repeat the procedure from 2B.

Answers
1. Do, do
2. Do, don't

> **MULTILEVEL STRATEGIES**
>
> Adapt 2B and 2C for your pre-level students.
>
> • **Pre-level** Provide these students with the answers to the exercises and have them practice reading the sentences to each other, or have them complete page 61 of the *Literacy Reproducible Activities Unit 7*.

D 1. Have students work with a partner to ask and answer one more question about the shopping lists in 2B and 2C.

2. Call on volunteers to share their original questions and answers with the class.

3 Ask about likes and needs

Presentation III
10–15 minutes

A 🔊 2-45 Play the audio. Have students repeat the questions and answers.

B 1. Direct students' attention to the pictures. Ask them to name the foods [cheese, pork, chicken, beef, eggs].

2. Have students work in pairs to take turns asking and answering the question about each of the pictures.

Communicative Practice
15–20 minutes

C 🔊 2-46 1. Direct students' attention to the pictures. Tell them to read the words on the shopping lists.

2. Play the audio. Have students repeat the questions and answers.

D 1. Model the activity with a volunteer.

2. Have students practice asking and answering the questions in pairs. Remind them to look at the shopping lists in the pictures in 3C.

3. Call on pairs to say questions and answers for the class.

E 1. Read the example sentences. Elicit a new sentence from the class.

2. Have students work independently to write sentences about the pictures in 3C. Ask volunteers to write one of their sentences on the board.

Evaluation
10–15 minutes

TEST YOURSELF

1. Direct students to look at the pictures in 2A. Read the example sentences. Tell them to write their own sentences about the pictures.

2. Collect and correct their work.

> **MULTILEVEL STRATEGIES**
>
> Target the *Test Yourself* to the level of your students.
>
> • **Pre-level** Provide these students with sentence frames:
>
> *I like/don't like _____.*
>
> *He/She needs/doesn't need _____.*
>
> Ask students to complete the frames.
>
> • **Higher-level** In addition to the two sentences, ask these students to write three questions and three answers about Barbara, the woman in the pictures on page 91.

> **EXTENSION ACTIVITY**
>
> **Picture Cards**
>
> 1. Provide each student with a picture card of a food item. (See pages 83–84 of *Multilevel Activities Introductory Level Unit 7*.)
>
> 2. Set a time limit (five minutes). Tell students to circulate around the room, asking *Do you like _____?* and answering *Yes, I do* or *No, I don't*. After they have practiced with one partner, have them exchange picture cards and move on to a new partner.

LESSON 4 EVERYDAY CONVERSATION

Lesson Overview

MULTILEVEL OBJECTIVES

On-, Pre-, and Higher-level: Ask for help in a store

LANGUAGE FOCUS

Grammar: Present tense *(I need apples.)*

Vocabulary: Food, *pound*

For vocabulary expansion, see these **Oxford Picture Dictionary** topics: Fruit, page 68; Vegetables, page 69; Meat and Poultry, page 70; Back from the Market, pages 66–67; A Grocery Store, pages 72–73

STRATEGY FOCUS

Identify price per pound and recognize the abbreviation for pound(s).

READINESS CONNECTION

In this lesson, students interpret food ads.

PACING

To compress this lesson: Conduct 1A–C as whole-class activities.

To extend this lesson: Practice with grocery store ads. (See end of lesson.)

And/or have students complete **Workbook Introductory Level page 48** and **Multilevel Activities Introductory Level Unit 7 page 81.**

Lesson Notes

CORRELATIONS

CCRS: RF.2.A Demonstrate understanding of spoken words, syllables, and sounds (phonemes). SL.1.A Participate in collaborative conversations with diverse partners in small and larger groups.	**ELPS:** 2. An ELL can participate in level-appropriate oral and written exchanges of information, ideas, and analyses, in various social and academic contexts, responding to peer, audience, or reader comments and questions. 9. An ELL can create clear and coherent level-appropriate speech and text.

Warm-up and Review
5 minutes (books closed)

Display or draw pictures of the food items from Lessons 1 and 2. Ask volunteers to write the names next to the pictures. Say and have students repeat all of the words.

Introduction
5 minutes

1. Make statements with *I need*, for example: *I need rice.* Have volunteers hand you (or point to) the correct pictures. Say: *Thank you.*

2. State the objective: *Today we'll learn to ask for help in a store. To begin, we are going to look at supermarket ads and listen for prices.*

1 Listen for prices

Listening Extension
20–25 minutes

A 🔊 **2-47** 1. Direct students to look at the ad. Say and have students repeat *pound*. Show pictures of various items (oranges, rice, milk, eggs) and discuss whether they are sold by the pound or not.

2. Read the instructions. Play the entire audio once and direct students to point to the food.

B 🔊 **2-47** 1. Play the audio, stopping after each item to give students time to write. Repeat the item if necessary.

2. Call on volunteers for the answers. Write them on the board.

Answers
apples: $3.87
oranges: $1.50
grapes: $1.10
bananas: 29¢

C 1. Direct students to look at the ads. Elicit the prices of the apples and the oranges. Point out the *Need help?* box and explain that *lbs.* means *pounds*.

2. Do a sample problem on the board: *I need 9 lbs. of apples. 3 lbs. × 3 = 9 lbs. $2 × 3 = $6.*

3. Read number 1 aloud. Direct students to work individually to complete number 2. Ask a volunteer to write the problems and answers on the board.

Answers
1. 4, 4
2. 2, 6, 6

2 Practice your pronunciation

Pronunciation Extension
10–15 minutes

A 🔊 **2-48** 1. Say: *Now we're going to practice the pronunciation of s.* Direct students to read and listen to the words in the chart.

2. Say the singular and plural forms of the words in the bottom row and clap out the syllables to demonstrate that *–es* adds a syllable. Direct students' attention to the *Need help?* box if *peaches* is a new word for them.

B 🔊 **2-49** Play the audio. Tell students to listen and check the sounds they hear. Go over the answers as a class.

Answers	1.	2.	3.	4.	5.
-s		✓	✓		✓
-es	✓			✓	

C 🔊 **2-49** Replay the audio and ask students to repeat the words.

3 Make conversation: ask for help in a store

Presentation
5–10 minutes

A 1. Direct students to look at the pictures. Ask: *What is the woman buying?* [apples]

2. Direct students to read the conversation silently. Elicit any questions.

B 🔊 **2-50** Play the audio. Have students read the conversation silently.

Guided Practice
5–10 minutes

C 🔊 **2-50** 1. Play the audio again and have students repeat the conversation.

2. Do a choral reading of the conversation in 3B. Divide the class in half. Have one side be the clerk and one side be Rosita, and then have the sides switch roles.

Communicative Practice and Application
15–20 minutes

D 1. Model the conversation with a volunteer. Then switch roles and model it with another volunteer. Direct students to look at the ad in 1A for ideas.

2. Elicit other ways to complete the conversation.

3. Set a time limit (five minutes). Ask students to practice the conversation with several partners. Encourage pantomime and improvisation.

4. Ask volunteer pairs to present their conversations to the class.

> **MULTILEVEL STRATEGIES**
>
> For 3D, adapt the practice to the level of your students.
>
> • **Pre-level** While other students are practicing the conversation, have these students complete page 62 in the *Literacy Reproducible Activities Unit 7*.
>
> • **Higher-level** Teach these students a negative response for B: *I'm sorry. We don't have ____.*

Evaluation
5 minutes

TEST YOURSELF

Model the activity with a volunteer. Set a time limit (three minutes). Have students practice with several partners. Monitor and provide feedback.

> **EXTENSION ACTIVITY**
> **Shopping Ads**
>
> 1. Seat students in mixed-level groups. Give each group several grocery-store circulars or printouts from online grocery stores.
>
> 2. Set a time limit (five minutes). Tell them to talk about the prices. *Is the food expensive? What are the good prices?*
>
> 3. Call on reporters from each group to share the good prices and the expensive prices.

LESSON 5 READING

Lesson Overview

MULTILEVEL OBJECTIVES

On- and Higher-level: Identify containers and read a shopping list

Pre-level: Recognize containers and read a shopping list

LANGUAGE FOCUS

Grammar: Simple present *yes/no* questions and short answers *(Do they need soup? Yes, they do.)*

Vocabulary: *Bottle, box, buy, can, cereal, coffee, juice, shopping, soup, tea, water*

For vocabulary expansion, see these **Oxford Picture Dictionary** topics: A Grocery Store, pages 72–73; Containers and Packaging, page 74

STRATEGY FOCUS

Interpret *true/false* statements.

READINESS CONNECTION

In this lesson, students interpret a shopping list.

PACING

To compress this lesson: Conduct 2B as a whole-class activity.

To extend this lesson: Have groups make a shopping list. (See end of lesson.)

And/or have students complete **Workbook Introductory Level page 49** and **Multilevel Activities Introductory Level Unit 7 page 82.**

Lesson Notes

CORRELATIONS

CCRS: L.6.A Use words and phrases acquired through conversations, reading and being read to, and responding to texts, including using frequently occurring conjunctions to signal simple relationships (e.g., *because*).

R.1.A Ask and answer questions about key details in the text.

R.7.A Use the illustrations and details in a text to describe its key ideas (e.g., maps, charts, photographs, political cartoons, etc.).

SL.2.A Confirm understanding of a text read aloud or information presented orally or through other media by asking and answering questions about key details and requesting clarification if something is not understood.

ELPS: 1. An ELL can construct meaning from oral presentations and literary and informational text through level-appropriate listening, reading, and viewing. 8. An ELL can determine the meaning of words and phrases in oral presentations and literary and informational text.

Warm-up and Review
10–15 minutes (books closed)

Bring in real containers for the items in 1A. Elicit any words that the students already know for the containers or the foods. Find out if students have any of the items at home.

Introduction
5 minutes

1. Name the items you brought: *a can of coffee, a box of cereal*, etc.

2. State the objective: *Today we'll learn about containers, and we'll read a shopping list.*

1 Get ready to read

Presentation I
10–15 minutes

 1. Tell students to look at the pictures and listen to the words. Play the audio.

2. Check comprehension of the words. If you brought the items in, number them and call out descriptions: *a can of soup*. Tell students to show you the correct number with their fingers. If you didn't bring items, do the activity using pictures on the board.

3. Replay the audio and tell students to listen and repeat.

Guided Practice I
10–15 minutes

 1. Play number 1. Ask students what they heard [a can of soup].

2. Play the rest of the audio and have students listen and circle *a* or *b*.

Answers	
1. a	4. a
2. b	5. b
3. b	6. a

> **MULTILEVEL STRATEGIES**
>
> Replay the audio from 1B to allow pre-level students to catch up while you provide a challenge for on- and higher-level students.
>
> • **Pre-level** Have these students listen again to circle the correct answer.
>
> • **On- and Higher-level** Ask these students to listen again and write the items they hear.

Presentation II
5–10 minutes

 1. Direct students to look at the pictures. Say and have students repeat the words.

2. Provide sample sentences to help students understand the difference between *buy* and *shopping*: *I go shopping at Save Mart. I like shopping. I go shopping on Saturdays. I buy fruit. I buy vegetables. I buy soup. I buy candy.*

 1. Have students work individually to check the box.

2. Ask for a show of hands to find out how many students like shopping.

2 Read a shopping list

Guided Practice II
15–20 minutes

 1. Direct students to look at the picture in 2A. Ask who the people are [presumably husband and wife] and where the man is going [food/grocery shopping; to the supermarket/grocery store]. Ask your students if they make shopping lists.

2. Draw their attention to the *Reading Note*. Say and have students repeat the words. Elicit the number of syllables in each word.

3. Give students a couple of minutes to read the shopping list silently.

 1. Read number 1. Direct students' attention to the *Need help?* box. Explain that *True* is *yes* (or thumbs up) and *False* is *no* (or thumbs down).

2. Have students work independently to circle *True* and *False*.

Answers	
1. True	5. True
2. False	6. False
3. False	7. True
4. False	8. False

> **MULTILEVEL STRATEGIES**
>
> Adapt 2B to the level of your students.
>
> • **Pre-level** Read the statements aloud to these students. Have them look for the answers in the shopping list. Give them time to circle the answer before moving on to the next question.
>
> • **Higher-level** Ask these students to write two *true/false* statements about the shopping list. Have volunteers put their statements on the board. Call on other students to identify them as true or false.

> **TIP**
>
> After 2B, provide more practice with foods and containers. Set up a "store" (or several stores) in the front of the classroom. Use real containers and plastic food or use pictures. For each store, assign one student the role of clerk. Have the other students line up as customers, and have them ask for items in the store. Customer: *I need a box of cereal.* Clerk: *Here you go.* When the clerk has "sold" all of the items, have the customers return them and continue with a new clerk.

Application
5–10 minutes

BRING IT TO LIFE

Give students the URL for an online grocery store. If they are going to look at the website outside of class, tell them to make a list of things they need and note the prices. If you're doing it together in class, show them how to add items to their shopping cart.

> **TIP**
>
> In preparation for *Teamwork & Language Review*, have students review the unit vocabulary. Provide them with pictures you have collected or use the Picture Cards on pages 83–84 of *Multilevel Activities Introductory Level Unit 7*. Pair students and have them use the pictures as flashcards for recognition practice, dictation, or sentence writing.

EXTENSION ACTIVITY

Shopping List

1. Put students in mixed-level groups. Tell them they are going to have a party. Ask them to make a shopping list of things they would like to eat. Encourage students to refer to *The Oxford Picture Dictionary* or another dictionary.

2. Have the groups share their lists with the class.

3. As a follow-up, have the students look up the prices for their lists online. Ask each group to share its "party budget" with the class.

TEAMWORK & LANGUAGE REVIEW

Lesson Overview

MULTILEVEL OBJECTIVES

On-, Pre-, and Higher-level: Expand upon and review unit language and content

LANGUAGE FOCUS

Grammar: Simple present negative statements (*She doesn't like cheese.*); simple present yes/no questions and short answers (*Does he like fruit? Yes, he does.*)

Vocabulary: Food

For vocabulary expansion, see these **Oxford Picture Dictionary** topics: Fruit, page 68; Vegetables, page 69; Meat and Poultry, page 70; Back from the Market, pages 66–67; A Grocery Store, pages 72–73; Containers and Packaging, page 74

STRATEGY FOCUS

Use teamwork to reinforce and expand vocabulary.

READINESS CONNECTION

In this review, students practice teamwork and determine how to improve poor eating habits.

PACING

To extend this review: Have students complete **Workbook Introductory Level page 50**, **Multilevel Activities Introductory Level Unit 7 pages 83–86**, and **Multilevel Grammar Exercises Introductory Level Unit 7.**

Lesson Notes

CORRELATIONS

CCRS: L.6.A Use words and phrases acquired through conversations, reading and being read to, and responding to texts, including using frequently occurring conjunctions to signal simple relationships (e.g., *because*).

R.7.A Use the illustrations and details in a text to describe its key ideas (e.g., maps, charts, photographs, political cartoons, etc.).

SL.1.A Participate in collaborative conversations with diverse partners in small and larger groups.

SL.4.A Describe people, places, things, and events with relevant details, expressing ideas and feelings clearly.

SL.6.A Speak audibly and express thoughts, feelings, and ideas clearly. Produce complete sentences when appropriate to task and situation.

ELPS: 9. An ELL can create clear and coherent level-appropriate speech and text.

Warm-up and Review
5–10 minutes (books closed)

1. Review the *Bring It to Life* assignment from Lesson 5.

2. Ask volunteers to read their shopping lists aloud. Ask other students questions about their classmates' lists: *Does he need rice? Does she need cabbage?*

Introduction and Presentation
5 minutes

1. Write several of the questions and answers from the warm-up on the board. Write several negative and affirmative statements: *Choi doesn't need milk. Norma needs a box of cereal.*

2. State the objective: *Today we're going to review unit vocabulary and the present tense.*

Communicative Practice
15–20 minutes

A 1. Tell students to take turns naming one thing they see in the picture. Have three volunteers help you model turn-taking.

2. Tell students to put their pencils down and listen to each other so that they don't repeat ideas. Direct them to go around the group until they have run out of ideas.

B 1. Have students work in the same groups from A. Assign roles: secretary, reporter, editor, and manager. Write the roles on the board. As you explain each role, pantomime the duties you expect the person taking that role to perform. Explain that students work with their groups to write the words. Verify comprehension of roles.

2. Set a time limit (five minutes) to complete the chart. Circulate and answer any questions.

3. Call on the reporters from each group to say the words from their chart. Write the words on the board. Go around the class until there are no more ideas.

Possible Answers				
Fruit	**Vegetables**	**Grains**	**Meat**	**Other**
bananas	broccoli	rice	chicken	cheese
grapes	corn	bread	fish	eggs
apples	lettuce		beef	box
orange				bag
				shopping list
				clock

C 1. Have the groups identify new words from the board and to look them up in a picture dictionary or a bilingual dictionary.

2. Tell students to add three new words to their chart. [New words might include: *bowl, carton, freezer, ketchup, mustard, refrigerator, shopping bag, window*.]

> **MULTILEVEL STRATEGIES**
>
> For A–C, use mixed-level groups.
>
> • **Pre-level** Assign these students the role of manager.
>
> • **On-level** Assign these students the role of secretary or reporter.
>
> • **Higher-level** Assign these students the role of editor.

D 1. Read number 1 aloud. Tell students to work independently to complete the questions and answers.

2. Call on volunteers to read the completed questions and answers aloud.

Answers	
1. Does	4. Do, don't
2. Do, don't	5. Does, does
3. Do, don't	6. Does, doesn't

F 1. Have students work independently to write two sentences.

2. Ask volunteers to write their sentences on the board. Correct them as a class.

PROBLEM SOLVING IN DAILY LIFE
15–20 minutes

A **2-53** 1. Tell students the pictures in A tell a story about a man named Duncan. He has a problem with food.

2. Direct students to look at the pictures. Ask what time it is in each picture [6 a.m.; 12 p.m.; 8 p.m.; 10 p.m.]. Ask where Duncan is eating [a donut shop; the office/at his desk; in the car].

3. Play the audio and have students listen and look at the pictures. Check comprehension. Ask: *What does Duncan eat?* [donuts, pizza, hamburgers] Write and have students repeat *donut, pizza,* and *hamburger*. Ask: *Are those good foods?*

B 1. Tell students to look at the pictures. Read the captions and talk about them. Explain that breakfast is the morning meal and lunch is the noon meal. Point out the differences between these meals and the ones in A. Say and have students repeat the word *walk*. Demonstrate its meaning.

2. Ask for a show of hands to see which solution the class likes best. Emphasize that there can be more than one correct answer.

Evaluation
20–25 minutes

To test students' understanding of the unit language and content, have them take the Unit 7 Test, available on the Teacher Resource Center.

UNIT 8: What's the Matter?

Unit Overview

This unit explores health problems, medical appointments, the verb *have*, and medicine labels.

KEY OBJECTIVES

Lesson 1	Identify parts of the body
Lesson 2	Identify common symptoms and ailments; describe health problems in an email
Lesson 3	Use *have* and *has* to describe symptoms and ailments
Lesson 4	Make medical appointments
Lesson 5	Interpret medical labels
Teamwork & Language Review	Review unit language

UNIT FEATURES

Academic Vocabulary	*label, medical*
Employability Skills	• Listen actively • Understand teamwork • Communicate information • Work with others • Cooperate with others • Interpret medicine labels • Determine how to handle obligations when sick

Resources	**Class Audio** CD2, Tracks 54–68
	Workbook Unit 8, pages 51–57
	Teacher Resource Center
	    Literacy Reproducible Activities Unit 8
	    Multilevel Activities Introductory Level Unit 8
	    Multilevel Grammar Exercises Introductory Level Unit 8
	    Unit 8 Test
	Oxford Picture Dictionary The Body, Symptoms and Injuries, Illnesses and Medical Conditions, Medical Care, Taking Care of Your Health

LESSON 1 VOCABULARY

Lesson Overview

MULTILEVEL OBJECTIVES

On-level: Identify parts of the body
Pre-level: Recognize parts of the body
Higher-level: Talk about parts of the body

LANGUAGE FOCUS

Grammar: Imperatives *(Point to your leg.)*
Vocabulary: *Arm, back, ear, eye, foot, hand, head, leg, nose, stomach*
For vocabulary expansion, see this **Oxford Picture Dictionary** topic: The Body, pages 104–105

STRATEGY FOCUS

To remember different parts of the body, it may help to categorize them by number, or how many of them we typically have.

READINESS CONNECTION

In this lesson, students work with others to practice words for parts of the body.

PACING

To compress this lesson: Conduct 2A as a whole-class activity.
To extend this lesson: Do a picture dictation. (See end of lesson.)
And/or have students complete **Workbook Introductory Level page 51** and **Multilevel Activities Introductory Level Unit 8 page 88.**

Lesson Notes

CORRELATIONS

CCRS: L.6.A Use words and phrases acquired through conversations, reading and being read to, and responding to texts, including using frequently occurring conjunctions to signal simple relationships (e.g., *because*).
SL.2.A Confirm understanding of a text read aloud or information presented orally or through other media by asking and answering questions about key details and requesting clarification if something is not understood.

ELPS: 1. An ELL can construct meaning from oral presentations and literary and informational text through level-appropriate listening, reading, and viewing.

Warm-up and Review
10–15 minutes (books closed)

Find out which words for body parts your students already know. Say *head* and touch your head. Then call out *arm, leg, hand, ear, eye,* and *nose* and ask your students to point to the ones they recognize.

Introduction
5 minutes

1. Say and point to each of these body parts: *head, eye, ear, nose, arm, hand, stomach, leg, foot.*

2. State the objective: *Today we're going to learn parts of the body.*

Lesson Plans Intro   Unit 8 Lesson 1 Vocabulary

1 Learn parts of the body

Presentation
20–25 minutes

A Direct students to look at the picture. Ask if the woman is sick [no].

B 🔊 **2-54** 1. Play the audio. Ask students to point to the correct part of the picture as they listen. Circulate and monitor.

2. Check comprehension. Point to your own body and ask: *Is this my arm? Is this my head?* Have students hold their thumbs up (*yes*) or thumbs down (*no*) in order to get a nonverbal response.

C 🔊 **2-54** 1. Tell students to listen and repeat the words.

2. Call out the numbers out of order and ask students to say the words.

Guided Practice I
15–20 minutes

D Direct students to take turns reading the words with a partner.

E 1. Model the activity with two volunteers. Direct one partner to point to the picture or say the numbers. Have the other partner cover the words in 1C and identify the parts of the body from memory.

2. Have students practice in pairs.

> **MULTILEVEL STRATEGIES**
>
> For 1E, pair same-level students together.
>
> • **Pre-level** Tell these students to practice together by pointing to the picture in 1B and saying the correct words.
>
> • **Higher-level** Tell these students to dictate the words to each other.

2 Talk about parts of the body

Guided Practice II
15–20 minutes

A 1. Direct students to look at the picture. Call out the numbers and ask students to identify the body parts.

2. Copy number 1 on the board and have students spell *head* aloud. Demonstrate how to write one letter on each line.

3. Tell students to work individually to complete the words.

4. Ask volunteers to spell the completed words aloud. Write the answers on the board. Read and have students repeat the words.

Answers	
1. h-e-a-d	6. a-r-m
2. e-a-r	7. s-t-o-m-a-c-h
3. e-y-e	8. b-a-c-k
4. n-o-s-e	9. f-o-o-t
5. h-a-n-d	10. l-e-g

B Give students time to copy the words into their notebooks. Monitor and check their writing.

C 🔊 **2-55** 1. Play the audio. Have students read along silently and point to their own bodies.

2. Play the audio again. Tell students to listen and repeat.

> **TIP**
>
> Before 2D, check comprehension by having all of the students stand and point to the parts of the body that you call out. Repeat any problem contrasts (for example, *head/hand*, *ear/eye*).

Communicative Practice and Application
10–15 minutes

D 1. Pair students. Have one pair model giving and following directions.

2. Set a time limit (five minutes) and have partners practice in both roles. Encourage students to use all of the words from 2A. Circulate and monitor. Provide feedback.

> **MULTILEVEL STRATEGIES**
>
> For 2D, seat students in mixed-level groups.
>
> • **Pre-level** Have these students listen and follow directions.
>
> • **On- and Higher-level** Have these students give directions.

Evaluation
10–15 minutes

TEST YOURSELF

Direct students to copy the chart into their notebooks. Ask them to work independently to complete their charts. Monitor and provide feedback.

> **MULTILEVEL STRATEGIES**
>
> Target the *Test Yourself* to the level of your students.
>
> • **Pre-level** Have these students complete the chart with their books open.
>
> • **Higher-level** Direct these students to close their books and write as many words as they can remember in the chart. Challenge them to include words not presented in the unit.

> **EXTENSION ACTIVITY**
>
> **Picture Dictation**
>
> 1. Draw a funny-looking creature on the board—for example, something with a big head, four eyes, one ear, and three arms. Tell students it's a monster. Elicit the number of eyes, ears, and arms.
>
> 2. Tell students they are going to draw a different monster. Dictate numbers and body parts and have the students draw what you are describing: *Two heads! Four arms!* For variety, teach the words *big* and *small* and incorporate them into your descriptions: *One big head, two small ears.*
>
> 3. As a follow-up, ask students to describe the monster back to you and write out the numbers and body parts on the board. Ask volunteers to display their monsters for the class.

LESSON 2 WRITING

Lesson Overview

MULTILEVEL OBJECTIVES

On- and Higher-level: Read and write about health problems

Pre-level: Recognize health problems

LANGUAGE FOCUS

Grammar: Has/have (He has a headache.)

Vocabulary: Cold, cough, earache, fever, flu, headache, sore throat, stomachache

For vocabulary expansion, see these **Oxford Picture Dictionary** topics: Symptoms and Injuries, page 110; Illnesses and Medical Conditions, pages 112–113

STRATEGY FOCUS

When addressing someone in a formal email, use *Dear*; when closing the email, use *Sincerely*.

READINESS CONNECTION

In this lesson, students listen actively for and communicate information about medical symptoms.

PACING

To compress this lesson: Assign the *Test Yourself* for homework.

To extend this lesson: Write a class composition. (See end of lesson.)

And/or have students complete **Workbook Introductory Level page 52** and **Multilevel Activities Introductory Level Unit 8 page 89.**

Lesson Notes

CORRELATIONS

CCRS: R.1.A Ask and answer questions about key details in the text.

R.7.A Use the illustrations and details in a text to describe its key ideas (e.g., maps, charts, photographs, political cartoons, etc.).

SL.2.A Confirm understanding of a text read aloud or information presented orally or through other media by asking and answering questions about key details and requesting clarification if something is not understood.

ELPS: 1. An ELL can construct meaning from oral presentations and literary and informational text through level-appropriate listening, reading, and viewing. 9. An ELL can create clear and coherent level-appropriate speech and text.

Warm-up and Review
10–15 minutes (books closed)

Review body parts. Point to your head, eye, ear, nose, arm, hand, stomach, leg, and foot. Ask volunteers to come to the board and write the words.

Introduction
5 minutes

1. Pantomime having a headache, an earache, and a stomachache. Say: *I'm sick. I have a headache. I have an earache. I have a stomachache.*

2. State the objective: *Today we're going to read and write about health problems.*

142 Unit 8 Lesson 2 Writing   Lesson Plans Intro

1 Learn about health problems

Presentation I
15–20 minutes

A Direct students to look at the picture. Ask if Paula is the mother or the daughter [mother]. Have students point to her husband, son, and daughter. Ask them to name some of the "problem" body parts [throat, ear, head].

B 🔊 **2-56** 1. Play the audio. Have students read along silently.

2. Check comprehension. Direct students to cover the words and look at the picture. Say the words out of order and have students call out the correct numbers. Then say the numbers and have students call out the words.

3. Replay the audio and ask students to repeat the words.

4. Act out the health problems and ask students to name them.

Guided Practice I
10–15 minutes

C 1. Read number 1 aloud. Ask students to find Adam in the picture.

2. Direct students to work independently to complete the sentences.

3. Have students read the completed sentences with a partner. Call on volunteers to read them aloud.

Answers	
1. earache	4. cold, cough
2. stomachache	5. flu
3. headache	6. sore throat

2 Prepare to write: email the doctor

Presentation II
10–15 minutes

A 🔊 **2-57** 1. Ask students to read the times aloud in number 1. Explain that they are appointment times. Play number one and ask which time they heard [12:00].

2. Play the rest of the audio and have students work independently to circle the times they hear.

Answers
1. a
2. b
3. a
4. a

B 🔊 **2-57** 1. Point out Daniela's name on the health form. Replay number 1 and elicit the answers.

2. Replay the rest of the audio one at a time and tell students to check the health problems.

3. Go over the answers as a class and replay the audio if necessary.

Answers
1. Daniela Lopez: cough, fever, sore throat
2. Charlie Foss: headache, earache
3. Julie Chan: flu
4. Colleen Rios: stomachache

C 🔊 **2-58** 1. Read the instructions aloud. Tell students to point to Paula in the picture in 1A.

2. Play the audio. Have students read along silently.

3. Replay the audio and have students point to the picture in 1A as they listen. If you have access to a projector, ask a volunteer to point to the correct area as you read the sentences.

4. Direct students' attention to the *Writer's Note*. Point out the commas after *Dear* and *Sincerely*. Point out that Paula uses her first and last names because this is formal communication.

MULTILEVEL STRATEGIES

For 2C, seat students in mixed-level groups. After the whole-group practice, ask students to take turns reading the sentences in the email aloud. Demonstrate turn-taking, with the first student reading the first sentence, the second the next sentence, and so on.

- **Pre-level** Tell students who don't want to read aloud to listen to their classmates and follow along silently.

Guided Practice II
15–20 minutes

 1. Read number 1 aloud. Tell students to work independently to complete the exercise.

2. Have students compare their answers with a partner. Say the answers and have students repeat each sentence.

Answers
1. a
2. b
3. b
4. b

3 Write about health problems

Communicative Practice
10–15 minutes

1. Introduce the new activity: *Now we are going to write an email to our doctors.*

2. Tell students to copy the email in their notebooks and to work individually to complete the sentences with their own ideas.

3. Remind students to review their sentences for commas, periods, and capital letters.

4. Have students read their email aloud to a partner. When they finish, ask them to read it to a new partner.

> **MULTILEVEL STRATEGIES**
>
> Adapt 3 to the level of your students.
>
> • **Pre-level** While on- and higher-level students are completing 3, work with these students in a group, or have them complete page 66 of the *Literacy Reproducible Activities Unit 8*.

AT WORK

Report sickness
10–15 minutes

 Direct students to look at the sickness report. Ask them to find the date [7/19/17, or July 19, 2017]. Direct them to look at the *Start* date and the *End* date. Ask: *Is Allie going to be absent from work for one day or two days?* [one day]

B 1. Tell students to look at the sickness report and work individually to complete the sentences.

2. Go over the answers as a class. Ask students to show where they found the answers in the report. [The answers to 1 and 2 are in the *Notes* section. The answer to 3 is in the date fields.]

3. Ask students how they report sickness at work.

Answers
1. daughter
2. morning
3. 7/19 (July 19th)

Evaluation
10 minutes

TEST YOURSELF

1. Have students turn to page 105. Tell them to work independently to complete the sentences. Remind them to include *a* or *an*.

2. Have volunteers write sentences on the board. Have students correct their own work.

> **MULTILEVEL STRATEGIES**
>
> Adapt the *Test Yourself* to the level of your students.
>
> • **Higher-level:** Show these students how to list multiple symptoms in a sentence: *Daniela has a cough, a fever, and a sore throat.* Ask them to write sentences about Harry in the picture on page 104.

> **EXTENSION ACTIVITY**
>
> **Class Composition**
>
> As a class, write an absence excuse note to a teacher.
>
> 1. Write sentence frames on the board:
>
> Dear _____,
>
> My _____ is sick today. He/She has a _____. _____ name is _____ (child's name).
>
> Thank you,
>
> _____ (student's name).
>
> 2. Elicit completions for the letter. Have students copy and complete it in their books.

LESSON 3 GRAMMAR

Lesson Overview

MULTILEVEL OBJECTIVES

On- and Higher-level: Use *have* and *has*

Pre-level: Recognize *have* and *has*

LANGUAGE FOCUS

Grammar: *Have* and *has* (*He has a headache. Do you have a headache?*)

Vocabulary: Health problems

For vocabulary expansion, see these **Oxford Picture Dictionary** topics: Illnesses and Medical Conditions, pages 112–113; Symptoms and Injuries, page 110

STRATEGY FOCUS

When responding to questions about illnesses, use short answers appropriately.

READINESS CONNECTION

In this lesson, students work with others and communicate information about medical symptoms.

PACING

To compress this lesson: Assign the *Test Yourself* for homework.

To extend this lesson: Do pantomime practice. (See end of lesson.)

And/or have students complete **Workbook Introductory Level pages 53–54, Multilevel Activities Introductory Level Unit 8 page 90,** and **Multilevel Grammar Exercises Introductory Level Unit 8.**

Lesson Notes

CORRELATIONS

CCRS: L.1.A Demonstrate command of the conventions of standard English grammar and usage when writing or speaking. e. Use verbs to convey a sense of past, present, and future (e.g., *Yesterday I walked home; Today I walk home; Tomorrow I will walk home.*). g. Use frequently occurring nouns and verbs.

SL.1.A Participate in collaborative conversations with diverse partners in small and larger groups.

ELPS: 10. An ELL can demonstrate command of the conventions of standard English to communicate in level-appropriate speech and writing.

Warm-up and Review
10–15 minutes (books closed)

Review health problems. Pass out cards with health problems on them. Ask students to act out the problem on the card. Have the class guess the ailment.

Introduction
5–10 minutes

1. Make statements about students who pantomimed ailments: *He has a cough. She has a stomachache. I have a headache.*

2. State the objective: *Today we'll practice using* have *and* has.

1 Use *have* and *has*

Presentation I
20–25 minutes

A 1. Direct students to look at the pictures. Ask them to identify the health problems [backache, toothache, the flu].

2. Read the captions aloud.

B 🔊 2-60 1. Play the audio. Tell students to read the chart and listen.

2. Demonstrate how to read the grammar chart as complete sentences. Read the chart through sentence by sentence. Then read it again, and have students repeat after you.

3. Direct students to re-read the sentences in 1A and underline *have* and *has*.

4. Assess students' understanding of the chart. Hold up pictures of people with health problems or act them out and elicit sentences with *He has, She has,* and *You have.*

Guided Practice I
15–20 minutes

C 1. Have students look at the pictures and complete the sentences independently.

2. Have them read their completed sentences with a partner. Call on individuals to read the completed sentences for the class.

Answers	
1. has	3. has
2. have	4. has

D Tell students to work independently to complete the sentences. Have two volunteers write their sentences on the board.

Answers
1. She has a headache.
2. He has a fever.

MULTILEVEL STRATEGIES

For 1C and 1D, seat pre-level students together.

• **Pre-level** While other students are completing 1C and 1D, work with these students on 1C. Read each sentence aloud and elicit the answer. Have students complete the answer before you move on to the next sentence.

2 Practice: *yes/no* questions with *have*

Presentation II
10–15 minutes

A 🔊 2-61 1. Direct students to look at the pictures. Ask them to identify the health problems [sore throat, fever].

2. Play the audio. Ask students to read along silently.

3. Replay the audio and tell students to listen and repeat.

4. Tell students to read the conversations with a partner.

Guided Practice II
10–15 minutes

B 1. Direct students to look at the picture. Elicit the health problems. Ask: *Does Leo have a cough?* [No, he doesn't.] *Does he have a stomachache?* [Yes, he does.]

2. Read number 1 aloud. Direct students to work individually to complete the rest of the questions and answers.

3. Call on volunteers to read the questions and answers aloud. Write the completions on the board.

4. Have students read the conversations in pairs.

Answers	
1. he does	5. Does, have
2. she doesn't	6. Does, have
3. she does	7. Does, have
4. they don't	8. Does, have

C Have students circulate and ask and answer the question with at least three partners.

3 Ask and answer questions about health problems

Communicative Practice and Application
20–25 minutes

 A 2-62 Direct students' attention to the pictures. Play the audio and have students repeat the conversations.

 B 1. Direct students to look at the pictures. Elicit the health problems.

2. Read the model conversation with a volunteer. Have two volunteers model it again using a different picture and making substitutions as necessary.

> **MULTILEVEL STRATEGIES**
>
> Adapt 3B for your pre-level students.
>
> • **Pre-level** Have these students work with an on-level or higher-level pair. Instruct the on-level students to practice the conversation together. After they have practiced each conversation, one on-level partner repeats the questions for the pre-level student to answer.

Evaluation
10–15 minutes

TEST YOURSELF

Have students work independently to write sentences. Collect and correct their work.

> **MULTILEVEL STRATEGIES**
>
> Target the *Test Yourself* to the level of your students.
>
> • **Higher-level** Show these students how to write negative sentences with *have* and tell them to write an affirmative and negative sentence about three of the pictures.

> **EXTENSION ACTIVITY**
>
> **Pantomime Practice**
>
> 1. Write on the board:
>   A: *Act out a health problem.*
>   B: *Ask a question.*
>   C: *Answer. Ask a new question.*
>   D: *Answer.*
>   *Switch roles.*
>
> Have four volunteers come to the front of the room to model the activity. Student A begins by pantomiming a health problem. Demonstrate that there are two questions: one should have a *yes* answer and one should have a *no* answer. After they have gone through the sequence, have them switch roles and model again with a new health problem.
>
> 2. Have the students practice in groups. Circulate and provide feedback.

LESSON 4 EVERYDAY CONVERSATION

Lesson Overview	Lesson Notes
MULTILEVEL OBJECTIVES	
On- Pre- and Higher-level: Make a doctor's appointment	
LANGUAGE FOCUS	
Grammar: Have (I have a stomachache.) **Vocabulary:** Health problems For vocabulary expansion, see these **Oxford Picture Dictionary** topics: Symptoms and Injuries, page 110; Illnesses and Medical Conditions, pages 112–113; Medical Care, page 111	
STRATEGY FOCUS	
Use a calendar to arrange an appointment time.	
READINESS CONNECTION	
In this lesson, students listen actively in order to complete a medical appointment calendar.	
PACING	
To compress this lesson: Have students practice 3D with only one partner. **To extend this lesson:** Extend the pronunciation practice. (See end of lesson.) And/or have students complete **Workbook Introductory Level page 55** and **Multilevel Activities Introductory Level page 91**.	
CORRELATIONS	
CCRS: SL.1.A Participate in collaborative conversations with diverse partners in small and larger groups. SL.2.A Confirm understanding of a text read aloud or information presented orally or through other media by asking and answering questions about key details and requesting clarification if something is not understood. RF.2.A Demonstrate understanding of spoken words, syllables, and sounds (phonemes).	**ELPS:** 2. An ELL can participate in level-appropriate oral and written exchanges of information, ideas, and analyses, in various social and academic contexts, responding to peer, audience, or reader comments and questions. 9. An ELL can create clear and coherent level-appropriate speech and text.

Warm-up and Review
5 minutes (books closed)

Pass out a few slips of paper with health problems written on them. Then ask students holding the slips: *Do you have a _____?* Instruct them to answer *No, I don't* until you guess the right health problem. Once you have demonstrated the activity, show students that you are also holding two or three slips of paper. Call on students to ask you *yes/no* questions until they guess each health problem.

Introduction
5 minutes

1. Tell students that when you have these problems, you go to the doctor.

2. State the objective: *Today we'll learn how to call the doctor's office.*

1 Listen for medical appointment information

Listening Extension
15–20 minutes

A 🔊 2-63 Introduce the topic: *To begin, we're going to listen for medical appointment information.* Play the audio. Direct students to look at the appointment book and point to the days they hear.

B 🔊 2-63 1. Play the audio. Tell students to check the correct day and time. Ask for a show of hands to see how students answered. Repeat the segment if necessary.

2. Have students say the days and times with a partner.

Answers			
Time	Wednesday	Thursday	Friday
8:00	✓		
8:30	✓		
9:00		✓	
9:30			✓

MULTILEVEL STRATEGIES

Replay the conversation to allow pre-level students to catch up while you provide a challenge for higher-level students.

- **Pre-level** Have these students listen again to check the day and time.
- **On- and Higher-level** Ask these students to write the health problem they hear for each patient. As you go over the answers to 1B, elicit the health problem.

2 Practice your pronunciation

Pronunciation Extension
10–15 minutes

A 🔊 2-64 1. Direct students to look at the chart.

2. Play the audio and ask students to read along silently.

B 🔊 2-65 1. Tell students to read the words in the box. Ask them to guess which words will go in which column in the chart in 2A.

2. Play the audio, stopping after each word. Tell students to write the word in the correct column.

Answers	
matter	*ache*
1. have	7. say
2. has	8. name
3. sad	9. plane
4. hand	10. grapes
5. happy	11. day
6. back	12. make

C 🔊 2-65 Replay the audio in 2B and have students check their answers. Call on volunteers for the answers.

3 Make conversation: make a doctor's appointment

Presentation
5–10 minutes

A 1. Direct students to look at the pictures. Ask: *Does she have a sore throat?* [no]

2. Have students read the conversation silently. Elicit any questions.

Guided Practice
5–10 minutes

B 🔊 2-66 Play the audio. Have students read the conversation silently. Ask: *What is a receptionist's job?* [to answer the phone, identify the problem, and schedule an appointment]

C 🔊 2-66 1. Play the audio again and have students repeat the conversation.

2. Do a choral reading of the conversation in 3B. Divide the class in half. Have one side be Kara and one side be the receptionist, and then have the sides switch roles.

Communicative Practice and Application
15–20 minutes

D 1. Model the conversation with a volunteer. Then have two volunteers model the conversation using one of the health problems from the *Need help?* box.

2. Elicit other ways to complete the conversation.

3. Set a time limit (five minutes). Tell students to practice the conversation with several partners. Encourage pantomime and improvisation.

4. Ask volunteer pairs to present their conversations to the class.

> **MULTILEVEL STRATEGIES**
>
> For 3D, seat pre-level students together.
>
> • **Pre-level** While other students are practicing the conversation, have these students complete page 68 in the *Literacy Reproducible Activities Unit 8.*
>
> • **Higher-level** Encourage these students to close their books and practice with several partners.

Evaluation
5 minutes

TEST YOURSELF

1. Model the activity with a volunteer.

2. Set a time limit (three minutes). Have students practice with a partner. Then have them switch partners and repeat.

> **EXTENSION ACTIVITY**
>
> **Pronunciation Practice**
>
> After 2C, provide more practice with the different sounds of *a*.
>
> 1. Draw a chart of two columns and six rows on the board with *matter* and *ache* as column headings. Ask students to copy it into their notebooks.
>
> 2. Write the following words on the board: *apples, pants, table, paper, state, lamp, family, date, age,* and *lamb*. Pronounce the words, and ask students to write them in the correct column of their chart.
>
> **Answers**
> **matter**: apples, pants, lamp, family, lamb
> **ache**: table, paper, state, date, age

LESSON 5 READING

Lesson Overview

MULTILEVEL OBJECTIVES

On- and Higher-level: Identify frequency expressions and read a medicine label

Pre-level: Recognize frequency expressions and read a medicine label

LANGUAGE FOCUS

Grammar: Have (I have medicine for coughs.)

Vocabulary: Frequency expressions, *label, medicine, tablespoon, tablet, teaspoon*

For vocabulary expansion, see this **Oxford Picture Dictionary** topic: Taking Care of Your Health, pages 116–117

STRATEGY FOCUS

Interpret abbreviations to identify the correct dosage on a medicine label.

READINESS CONNECTION

In this lesson, students interpret medicine labels.

PACING

To compress this lesson: Conduct 2B as a whole-class activity.

To extend this lesson: Practice a conversation about medicine. (See end of lesson.)

And/or have students complete **Workbook Introductory Level page 56** and **Multilevel Activities Introductory Level Unit 8 page 92**.

Lesson Notes

CORRELATIONS

CCRS: R.1.A Ask and answer questions about key details in the text.

R.7.A Use the illustrations and details in a text to describe its key ideas (e.g., maps, charts, photographs, political cartoons, etc.).

L.6.A Use words and phrases acquired through conversations, reading and being read to, and responding to texts, including using frequently occurring conjunctions to signal simple relationships (e.g., *because*).

ELPS: 1. An ELL can construct meaning from oral presentations and literary and informational text through level-appropriate listening, reading, and viewing. 8. An ELL can determine the meaning of words and phrases in oral presentations and informational text.

Warm-up and Review
10–15 minutes (books closed)

Review times. Use a clock with movable hands, show various times, and ask students: *What time is it?*

Introduction
5 minutes

1. Show students an over-the-counter medicine bottle. Say: *When I have _____, I take this medicine in the morning and in the evening. I take it twice a day.*

2. State the objective: *Today we'll learn frequency words, and we'll read a medicine label.*

1 Get ready to read

Presentation I
10–15 minutes

 A 🔊 2-67 1. Tell students to look at the calendars. Ask how many days they see on each calendar [7, 7, 7, 1, 1]. Play the audio.

2. Check comprehension of the words. Say: *I take medicine at 9 a.m. and 9 p.m. Is that twice a day or three times a day?* [twice a day]

3. Replay the audio and tell students to listen and repeat.

Guided Practice I
15–20 minutes

 B 1. Read number 1 aloud. Use a clock with movable hands to show the times in letter *c*. Have students count the hours between each time. Tell them to work individually to complete the exercise.

2. Call on volunteers for the answers. Write the answers on the board.

Answers
1. c
2. e
3. b
4. a
5. d

> **TIP**
>
> For more practice with frequency expressions after 1B, pantomime actions and ask students to tell you an appropriate frequency expression. Possible actions to pantomime: eating, brushing teeth, showering, exercising, talking on the phone, washing the car, and sweeping.

Presentation II
10–15 minutes

 C 1. Direct students to look at the medicine labels. Say and have students repeat the words.

2. Bring in over-the-counter medicine, a teaspoon, and a tablespoon to demonstrate the vocabulary.

 D Ask students to check the sentences about themselves. Call on volunteers to read their sentences aloud.

2 Read medicine labels

Guided Practice II
15–20 minutes

 A 1. Direct students to look at the medicine labels. Ask them which medicines they think are for a cough, a headache, and a cold.

2. Tell students to read the labels silently. Ask if there are any questions about the reading.

3. Check students' comprehension. Ask *or* questions: *Do you take the cough medicine every four hours or every six hours?* [every six hours]

4. Draw students' attention to the *Reading Note*. Ask them to identify which medicines use tablespoons [1 and 4] and which uses teaspoons [3].

 B 1. Read the answers choices for number 1 and show students where to find the answer. Direct students to work individually to circle *a* or *b*.

2. Call on volunteers for the answers. Write them on the board.

Answers
1. b
2. b
3. a
4. a
5. a

> **MULTILEVEL STRATEGIES**
>
> Adapt 2B for your pre-level students.
>
> • **Pre-level** While other students are completing the exercise, work with these students. Help them find and circle the words on the labels that match the words in the answer choices.

Application
5–10 minutes

BRING IT TO LIFE

Read the instructions aloud. Show students several examples of medicine bottles or boxes. Point out that the information is also on the box, so it's fine to bring in only the box.

TIP

In preparation for *Teamwork & Language Review*, have students review the unit vocabulary. Provide them with pictures you have collected or use the Picture Cards on pages 93–94 of *Multilevel Activities Introductory Level Unit 8*. Pair students and have them use the pictures as flashcards for recognition practice, dictation, or sentence writing.

EXTENSION ACTIVITY

Conversation

For more practice with medicine labels after 2B, have students practice a conversation using the labels in 2A.

A: What's the matter?

B: I have a _____.

A: (pointing) Take this medicine. Take (two tablespoons every six hours).

Write sentence frames for the conversation on the board and model it with several volunteers. Set a time limit (five minutes) and have students practice it with a partner.

TEAMWORK & LANGUAGE REVIEW

Lesson Overview

MULTILEVEL OBJECTIVES

On-, Pre-, and Higher-level: Expand upon and review unit language and content

LANGUAGE FOCUS

Grammar: *Have* and *has* (*He has a headache. Do you have a headache?*)

Vocabulary: Health problems

For vocabulary expansion, see these **Oxford Picture Dictionary** topics: Symptoms and Injuries, page 110; Illnesses and Medical Conditions, pages 112–113; Taking Care of Your Health, pages 116–117

STRATEGY FOCUS

Use teamwork to reinforce and expand vocabulary.

READINESS CONNECTION

In this review, students work with a team to determine how to handle obligations when sick.

PACING

To extend this review: Have students complete **Workbook Introductory Level page 57**, **Multilevel Activities Introductory Level Unit 8 pages 93–96**, and **Multilevel Grammar Exercises Introductory Level Unit 8.**

Lesson Notes

CORRELATIONS

CCRS: L.6.A Use words and phrases acquired through conversations, reading and being read to, and responding to texts, including using frequently occurring conjunctions to signal simple relationships (e.g., *because*).

R.7.A Use the illustrations and details in a text to describe its key ideas (e.g., maps, charts, photographs, political cartoons, etc.).

SL.1.A Participate in collaborative conversations with diverse partners in small and larger groups.

SL.4.A Describe people, places, things, and events with relevant details, expressing ideas and feelings clearly.

SL.6.A Speak audibly and express thoughts, feelings, and ideas clearly. Produce complete sentences when appropriate to task and situation.

ELPS: 2. An ELL can participate in level-appropriate oral and written exchanges of information, ideas, and analyses, in various social and academic contexts, responding to peer, audience, or reader comments and questions.

Warm-up and Review
5–10 minutes (books closed)

1. Review the *Bring It to Life* assignment from Lesson 5.

2. Have students who brought medicine bottles or boxes read the amounts and frequencies on the labels. Tell other students to write the information on the board.

Introduction and Presentation
5 minutes

1. Use some of the medicines from the warm-up to bring up health problems: *Those tablets are for headaches. This is for a cough.* Write sentences on the board: *I have a headache. He has a cough.* Write and ask students questions: *Do you have a stomachache? Does she have the flu?* Write the questions and answers on the board.

2. State the objective: *Today we're going to review* have *and* has *to talk about health problems.*

Communicative Practice
15–20 minutes

A 1. Tell students to take turns naming one thing they see in the picture. Have three volunteers help you model turn-taking.

2. Tell students to put their pencils down and listen to each other so that they don't repeat ideas. Direct them to go around the group until they have run out of ideas.

B 1. Have students work in the same groups from A. Assign roles: secretary, reporter, editor, and manager. Write the roles on the board. As you explain each role, pantomime the duties you expect the person taking that role to perform. Explain that students work with their groups to write the words. Verify comprehension of roles.

2. Set a time limit (five minutes) to complete the chart. Circulate and answer any questions.

3. Call on the reporters from each group to say the words from their chart. Write the words on the board. Go around the class until there are no more ideas.

Possible Answers		
Parts of the body	**Health problems**	**Other**
head	fever	medicine
hands	sick	tablespoon
arms	cold	doctor
legs	flu	appointment
nose	cough	time
eyes		bed

C 1. Have the groups identify new words from the board and to look them up in a picture dictionary or a bilingual dictionary.

2. Tell students to add three new words to their chart. [New words might include: *tissues, alarm clock, slippers, thermometer.*]

MULTILEVEL STRATEGIES

For A–C, use mixed-level groups.

• **Pre-level** Assign these students the role of manager.

• **On-level** Assign these students the role of secretary or reporter.

• **Higher-level** Assign these students the role of editor.

D 1. Read number 1 aloud. Point to Lucas in the picture. Tell students to work independently to complete the sentences.

2. Call on volunteers to read the completed sentences aloud. Write the answers on the board.

Answers	
1. sick	5. work
2. has	6. doctor
3. medicine	7. appointment
4. tablespoon	

MULTILEVEL STRATEGIES

Adapt D to the level of your students.

• **Pre-level** Have these students work with an on-level student to complete the exercises. The on-level student helps with the answers. The pre-level student reads the completed sentences aloud.

• **Higher-level** Challenge these students to write three questions about the picture. For example: *Does Lucas have a cough? Is Lucas sick? When is his appointment?*

PROBLEM SOLVING
15–20 minutes

A 1. Tell students the pictures in A tell a story about a woman named Orane. She has a health problem.

2. Direct students to look at the pictures. Ask: *Is she sick?* [yes] *Does she have the flu?* [no; She doesn't have a fever.]

3. Play the audio and have students listen and look at the pictures. Check comprehension. Ask: *What's the matter with Orane?* [She has a cold.]

B 1. Tell students to look at the pictures. Read the captions and talk about them. Find out how many students come to work or school when they have a cold. Find out how many go to the doctor. Use pantomime and drawing to help students express their ideas about the best course of action.

2. Ask for a show of hands to see which solution the class likes best. Emphasize that there can be more than one correct answer.

Evaluation
20–25 minutes

To test students' understanding of the unit language and content, have them take the Unit 8 Test, available on the Teacher Resource Center.

UNIT 9 What Size?

Unit Overview

This unit explores descriptions of clothing, shopping for clothing, and weather conditions.

	KEY OBJECTIVES
Lesson 1	Identify colors
Lesson 2	Identify clothes; describe what you are wearing today
Lesson 3	Use the present continuous to describe clothes
Lesson 4	Shop for clothes; interpret basic sizes
Lesson 5	Identify weather conditions
Teamwork & Language Review	Review unit language

	UNIT FEATURES
Academic Vocabulary	*dress code*
Employability Skills	• Understand teamwork • Cooperate with others • Communicate information • Work with others • Communicate verbally • Interpret a receipt • Decide what to do with an unwanted gift

Resources	**Class Audio** CD3, Tracks 02–20
	Workbook Unit 9, pages 58–64
	Teacher Resource Center
	    Literacy Reproducible Activities Unit 9
	    Multilevel Activities Introductory Level Unit 9
	    Multilevel Grammar Exercises Introductory Level Unit 9
	    Unit 9 Test
	Oxford Picture Dictionary Colors, Seasonal Clothing, Everyday Clothes, Describing Clothes, Weather

LESSON 1 VOCABULARY

Lesson Overview

MULTILEVEL OBJECTIVES

On-level: Identify colors
Pre-level: Recognize colors
Higher-level: Talk about colors

LANGUAGE FOCUS

Grammar: The verb *be* (*It's red.*)

Vocabulary: *Black, blue, brown, green, orange, purple, red, white, yellow*

For vocabulary expansion, see this **Oxford Picture Dictionary** topic: Colors, page 24

STRATEGY FOCUS

Remember vocabulary by talking about how it relates to you (favorite colors).

READINESS CONNECTION

In this lesson, students communicate verbally about their favorite colors.

PACING

To compress this lesson: Conduct 2A as a whole-class activity.

To extend this lesson: Practice describing clothing in pairs. (See end of lesson.)

And/or have students complete **Workbook Introductory Level page 58** and **Multilevel Activities Introductory Level Unit 9 page 98.**

Lesson Notes

CORRELATIONS

CCRS: L.6.A Use words and phrases acquired through conversations, reading and being read to, and responding to texts, including using frequently occurring conjunctions to signal simple relationships (e.g., *because*).

SL.1.A Participate in collaborative conversations with diverse partners in small and larger groups.

ELPS: 1. An ELL can construct meaning from oral presentations and literary and informational text through level-appropriate listening, reading, and viewing.

Warm-up and Review
10–15 minutes (books closed)

On the board, post color pictures of already learned clothing items (*jacket, pants, shirt, shoes, socks,* and *sweater*). Elicit and write the words. Ask if anyone is wearing a sweater today.

Introduction
5 minutes

1. Describe the items on the board: *These are blue pants. This is a white shirt.*

2. State the objective: *Today we'll practice the colors.*

1 Learn colors

Presentation
20–25 minutes

A Direct students to look at the picture. Ask them to count the shoes [nine pairs].

B 🔊 3-02 1. Play the audio. Tell students to point to the correct part of the picture as they listen. Circulate and monitor.

2. Check comprehension. Point to each picture and ask: *Are they blue? Are they red?* Have students hold their thumbs up (*yes*) or thumbs down (*no*) in order to get a nonverbal response.

C 🔊 3-02 1. Tell students to listen and repeat the colors.

2. Write the words on the board and help students sound out and pronounce each one.

3. Call out the numbers out of order and ask students to say the colors.

Guided Practice I
15–20 minutes

D Direct students to take turns reading the words with a partner.

E 1. Model the activity with two volunteers. Direct one partner to point to the pictures or say the numbers. Have the other partner cover the words in 1C and identify the colors from memory.

2. Have students practice in pairs.

> **MULTILEVEL STRATEGIES**
>
> For 1E, pair same-level students together.
>
> • **Pre-level** Tell these students to practice together by pointing to the pictures in 1B and saying the correct colors.
>
> • **Higher-level** Tell these students to dictate the words to each other.

2 Talk about colors

Guided Practice II
15–20 minutes

A 1. Direct students to look at the picture. Call out the numbers and ask students to identify the colors.

2. Copy number 1 on the board and have students spell *red* aloud. Demonstrate how to write one letter on each line.

3. Tell students to work individually to complete the words.

4. Ask volunteers to spell the completed words aloud. Write the answers on the board. Read and have students repeat the words.

Answers	
1. r-e-d	6. o-r-a-n-g-e
2. g-r-e-e-n	7. y-e-l-l-o-w
3. w-h-i-t-e	8. b-l-u-e
4. b-l-a-c-k	9. p-u-r-p-l-e
5. b-r-o-w-n	

B Give students time to copy the words into their notebooks. Monitor and check their writing.

C 🔊 3-03 1. Play the audio. Have students read along silently and point to the picture.

2. Play the audio again. Tell students to listen and repeat.

Communicative Practice and Application
10–15 minutes

D 1. Pair students. Have one pair model completing the dialogue about an article of clothing in 2A.

2. Set a time limit (five minutes) and have partners practice in both roles. Encourage students to use all of the words from 2A. Circulate and monitor. Provide feedback.

> **TIP**
>
> Have students extend the conversation in 2D to include other items in the room: *What color is this book? What color is this pencil?*

E 1. Model the conversation with a volunteer. Switch roles and repeat the conversation.

2. Tell students to talk to three classmates to find out their favorite colors.

3. Invite students to report back to the class. Keep track of how many people prefer each color on the board to find out which one is the most popular.

Evaluation
10–15 minutes

TEST YOURSELF

1. Give students five to ten minutes to test themselves by writing the words they recall from the lesson.

2. Call "time" and have students check their spelling in the unit or in a dictionary. Circulate and provide feedback.

MULTILEVEL STRATEGIES

Target the *Test Yourself* to the level of your students.

- **Pre-level** Display or distribute to these students four pictures of the colors listed in 1C. Have students open their books to page 116, identify the correct words to match the pictures, and copy them.

- **Higher-level** Direct these students to close their books and write as many colors as they can remember. Challenge them to include words not presented in the unit.

EXTENSION ACTIVITY

Describe Your Clothing

Have students make *this* and *these* statements about their own clothing: *This is a white shirt. These are black shoes.* Direct them to say their statements to a partner. Then call on volunteers to tell the class.

LESSON 2 WRITING

Lesson Overview

MULTILEVEL OBJECTIVES
On- and Higher-level: Read and write about clothes
Pre-level: Recognize words for clothes

LANGUAGE FOCUS
Grammar: Present continuous (*I'm wearing shorts.*)
Vocabulary: *Belt, boots, cap, coat, dress, jacket, shorts, T-shirt*

For vocabulary expansion, see these **Oxford Picture Dictionary** topics: Seasonal Clothing, page 90; Weather, page 13

STRATEGY FOCUS
Use commas in a list of three.

READINESS CONNECTION
In this lesson, students communicate information about clothing and weather.

PACING
To compress this lesson: Assign the *Test Yourself* for homework.

To extend this lesson: Have a fashion show. (See end of lesson.)

And/or have students complete **Workbook Introductory Level page 59** and **Multilevel Activities Introductory Level Unit 9 page 99.**

Lesson Notes

CORRELATIONS

CCRS: L.6.A Use words and phrases acquired through conversations, reading and being read to, and responding to texts, including using frequently occurring conjunctions to signal simple relationships (e.g., *because*).

R.1.A Ask and answer questions about key details in the text.

R.7.A Use the illustrations and details in a text to describe its key ideas (e.g., maps, charts, photographs, political cartoons, etc.).

SL.2.A Confirm understanding of a text read aloud or information presented orally or through other media by asking and answering questions about key details and requesting clarification if something is not understood.

ELPS: 1. An ELL can construct meaning from oral presentations and literary and informational text through level-appropriate listening, reading, and viewing. 9. An ELL can create clear and coherent level-appropriate speech and text.

Warm-up and Review
10–15 minutes (books closed)

Point to items of clothing that students are wearing and ask the class to call out the colors. Write the colors on the board.

Introduction
5 minutes

1. Tell the class what you are wearing: *I'm wearing a red shirt. I'm wearing black pants.*

2. State the objective: *Today we'll read and write about clothes.*

1 Learn about clothes

Presentation I
15–20 minutes

A Direct students to look at the pictures. Ask them to say the months. Then ask them to name the clothes they see. [Responses might include the following: red T-shirt, white shorts, pink shoes, blue hat, purple jacket, dress, blue shoes, yellow coat, red sweater, green pants, white belt, brown boots.]

B 🔊 **3-04** 1. Play the audio. Have students read along silently.

2. Check comprehension. Direct students to cover the words and look at the pictures. Say the words out of order and have students call out the correct numbers. Then say the numbers and have students call out the words.

3. Replay the audio and ask students to repeat the words.

4. Look and see if students are wearing any of these clothing items. Point to them and have them say the color and the item, for example, *a brown jacket*.

Guided Practice I
10–15 minutes

C 1. Read the beginning of number 1 aloud. Ask students to find Justine's white shorts in the picture.

2. Direct students to work independently to complete the sentences.

3. Have students read the completed sentences with a partner. Call on volunteers to read them aloud.

Answers
1. shorts, T-shirt, hat
2. dress, jacket
3. coat, belt, boots

2 Prepare to write: my clothes

Presentation II
10–15 minutes

A 🔊 **3-05** 1. Introduce the topic: *Now we're going to listen for clothes, colors, and temperature.*

2. Direct students to look at the pictures. Elicit the clothing items and colors.

3. Play number 1 and elicit what students heard. Continue the audio, stopping after each number. Ask for a show of hands to see if students caught the answers. Repeat the segment if necessary.

4. Call on volunteers for the answers.

Answers
1. a
2. b
3. a
4. a

B 1. Ask a volunteer to make a statement about one of the items in 1A. Ask another to say something about one of the items in 2A.

2. Set a time limit (five minutes). Ask students to talk about the pictures with their partners.

C 🔊 **3-06** 1. Direct students to look at the pictures. Ask about each picture: *What is she wearing? What month do you think it is?*

2. Play the audio. Have students read along silently.

3. Replay the audio and have students repeat the sentences. Ask about the weather now: *Is it hot today? Is it cold?*

Guided Practice II
15–20 minutes

D 1. Tell students to work independently to complete the exercise.

2. Have students compare their answers with a partner.

3. Conduct a class poll. Ask students to raise their hands for their favorite weather choice.

E 🔊 **3-07** 1. Read the instructions aloud. Tell students to point to Justine in the picture in 1A.

2. Play the audio. Have students read along silently.

3. Draw students' attention to the *Writer's Note*. Have them point out the commas in Justine's story. Write on the board: *I'm a wearing shorts and a T-shirt. I'm wearing shorts a T-shirt and a hat.* Ask students to tell you which sentence needs commas and where. [*I'm wearing shorts, a T-shirt, and a hat.*]

F 🔊 **3-08** 1. Direct students to look at the picture. Say and have them repeat *Ben*. Read the instructions aloud.

2. Play number 1 and elicit the answer. Play the rest of the audio and ask students to circle the correct word.

3. Replay the entire audio so students can check their work. Go over the answers as a class.

Answers
1. a
2. a
3. a, a

3 Write about your clothes

Communicative Practice
10–15 minutes

A 1. Introduce the new activity: *Now we are going to write about our clothes.*

2. Tell students to copy the sentence frames in their notebooks and to work individually to complete the sentences with their own ideas.

3. Remind students to review their sentences for commas, periods, and capital letters.

B Have students read their sentences aloud to a partner. When they finish, tell them to read them to a new partner.

> **MULTILEVEL STRATEGIES**
>
> Adapt 3A and 3B to the level of your students.
>
> • **Pre-level** While on- and higher-level students are completing 3A and 3B, work with these students in a group, or have them complete page 72 of the *Literacy Reproducible Activities Unit 9*.

AT WORK

Dress codes
10–15 minutes

A 1. Write *dress code* on the board. Using gestures, describe what it means: *I'm a teacher. Do I wear shorts to school? I don't wear shorts because the school has a dress code.* Ask the students who work if there is a dress code at their jobs.

2. Point to the men in the pictures. Elicit their job [salesperson]. Explain that they're going to read a company's dress code for salespeople. Give students time to read the memo silently.

B 1. Tell students to look at the pictures and check the salesperson who is following the dress code.

2. Go over the answer as a class. Ask students to show where they found the answer in the dress code.

3. Have students describe their dress code at work or their children's dress codes at school.

Answer
Kevin

Evaluation
10 minutes

TEST YOURSELF

1. Ask students for example answers to complete the sentence frame.

2. Have students copy the frame into their notebooks and complete it.

3. Collect and correct students' work.

> **EXTENSION ACTIVITY**
>
> **Fashion Show**
>
> Have a fashion show. Pass out clothing items (caps, belts, jackets, sweaters, large T-shirts) and ask volunteers to model for the class. Ask the class to call out what the person is wearing (item and color).

LESSON 3 GRAMMAR

Lesson Overview

MULTILEVEL OBJECTIVES

On- and Higher-level: Use present continuous statements and questions

Pre-level: Recognize present continuous statements and questions

LANGUAGE FOCUS

Grammar: Present continuous statements *(He's wearing a coat.)*; present continuous questions *(Is she wearing a sweater?)*

Vocabulary: Clothing and colors

For vocabulary expansion, see these **Oxford Picture Dictionary** topics: Seasonal Clothing, page 90; Everyday Clothes, pages 86–87; Colors, page 24

STRATEGY FOCUS

To sound more fluent while speaking, remember that you can use contractions with the present continuous.

READINESS CONNECTION

In this lesson, students work with others to describe what people are wearing.

PACING

To compress this lesson: Conduct 2C and 3C as whole-class activities.

To extend this lesson: Do group question-and-answer practice. (See end of lesson.)

And/or have students complete **Workbook Introductory Level pages 60–61, Multilevel Activities Introductory Level Unit 9 page 100,** and **Multilevel Grammar Exercises Introductory Level Unit 9.**

Lesson Notes

CORRELATIONS

CCRS: L.1.A Demonstrate command of the conventions of standard English grammar and usage when writing or speaking. e. Use verbs to convey a sense of past, present, and future (e.g., *Yesterday I walked home; Today I walk home; Tomorrow I will walk home.*).

SL.1.A Participate in collaborative conversations with diverse partners in small and larger groups.

SL.3.A Ask and answer questions in order to see help, get information, or clarify something that is not understood.

ELPS: 10. An ELL can demonstrate command of the conventions of standard English to communicate in level-appropriate speech and writing.

Warm-up and Review
10–15 minutes (books closed)

Post color pictures of people wearing previously studied clothing items in various colors. Ask volunteers to come to the board and write the clothing/color combination.

Introduction
5–10 minutes

1. Make statements about yourself and about the students: *I am wearing brown pants. She is wearing a green jacket.*

2. State the objective: *Today we'll use the present continuous to talk about clothing.*

1 Use statements with the present continuous

Presentation I
20–25 minutes

A 🔊 3-09 1. Direct students to look at the pictures. Ask them to identify the clothing in the pictures. [Responses might include the following: yellow shirt, black pants, blue dress, brown shorts, blue T-shirt, green T-shirt.]

2. Read the captions aloud.

B 🔊 3-10 1. Play the audio. Ask students to read the chart and listen.

2. Demonstrate how to read the grammar chart as complete sentences. Read the chart through sentence by sentence. Then read it again, and have students repeat after you.

3. Direct students to re-read the sentences in 1A and underline the verbs.

4. Assess students' understanding of the chart. Elicit statements about the pictures from the warm-up: *He's wearing _____. She's wearing _____.* Write one of these statements on the board without a contraction.

5. Direct students' attention to the *Need help?* box. Ask a volunteer to change the sentence on the board to a contraction.

Guided Practice I
15–20 minutes

C 1. Read number 1 aloud. Show students how to refer to the chart to find the answer. Direct students to work individually to complete the sentences.

2. Call on volunteers to read the completed sentences aloud. Write the answers on the board.

Answers	
1. b	3. a
2. b	4. b

D 1. Have volunteers model the activity, taking turns to make statements about themselves and people in the class.

2. Tell students to work in pairs. Circulate and provide feedback.

> **MULTILEVEL STRATEGIES**
>
> For 1C and 1D, seat pre-level students together.
> - **Pre-level** Sit with these students and help them make statements about their classmates.
> - **Higher-level** When these students finish speaking with their partners, have them write a sentence about a classmate on the board.

2 Practice: *yes/no* questions with the present continuous

Presentation II
10–15 minutes

A 🔊 3-11 1. Direct students to look at the pictures. Have them make statements about what the people are wearing. Write some of the statements on the board. [For example: She is wearing a blue T-shirt.]

2. Play the audio. Tell students to read along silently.

3. Tell students to look at number 2. Point out the *ing* ending on *reading*. Have students read and repeat *sleeping*. Pantomime sleeping. Ask: *Are you sleeping?*

4. Direct students' attention to the statements on the board. Elicit how to turn the statements into questions.

5. Have students work with a partner to read the questions and answers aloud.

Guided Practice II
10–15 minutes

B 1. Direct students to look at the pictures. Elicit a couple of the clothing items. Ask: *What is Kip wearing?* [a black hat, an orange T-shirt, blue shorts]

2. Read number 1 aloud. Tell students to work individually to complete the rest of the questions.

3. Elicit the answers. Write them on the board.

Answers	
1. Is	4. reading
2. Is	5. wearing
3. Are	6. wearing

C Have students ask and answer the questions with a partner. Encourage them to make new questions about the pictures.

3 Ask and answer questions about clothing

Communicative Practice and Application
20–25 minutes

A **3-12** Direct students' attention to the pictures. Play the audio and have students repeat the conversations. Ask which pictures the conversations are referring to [1 and 4].

B 1. Read the model conversation with a volunteer. Have two volunteers model it again using a different picture and making substitutions as necessary.

2. Set a time limit (five minutes). Have students practice in pairs.

> **MULTILEVEL STRATEGIES**
>
> Adapt 3B for your pre- and higher-level students.
>
> • **Pre-level** Have these students work with an on-level pair. Instruct the on-level students to practice the conversations together. After they have practiced each conversation, one on-level partner repeats the questions for the pre-level student to answer.
>
> • **Higher-level** Teach these students the names of the occupations presented in the photos: *engineer, police officer, babysitter, model, homemaker, soldier*. Have them practice the conversation using the occupation names.

C 1. Model the activity with two volunteers.

2. Seat students in groups of three and direct them to take turns closing their eyes and asking a question. Set a time limit (five minutes).

Evaluation
10–15 minutes

TEST YOURSELF

Have students work in pairs to write questions and answers. Circulate and provide feedback.

> **MULTILEVEL STRATEGIES**
>
> Target the *Test Yourself* to the level of your students.
>
> • **Pre-level** Provide these students with sentence frames:
>
>   Is _____ wearing a dress? No, she isn't.
>
>   Is _____ wearing pants? Yes, he is.
>
> Tell students to complete the frames with names of their classmates.

> **EXTENSION ACTIVITY**
>
> **Group Practice**
>
> Have students practice present continuous questions and answers in a group. Seat students in mixed-level groups. Direct them to take turns asking questions about another group member and having a third group member answer. Allow less verbal students to answer questions but not ask them.

LESSON 4 EVERYDAY CONVERSATION

Lesson Overview

MULTILEVEL OBJECTIVES

On- and Higher-level: Ask and answer questions about clothing purchases

Pre-level: Answer questions about clothing purchases

LANGUAGE FOCUS

Grammar: Present continuous (*I'm looking for a shirt.*)

Vocabulary: Clothes, *extra-large, large, medium, size, small*

For vocabulary expansion, see these **Oxford Picture Dictionary** topics: Everyday Clothes, pages 86–87; Describing Clothes, pages 96–97

STRATEGY FOCUS

Use *I'm looking for* to make a polite request for help in a store.

READINESS CONNECTION

In this lesson, students interpret a receipt and communicate verbally about sizes and prices.

PACING

To compress this lesson: Have students practice 3D with only one partner.

To extend this lesson: Play *Go Fish*. (See end of lesson.)

And/or have students complete **Workbook Introductory Level page 62** and **Multilevel Activities Introductory Level Unit 9 page 101.**

Lesson Notes

CORRELATIONS

CCRS: L.6.A Use words and phrases acquired through conversations, reading and being read to, and responding to texts, including using frequently occurring conjunctions to signal simple relationships (e.g., *because*).

SL.1.A Participate in collaborative conversations with diverse partners in small and larger groups.

SL.2.A Confirm understanding of a text read aloud or information presented orally or through other media by asking and answering questions about key details and requesting clarification if something is not understood.

RF.2.A Demonstrate understanding of spoken words, syllables, and sounds (phonemes).

ELPS: 2. An ELL can participate in level-appropriate oral and written exchanges of information, ideas, and analyses, in various social and academic contexts, responding to peer, audience, or reader comments and questions. 9. An ELL can create clear and coherent level-appropriate speech and text.

Warm-up and Review
5 minutes (books closed)

Put up letters on the board. Tell students they are the first letters of words for clothes. Ask volunteers to complete the words. [Possible letters: *sh, T, p, sw, c, j, b, d*. Possible answers: shirt, T-shirt, pants, sweater, coat, jacket, boots, dress.]

Introduction
5 minutes

1. Read the words students came up with and correct spelling if necessary.

2. State the objective: *Today we'll learn about shopping for clothes. To begin, we're going to listen for sizes.*

1 Listen for sizes and prices

Listening Extension
15–20 minutes

A Direct students to look at the picture. Ask the questions in the directions. [The T-shirts are blue, yellow, green, and purple. Yes, they are on sale. They are 20% off.]

B 🔊 3-13 1. Play number 1 on the audio. Elicit what students heard. Play the rest of the audio and ask students to circle *a* or *b*.

2. Call on volunteers for the answers.

Answers
1. b
2. b
3. a
4. b

C 🔊 3-14 1. Play number 1 on the audio. Elicit what students heard. Play the rest of the audio, stopping after each item to give students time to write. Repeat the item if necessary.

2. Ask volunteers to write the answers on the board.

Answers
dress $35.00
jacket $30.00
sub-total $65.00
tax 5% $3.25

MULTILEVEL STRATEGIES

Replay 1C to allow pre-level students to catch up while you provide a challenge for higher-level students.

- **Pre-level** Have these students listen again to write the prices.
- **On- and Higher-level** Ask these students to listen again and write the colors and clothing items they hear.

D Give students a moment to calculate the total. Tell them to add the number and write the total on the receipt. Elicit the answer and write it on the board [$68.25].

TIP
After 1D, have students re-figure the bill using the sales tax from your area.

2 Practice your pronunciation

Pronunciation Extension
10–15 minutes

A 🔊 3-15 1. Direct students to look at the chart.

2. Play the audio and tell students to read along silently.

B 🔊 3-16 Play the audio. Tell students to circle the form they hear.

Answers	
1. I'm	4. I'm
2. I	5. I
3. I'm	6. I'm

C Replay the audio in 2B. Stop after each item and have students repeat. Write the answers on the board and demonstrate the mouth position for each one.

3 Make conversation: shopping for clothes

Presentation
5–10 minutes

A 1. Direct students to look at the pictures. Ask where the people are [a clothing store] and what Hector is buying [an orange T-shirt]. Explain that a clerk is a salesperson (not a name).

2. Have students read the conversation silently. Elicit any questions.

Guided Practice
5–10 minutes

B 🔊 3-17 Play the audio. Have students read the conversation silently. Ask: *What is Hector looking for?* [a small orange T-shirt] *Does the clerk give him an orange T-shirt?* [No, he gives him an orange and purple T-shirt.]

C 🔊 3-17 1. Play the audio again and have students repeat the conversation.

2. Do a choral reading of the conversation in 3B. Divide the class in half. Have one side be Hector and one side be the clerk, and then have the sides switch roles.

Communicative Practice and Application

15–20 minutes

 1. Model the conversation with a volunteer. Then have two volunteers model the conversation using one of the clothing items from the *Need help?* box.

2. Elicit other ways to complete the conversation.

3. Set a time limit (five minutes). Ask students to practice the conversation with several partners. Encourage pantomime and improvisation.

4. Ask volunteer pairs to present their conversations to the class.

> **MULTILEVEL STRATEGIES**
>
> For 3D, seat pre-level students together.
>
> • **Pre-level** While other students are practicing the conversation, have these students complete page 74 in the *Literacy Reproducible Activities Unit 9*.
>
> • **Higher-level** Add lines to the conversation for these students. Have the clerk ask, *What color?*, and have the customer ask, *How much?*

Evaluation

5 minutes

TEST YOURSELF

1. Model the activity with a volunteer.

2. Set a time limit (three minutes). Have students practice with a partner. Then have them switch partners and repeat.

> **EXTENSION ACTIVITY**
> **Go Fish**
>
> 1. Group students and give four sets of clothing picture cards to each group. (See Picture Cards 9.1–9.8 on page 103 of *Multilevel Activities Introductory Level Unit 9*.) Have a group leader "shuffle" and deal five cards to each member of the group. Direct them to put the rest of the cards in a pile.
>
> 2. The goal of the game is to get four of a kind. Students should take turns requesting cards from the person on their left: *I'm looking for _____.* That person should hand over any of those cards that he or she has or say, *I'm sorry.* If the partner doesn't have the card, the first person draws a card from the pile, and it's the next player's turn.
>
> 3. Set a time limit (10 to 15 minutes) and call "time." The student with the most sets of four of a kind is the winner.

LESSON 5 READING

Lesson Overview

MULTILEVEL OBJECTIVES

On- and Higher-level: Identify weather and read a weather website

Pre-level: Recognize weather and read a weather website

LANGUAGE FOCUS

Grammar: Present continuous *(They're playing soccer.)*

Vocabulary: *Cloudy, cold, cool, hot, raining, snowing, soccer, sunny*

For vocabulary expansion, see these **Oxford Picture Dictionary** topics: Seasonal Clothing, page 90; Everyday Clothes, pages 86–87; Weather, page 13

STRATEGY FOCUS

Understand the x- and y-axes on bar graphs.

READINESS CONNECTION

In this lesson, students communicate information about the weather.

PACING

To compress this lesson: Assign 2C as homework or conduct it as a whole-class activity.

To extend this lesson: Conduct a categorization exercise. (See end of lesson.)

And/or have students complete **Workbook Introductory Level page 63** and **Multilevel Activities Introductory Level Unit 9 page 102.**

Lesson Notes

CORRELATIONS

CCRS: L.6.A Use words and phrases acquired through conversations, reading and being read to, and responding to texts, including using frequently occurring conjunctions to signal simple relationships (e.g., *because*).

R.1.A Ask and answer questions about key details in the text.

R.7.A Use the illustrations and details in a text to describe its key ideas (e.g., maps, charts, photographs, political cartoons, etc.).

ELPS: 1. An ELL can construct meaning from oral presentations and literary and informational text through level-appropriate listening, reading, and viewing. 8. An ELL can determine the meaning of words and phrases in oral presentations and informational text.

Warm-up and Review
10–15 minutes (books closed)

Draw a sun and a rain cloud on the board. Pass out word cards to students (*boots, sweater, coat, jacket, shorts, T-shirt, cap*). Ask students to place the cards under the appropriate picture [sun: shorts, T-shirt, cap; rain cloud: boots, sweater, coat, jacket].

Introduction
5 minutes

1. Talk about the information on the board: *When it's sunny, I wear a T-shirt, shorts, and a cap. When it's cool or rainy, I wear boots, a sweater, and a coat or a jacket.*

2. State the objective: *Today we'll learn words for weather and read about the weather.*

1 Get ready to read

Presentation I
10–15 minutes

 1. Tell students to look at the pictures and listen to the sentences.

2. Check comprehension of the words. Ask how the weather is in your area today, how it is in December, and how it is in June.

3. Replay the audio and tell students to listen and repeat.

Guided Practice I
15–20 minutes

B 1. Direct students to look at the pictures. Elicit the weather in each picture.

2. Read number 1 aloud. Tell students to work individually to complete the sentences. Have volunteers write the answers on the board.

3. Point out the word *soccer*. Soccer is called *football* in most countries. Tell students that Americans are referring to a different game when they say *football*.

4. Ask students to take turns reading the sentences aloud with a partner.

Answers
1. sunny
2. raining
3. cloudy
4. snowing

Presentation II
10–15 minutes

C 1. Direct students to look at the weather website. Say and have students repeat the words. Ask students if they look at a site or an app with weather information.

2. Identify the cities from the website on a map. Write a sentence frame on the board: *It's _____ and _____ in _____.* Call on students to make statements about each city according to the picture: *It's sunny and hot in Miami.*

D Have students check the words about today's weather. Call on volunteers to read their answers as a sentence using the frame on the board.

TIP

For more practice with these words, post pictures of various weather conditions. Ask students to write a description of each picture: *It's snowing and cold. It's sunny and warm*, etc. Have volunteers write their sentences on the board and discuss them as a class. Alternatively, pass out a one-month calendar page to each student. Call out weather forecasts: *Sunday the 21st. It'll be warm and sunny.* Direct students to write or draw the weather on the correct day. To follow up, call out the dates and have students tell you the weather.

2 Read about weather in Seattle, Washington

Guided Practice II
15–20 minutes

A 1. Point out Seattle on a map. Direct students to look at the paragraph and the bar graph. Point out the increments on the y-axis. Ask students to show you how much 1 inch and 6 inches are. Point out the months on the x-axis. Ask students which month has a small amount of rain [July].

2. Tell students to read the paragraph silently. Ask if there are any questions about the reading.

3. Check students' comprehension. Ask: *When is there a lot of rain in Seattle?* [winter] *When is it warm and sunny in Seattle?* [summer]

B Play the audio and have students read the paragraph silently.

C 1. Read the answer choices for number 1 and show students where to find the answer. Direct students to work individually to circle the answers.

2. Call on volunteers for the answers. Write them on the board.

Answers
1. December
2. January
3. September
4. February
5. summer

MULTILEVEL STRATEGIES

Adapt 2C for your pre-level students.

- **Pre-level** While other students are completing the exercise, work with these students. Show them how to read the bar graph.

TIP

If you have the means of projecting or displaying a computer screen to students, show them a weather website. Ask students to predict the weather in their home country or hometown. Type the capital-city names or the names of your students' hometowns into the site and check their predictions.

Application
5–10 minutes

BRING IT TO LIFE

If students don't have a weather app on their phones, provide them with a URL where they can find the weather.

TIP

In preparation for *Teamwork & Language Review*, have students review the unit vocabulary. Provide them with pictures you have collected or use the Picture Cards on pages 103–104 of *Multilevel Activities Introductory Level Unit 9*. Pair students and have them use the pictures as flashcards for recognition practice, dictation, or sentence writing.

EXTENSION ACTIVITY

Categorization

1. Make a set of large word cards. Include *December, April, July*, clothing items, and weather words. Distribute the cards and ask all students with a card to stand at the front of the room displaying their cards.

2. Tell the rest of the class to categorize the students with the word cards into three groups. For example: *1) April, cool, cloudy, raining, jacket; 2) December, snowing, cold, boots, coat; 3) July, hot, warm, sunny, shorts, T-shirt.*

TEAMWORK & LANGUAGE REVIEW

Lesson Overview

MULTILEVEL OBJECTIVES

On-, Pre-, and Higher-level: Expand upon and review unit language and content

LANGUAGE FOCUS

Grammar: Present continuous statements (*He's wearing a coat.*); present continuous questions (*Is she wearing a sweater?*)

Vocabulary: Clothes and weather

For vocabulary expansion, see these **Oxford Picture Dictionary** topics: Colors, page 24; Seasonal Clothing, page 90; Everyday Clothes, pages 86–87; Describing Clothes, pages 96–97

STRATEGY FOCUS

Use teamwork to reinforce and expand vocabulary.

READINESS CONNECTION

In this review, students work with a team to decide what to do with an unwanted gift.

PACING

To extend this review: Have students complete **Workbook Introductory Level page 64**, **Multilevel Activities Introductory Level Unit 9 pages 103–106**, and **Multilevel Grammar Exercises Introductory Level Unit 9.**

Lesson Notes

CORRELATIONS

CCRS: L.6.A Use words and phrases acquired through conversations, reading and being read to, and responding to texts, including using frequently occurring conjunctions to signal simple relationships (e.g., *because*).

R.7.A Use the illustrations and details in a text to describe its key ideas (e.g., maps, charts, photographs, political cartoons, etc.).

SL.1.A Participate in collaborative conversations with diverse partners in small and larger groups.

SL.4.A Describe people, places, things, and events with relevant details, expressing ideas and feelings clearly.

SL.6.A Speak audibly and express thoughts, feelings, and ideas clearly. Produce complete sentences when appropriate to task and situation.

ELPS: 2. An ELL can participate in level-appropriate oral and written exchanges of information, ideas, and analyses, in various social and academic contexts, responding to peer, audience, or reader comments and questions.

Warm-up and Review
5–10 minutes (books closed)

1. Review the *Bring It to Life* assignment from Lesson 5.

2. Ask students to describe today's weather.

Introduction and Presentation
5 minutes

1. Write a sentence about the weather and what you are wearing: *It's _____. I'm wearing _____.* Write statements about what some of the students are doing: *Luis is reading. Sanam is writing.* Elicit questions based on your sentences: *Are you wearing a jacket? Is he reading?* Write them on the board. Elicit

short answers and write the questions and answers on the board.

2. State the objective: *Today we're going to review the present continuous and words for clothing and weather.*

Communicative Practice
15–20 minutes

A 1. Tell students to take turns naming one thing they see in the picture. Have three volunteers help you model turn-taking.

2. Tell students to put their pencils down and listen to each other so that they don't repeat ideas. Direct them to go around the group until they have run out of ideas.

B 1. Have students work in the same groups from A. Assign roles: secretary, reporter, editor, and manager. Write the roles on the board. As you explain each role, pantomime the duties you expect the person taking that role to perform. Explain that students work with their groups to write the words. Verify comprehension of the roles.

2. Set a time limit (five minutes) to complete the chart. Circulate and answer any questions.

3. Call on the reporters from each group to say the words from their chart. Write the words on the board. Go around the class until there are no more ideas.

Possible Answers		
Colors	**Clothes**	**Other**
black	shirt	men
white	dress	women
blue	pants	
green	T-shirt	
red	hat	
brown	shoes	
orange	belt	

C 1. Have the groups identify new words from the board and to look them up in a picture dictionary or a bilingual dictionary.

2. Tell students to add three new words to their chart. [New words might include: *purse, tie, suit, shoelaces*.]

MULTILEVEL STRATEGIES

For A–C, use mixed-level groups.
• **Pre-level** Assign these students the role of manager.
• **On-level** Assign these students the role of secretary or reporter.
• **Higher-level** Assign these students the role of editor.

D 1. Read number 1 aloud. Point to Al in the picture. Tell students to work independently to complete the sentences.

2. Call on volunteers to read the completed sentences aloud. Write the answers on the board.

Answers
1. Yes, he is.
2. No, he's not./No, he isn't.
3. No, she's not./No, she isn't.
4. Is Jody/she wearing
5. Is Al/he wearing
6. Is Mary/she wearing

E 1. Have students work independently to write two questions and answers.

2. Ask volunteers to write their questions and answers on the board. Correct them as a class.

MULTILEVEL STRATEGIES

Adapt D and E to the level of your students.
• **Pre-level** Have these students work together to complete exercise D. Assist as necessary. After on- and higher-level students write questions on the board for E, have these students copy them into their notebooks.

PROBLEM SOLVING
15–20 minutes

A 🔊 **3-20** 1. Draw a present on the board and teach students the word *present*. Tell students the pictures in A tell a story about a man named Ethan. He has a problem with a birthday present.

2. Direct students to look at the pictures. Ask who the people in the pictures are [presumably husband and wife].

3. Play the audio and have students listen and look at the pictures. Check comprehension. Ask: *What is the present?* [a shirt] *What color is it?* [yellow with green, orange, and red flowers] *Does Ethan like the shirt?* [no]

B

1. Tell students to look at the pictures. Read the captions and talk about them. For each choice, direct students to look at the picture and say how the man and woman feel. For picture *b,* ask students if they think Ethan will wear the shirt. For *c,* ask students if they ever return clothes to the store.

2. Elicit students' ideas for option *d.* Possibilities include gently telling his wife the truth, giving it to someone else, selling it, and telling his wife he lost it. Use pantomime and drawing to help students express their ideas.

3. Ask for a show of hands to see which solution the class likes best. Emphasize that there can be more than one correct answer.

Evaluation
20–25 minutes

To test students' understanding of the unit language and content, have them take the Unit 9 Test, available on the Teacher Resource Center.

> **TIP**
>
> Encourage students to reflect on what they have learned in this unit. Write these topics in a list on the board and elicit words, phrases, and sentences that students learned for each topic: *a) Colors; b) Clothing; c) Present continuous; d) Shopping; e) Weather.* Congratulate students on their progress.

UNIT 10 This Is My Home

Unit Overview

This unit explores rooms and things in a home, possessive 's, prepositions of location, housing rentals, and housing ads.

\	KEY OBJECTIVES
Lesson 1	Identify rooms and things in the home
Lesson 2	Identify parts of an apartment building; describe your house
Lesson 3	Use possessive 's; use prepositions to describe a home
Lesson 4	Ask for information about a home for rent
Lesson 5	Identify different types of housing; interpret classified ads
Teamwork & Language Review	Review unit language

\	UNIT FEATURES
Employability Skills	• Listen actively • Understand teamwork • Speak so others can understand • Communicate information • Work with others • Communicate verbally • Interpret classified housing ads • Decide what to do when electric power is out

Resources	**Class Audio** CD3, Tracks 21–39
	Workbook Unit 10, pages 65–71
	Teacher Resource Center
	    Literacy Reproducible Activities Unit 10
	    Multilevel Activities Introductory Level Unit 10
	    Multilevel Grammar Exercises Introductory Level Unit 10
	    Unit 10 Test
	Oxford Picture Dictionary A Bedroom, A Kitchen, A Living Room, A Bathroom, Different Places to Live, Numbers

Lesson Plans Intro

LESSON 1 VOCABULARY

Lesson Overview

MULTILEVEL OBJECTIVES
On-level: Identify things in the home
Pre-level: Recognize things in the home
Higher-level: Talk about things in the home

LANGUAGE FOCUS
Grammar: The verb *be + in* (*It's in the kitchen.*)
Vocabulary: Bed, dresser, furniture, refrigerator, room, sofa, stove, TV, window

For vocabulary expansion, see these **Oxford Picture Dictionary** topics: A Bedroom, page 58; A Kitchen, page 54; A Living Room, page 56

STRATEGY FOCUS
Remember vocabulary by categorizing.

READINESS CONNECTION
In this lesson, students speak so others can understand about locations of items in a home.

PACING
To compress this lesson: Conduct 2A as a whole-class activity.
To extend this lesson: Interview a partner. (See end of lesson.)
And/or have students complete **Workbook Introductory Level page 65** and **Multilevel Activities Introductory Level Unit 10 page 108.**

CORRELATIONS
CCRS: L.6.A Use words and phrases acquired through conversations, reading and being read to, and responding to texts, including using frequently occurring conjunctions to signal simple relationships (e.g., *because*).
SL.1.A Participate in collaborative conversations with diverse partners in small and larger groups.

ELPS: 1. An ELL can construct meaning from oral presentations and literary and informational text through level-appropriate listening, reading, and viewing.

Lesson Notes

Warm-up and Review
10–15 minutes (books closed)

Tell students to look around the room and write the names of as many things as they can. Elicit their words and write them on the board.

Introduction
5 minutes

1. Circle any room or furniture words students came up with during the warm-up (such as *table*, *chair*, or *desk*). Ask if they have these items at home.

2. State the objective: *Today we'll learn more words for things in the home.*

TIP

Throughout this unit, be sensitive to the fact that students may not want to share information about their living conditions with the class. Address questions about students' homes to the class at large and call on volunteers for answers.

MULTILEVEL STRATEGIES

For 1E, pair same-level students together.
- **Pre-level** Tell these students to practice together by pointing to the pictures in 1B and saying the correct words.
- **Higher-level** Tell these students to dictate the words to each other.

1 Learn about rooms and things in the home

Presentation
20–25 minutes

A Direct students to look at the pictures. Ask them to say the words they know. Ask them to look at picture 8 and say what food items they see [bananas, bread].

B 🔊 3-21 1. Play the audio. Tell students to point to the correct picture as they listen. Circulate and monitor.

2. Check comprehension by asking *yes/no* questions. Point to each picture and ask, for example: *Is this the dresser?* Have students use thumbs up (*yes*) or thumbs down (*no*) to respond.

C 🔊 3-21 1. Tell students to listen and repeat the words.

2. Write *refrigerator* on the board and help students pronounce it one syllable at a time. Clap out the syllables. Show students how it is stressed on the second syllable.

3. Call out the numbers out of order and ask students to say the words.

Guided Practice I
10–15 minutes

D Direct students to take turns reading the words with a partner.

E 1. Model the activity with two volunteers. Direct one partner to point to the pictures or say the numbers. Have the other partner cover the words in 1C and identify the pictures from memory.

2. Have students practice in pairs.

2 Talk about a home

Guided Practice II
20–25 minutes

A 1. Direct students to look at the pictures. Say and have students repeat the names of the rooms. Call out words and ask students to say which room it's in.

2. Copy number 1 on the board and have students spell *room* aloud. Demonstrate how to write one letter on each line.

3. Tell students to work individually to complete the words.

4. Ask volunteers to spell the completed words aloud. Write the answers on the board. Read and have students repeat the words.

Answers	
1. r-o-o-m	6. f-u-r-n-i-t-u-r-e
2. r-e-f-r-i-g-e-r-a-t-o-r	7. w-i-n-d-o-w
3. s-t-o-v-e	8. T-V
4. d-r-e-s-s-e-r	9. s-o-f-a
5. b-e-d	

B Give students time to copy the words into their notebooks. Monitor and check their writing.

C 🔊 3-22 1. Play the audio. Have students read along silently.

2. Play the audio again. Tell students to listen and repeat.

Communicative Practice and Application
10–15 minutes

D 1. Model the conversation with a volunteer. Show students how to use the pictures in 2A. Switch roles and model the conversation with another volunteer.

2. Pair students. Have one pair model the conversation.

3. Set a time limit (five minutes) and have the partners practice the conversation in both roles. Encourage students to use all of the words. Circulate and monitor. Provide feedback.

Evaluation
10–15 minutes

TEST YOURSELF

1. Have students copy the chart in their notebooks.

2. Have students work independently to complete the chart. Monitor and provide feedback.

> **MULTILEVEL STRATEGIES**
>
> Target the *Test Yourself* to the level of your students.
>
> • **Pre-level** Have these students work with their books open.
>
> • **Higher-level** Have these students close their books. Challenge them to include words not presented in the unit. Have them check their answers in a picture dictionary.

> **EXTENSION ACTIVITY**
>
> **Interview**
>
> Have students interview a partner about their own home. Elicit questions they can ask: *What color is your sofa? Where is your TV?* Write the questions on the board. Have partners take turns asking and answering the questions.

LESSON 2 WRITING

Lesson Overview

MULTILEVEL OBJECTIVES

On- and Higher-level: Read and write about a home
Pre-level: Recognize words for parts of a home

LANGUAGE FOCUS

Grammar: Have/has (My apartment has two bedrooms.)
Vocabulary: Apartment building, bathroom, caution sign, door, fire extinguisher, floor, garage, large, small, smoke alarm, stairs
For vocabulary expansion, see this **Oxford Picture Dictionary** topic: Different Places to Live, page 52

STRATEGY FOCUS

Give your story a title.

READINESS CONNECTION

In this lesson, students communicate information about their homes.

PACING

To compress this lesson: Assign the *Test Yourself* for homework.
To extend this lesson: Describe pictures. (See end of lesson.)
And/or have students complete **Workbook Introductory Level page 66** and **Multilevel Activities Introductory Level Unit 10 page 109.**

Lesson Notes

CORRELATIONS

CCRS: L.6.A Use words and phrases acquired through conversations, reading and being read to, and responding to texts, including using frequently occurring conjunctions to signal simple relationships (e.g., *because*).

R.1.A Ask and answer questions about key details in the text.

R.7.A Use the illustrations and details in a text to describe its key ideas (e.g., maps, charts, photographs, political cartoons, etc.).

SL.1.A Participate in collaborative conversations with diverse partners in small and larger groups.

SL.2.A Confirm understanding of a text read aloud or information presented orally or through other media by asking and answering questions about key details and requesting clarification if something is not understood.

ELPS: 1. An ELL can construct meaning from oral presentations and literary and informational text through level-appropriate listening, reading, and viewing. 9. An ELL can create clear and coherent level-appropriate speech and text.

Warm-up and Review
10–15 minutes (books closed)

Write scrambled words on the board and tell students they are things in the home (*mroo, woinwd, tfniureur, saof, bde, sedsrre, sevto, gerfrireatro, ihcar, etbla, sdek*). Give them a few minutes to unscramble the words. Then call on volunteers for the answers. Ask volunteers with the correct answers to write them on the board [room, window, furniture, sofa, bed, dresser, stove, refrigerator, chair, table, desk].

Introduction
5 minutes

1. Say and have students repeat the words on the board.

2. State the objective: *Today we'll read and write about a home.*

1 Learn about an apartment building

Presentation I
15–20 minutes

A Have students look at the picture. Tell them to count the windows in the apartment building [four, not counting the smaller ones above and on the doors that cannot be opened or closed].

B 🔊 3-23 1. Play the audio. Have students read along silently.

2. Check comprehension. Say the words out of order and have students call out the correct numbers.

3. Replay the audio and tell students to repeat the words.

4. Say the numbers and have students call out the words.

Guided Practice I
5–10 minutes

C 1. Read the instructions aloud. Tell students to point to Peter in the picture in 1A.

2. Tell students to work independently to complete the sentences.

3. Have students read their completed sentences with a partner. Call on individuals for the answers and write them on the board.

Answers	
1. apartment building	5. door
2. second floor	6. bathroom
3. first floor	7. apartment
4. stairs	8. garage

2 Prepare to write: my home

Presentation II
25–30 minutes

A 🔊 3-24 Direct students to look at the floor plans. Ask: *Who has an apartment?* [Jill] *Who lives in a house?* [Ken]

2. Play the audio. Have students listen silently and look at the floor plans. Tell them to point to the rooms they hear as they listen.

B 1. Read number 1 aloud. Show students how to find the answer by looking at the words in the box and then looking at the floor plan for Jill's apartment. Have students work independently to complete the sentences, referring to both of the floor plans in 2A.

2. Ask students to read the completed sentences in pairs. Call on individuals to read the answers aloud.

Answers	
1. living room	4. floor
2. small	5. bedrooms
3. large	6. bathroom

C 🔊 3-25 1. Read the instructions aloud.

2. Read the *Writer's Note*. Ask students to read the story silently.

3. Play the audio. Have students read along silently. Check comprehension: *Is Peter's apartment small or large?* [small] *Is his kitchen small or large?* [small] *Does Peter like his apartment?* [yes]

> **MULTILEVEL STRATEGIES**
>
> For 2C, seat students in mixed-level groups. After the whole-group practice, ask students to take turns reading the sentences aloud. Demonstrate turn-taking, with the first student reading number 1, the second number 2, and so on.
>
> • **Pre-level** Tell students who don't want to read aloud to listen to their classmates and follow along silently.

Guided Practice II
10–15 minutes

D 🔊 3-26 1. Direct students to look at the picture. Say and have them repeat *Meg*. Read the instructions aloud.

2. Pause after the first sentence and elicit the answer. Play the rest of the audio and tell students to circle the correct words in the rest of the story.

3. Replay the entire audio so students can check their work. Go over the answers as a class.

Answers
a, b, a, b

3 Write about your home

Communicative Practice
10–15 minutes

A 1. Introduce the new activity: *Now you are going to write about your home.*

2. Call on volunteers to complete the sentences aloud.

3. Tell students to work individually to complete the sentences with their own information.

4. Remind students to give their story a title.

B 1. Have students read their titles and sentences aloud to a partner. Tell them to correct any mistakes they notice. When they finish, ask them to read the stories to a new partner.

2. Have students copy their stories into their notebooks.

> **MULTILEVEL STRATEGIES**
>
> Adapt 3A and 3B to the level of your students.
>
> • **Pre-level** While on- and higher-level students are completing 3A and 3B, work with these students in a group, or have them complete page 78 of the *Literacy Reproducible Activities Unit 10*.

AT WORK

Safety

10–15 minutes

A 1. Direct students to look at the pictures. Ask if they have these items at work.

2. Play the audio and ask students to read along silently.

3. Say and have students repeat the new vocabulary: *smoke alarm*, *fire extinguisher*, and *caution sign*. Ask them to point to the smoke alarm and fire extinguisher in the room. Ask where they see a caution sign sometimes.

B 1. Have students read the sentences in A with a partner. Tell them to ask and answer the questions. Tell them to ask *Where is it?* if their partner says *yes*.

2. Call on pairs of students to ask and answer the questions.

Evaluation
10 minutes

TEST YOURSELF

1. Have students copy the sentence frames into their notebooks. Tell them to look at the floor plans in 2A and complete the sentences.

2. Collect and correct students' work.

> **EXTENSION ACTIVITY**
>
> **Picture Prompt**
>
> Seat students in groups and give each group a picture of a house interior (from a magazine or the Internet). Tell the group members to take turns writing as many sentences as they can about the picture. Set a time limit (five minutes). Call on a reporter from each group to read their sentences aloud.

LESSON 3 GRAMMAR

Lesson Overview

MULTILEVEL OBJECTIVES

On- and Higher-level: Use possessive 's and prepositions of location

Pre-level: Recognize possessive 's and prepositions of location

LANGUAGE FOCUS

Grammar: Possessive 's *(Karen's bedroom is green.)*; prepositions of location *(The shirt is on the dresser.)*

Vocabulary: Things in the home

For vocabulary expansion, see these **Oxford Picture Dictionary** topics: A Bathroom, page 57; A Bedroom, page 58; A Kitchen, page 54; A Living Room, page 56.

STRATEGY FOCUS

To use prepositions correctly, identify where the first item in the sentence is in relation to the second (and third).

READINESS CONNECTION

In this lesson, students communicate verbally about the locations of things in a home.

PACING

To compress this lesson: Assign 1C and the *Test Yourself* for homework.

To extend this lesson: Do a picture dictation. (See end of lesson.)

And/or have students complete **Workbook Introductory Level pages 67–68, Multilevel Activities Introductory Level Unit 10 page 110,** and **Multilevel Grammar Exercises Introductory Level Unit 10.**

CORRELATIONS

CCRS: L.1.A Demonstrate command of the conventions of standard English grammar and usage when writing or speaking. b. Use common, proper, and possessive nouns. f. Use frequently occurring adjectives. j. Use frequently occurring prepositions (e.g., *during, beyond, toward*).

R.1.A Ask and answer questions about key details in the text.

R.7.A Use the illustrations and details in a text to describe its key ideas (e.g., maps, charts, photographs, political cartoons, etc.).

SL.1.A Participate in collaborative conversations with diverse partners in small and larger groups.

ELPS: 10. An ELL can demonstrate command of the conventions of standard English to communicate in level-appropriate speech and writing.

Lesson Notes

Warm-up and Review
10–15 minutes (books closed)

Ask students about things in their homes and write sentences on the board with possessive adjectives: *His sofa is green. Her TV is small. Their apartment is big.*

Introduction
5–10 minutes

1. Re-state the sentences on the board with the students' names: *(Felipe's) sofa is green. (Greta's) TV is small. (Mr. and Mrs. Lee's) apartment is big.*

2. State the objective: *Today we'll learn possessives and prepositions.*

1 Explore possessive 's

Presentation I
20–25 minutes

 A 🔊 3-28 1. Direct students to look at the pictures. Ask them to name the furniture they see [chair, table, bed, TV, sofa].

2. Play the audio and tell students to read the captions. Draw students' attention to the *'s*.

3. Have students look at the sentences on the board from the warm-up. Elicit the names that belong with the sentences. Erase the possessive adjectives and write the students' names in possessive form.

B 1. Read number 1 aloud. Show students that sentence *c* has the same meaning. Tell them to work individually to match the rest of the sentences.

2. Call on volunteers for the answers. Write them on the board.

Answers
1. c
2. e
3. d
4. b
5. a

Guided Practice I
5–10 minutes

 C 1. Direct students to look at the pictures. Ask them where each person is. [Min is in the kitchen. Alba is in the living room. Taylor is in the living room. Mr. and Mrs Brown are in the kitchen.]

2. Direct students to work individually to complete the sentences. Call on volunteers to write the answers on the board.

Answers
1. Taylor's
2. Mr. and Mrs. Brown's
3. Min's
4. Alba's

MULTILEVEL STRATEGIES
For 1C, seat higher-level students together. • **Higher-level** After these students complete 1C, have them write two sentences about someone's house using possessive *'s*.

Communicative Practice I
5–10 minutes

 D 1 Read the example sentences aloud. Elicit the names of things they might describe and write them on the board (for example: *refrigerator, bathroom, kitchen table, notebook, desk*).

2. Set a time limit (five minutes). Ask students to work with a partner and talk about the homes and belongings of people they know. Remind them to pronounce the *'s*. Circulate and provide feedback.

2 Learn about prepositions of location

Presentation II
10–15 minutes

 A 🔊 3-29 1. Direct students to look at the pictures. Ask them to identify the rooms [1, 2: bedroom; 3, 4: kitchen; 5, 6: living room].

2. Introduce the new topic: *Now we're going to learn about prepositions of location.*

3. Play the audio. Have students read the captions silently.

4. Check comprehension: *In number 2, is the shirt in the dresser?* [Yes, it is.] *In number 4, is the refrigerator next to the sink?* [No, it's not.]

5. Replay the audio and have students repeat the sentences.

Guided Practice II
10–15 minutes

 B 1. Direct students to look at the picture and ask: *Is the book on the bed?* [No, it's not. The book is on the dresser.]

2. Tell students to work individually to complete the sentences

3. Have students read their completed sentences with a partner. Call on individuals to read the sentences for the class.

Answers	
1. a	5. b
2. a	6. a
3. b	7. a
4. b	8. b

3 Ask about locations

Presentation III
10–15 minutes

 1. Direct students' attention to the pictures. Ask them to name the rooms and the things they see. Point out the name labels in each of the pictures.

2. Have students work independently to complete the sentences. Tell them to use the names they see in each of the pictures.

3. Tell them to read the sentences with a partner. Have volunteers write the answers on the board.

Answers
1. Mario's
2. Jill's
3. Ben's
4. Kip's
5. Beth's
6. Alana's

Communicative Practice II
15–20 minutes

 3-30 Play the audio. Have students repeat the questions and answers.

 1. Model the activity with a volunteer.

2. Have students practice asking and answering the questions in pairs. Encourage them to talk about all of the pictures.

3. Call on pairs to say questions and answers for the class.

Evaluation
10–15 minutes

TEST YOURSELF

1. Read the example sentences. Have students work independently to write sentences.

2. Collect and correct their work.

MULTILEVEL STRATEGIES

Target the *Test Yourself* to the level of your students.

• **Pre-level** Provide these students with sentence frames that work for things in your classroom, leaving only the name or preposition blank. For example: ___ *book is on the table. Sara's desk is ___ the window.* Provide the answers separately and ask students to copy them into the correct frame.

• **Higher-level** In addition to the three sentences, ask these students to write one true and one false sentence on the board using possessive 's and prepositions. Have the class say which sentences are true or false.

EXTENSION ACTIVITY

Picture Dictation

1. Draw a rectangle on the board and draw a very simple sofa in the middle of it. Have students copy it. Explain that you're going to tell them where to put the furniture. Say: *Draw a chair next to the sofa. Draw a cap on the chair. Draw a window over the sofa. Draw a clock next to the window. Draw a table next to the sofa. Draw an apple on the table.*

2. Circulate and monitor. After every sentence or two, hold up good examples and have the class make statements about the picture: *The chair is next to the sofa. The cap is on the chair,* etc.

LESSON 4 EVERYDAY CONVERSATION

Lesson Overview

MULTILEVEL OBJECTIVES
On-, Pre-, and Higher-level: Ask about a home for rent

LANGUAGE FOCUS
Grammar: Questions with *Is there* and *How much* (*Is there an apartment for rent? How much is the rent?*)

Vocabulary: Large numbers, *deposit, first month's rent, for rent, last month's rent*

For vocabulary expansion, see these **Oxford Picture Dictionary** topics: Numbers, page 16; Different Places to Live, page 52

STRATEGY FOCUS
Use addition to calculate initial expenses for an apartment.

READINESS CONNECTION
In this lesson, students listen actively for large numbers.

PACING
To compress this lesson: Conduct 1C as a whole-class activity.

To extend this lesson: Discuss local prices. (See end of lesson.)

And/or have students complete **Workbook Introductory Level page 69** and **Multilevel Activities Introductory Level Unit 10 page 111**.

Lesson Notes

CORRELATIONS

CCRS: SL.1.A Participate in collaborative conversations with diverse partners in small and larger groups.

SL.2.A Confirm understanding of a text read aloud or information presented orally or through other media by asking and answering questions about key details and requesting clarification if something is not understood.

RF.2.A Demonstrate understanding of spoken words, syllables, and sounds (phonemes).

ELPS: 2. An ELL can participate in level-appropriate oral and written exchanges of information, ideas, and analyses, in various social and academic contexts, responding to peer, audience, or reader comments and questions. 9. An ELL can create clear and coherent level-appropriate speech and text.

Warm-up and Review
5 minutes (books closed)

Write numbers on the board: *3, 30, 300*. Ask students to pronounce them. Then write *3,000, 30,000,* and *300,000* and elicit the pronunciation, helping as necessary. Repeat with other numbers.

Introduction
5 minutes

1. Point to the numbers on the board and ask *How much* questions: *How much is a notebook: three dollars or thirty dollars?* [three dollars] *How much is a house: three thousand dollars or three hundred thousand dollars?* [three hundred thousand dollars]

2. State the objective: *Today we'll learn to ask about an apartment. To begin, we are going to practice large numbers.*

1 Listen for large numbers

Listening Extension
20–25 minutes

A 🔊 **3-31** Play the audio and have students repeat the numbers. Repeat if necessary.

B 🔊 **3-32** 1. Play number 1. Ask students which number they heard.

2. Play the rest of the audio. Have students work independently to check the answers. Ask volunteers to write the answers on the board.

3. Say the numbers on the board together as a class.

Answers
1. 250
2. 6,000
3. 1,250
4. 3,100
5. 180,000
6. 1,520

C 🔊 **3-33** 1. Direct students to look at the ad. Have them read the ad. Explain the meaning of *rent* and *deposit*: *You pay the rent every month. You pay the deposit once.* Use pantomime to help explain that a deposit is usually returned. *I pay the deposit. I live in the apartment. I clean the apartment. I get the deposit back. If I don't clean the apartment, I don't get the deposit!*

2. Tell students that they need to listen for three numbers: the first month's rent, the last month's rent, and the cleaning deposit. Play the audio and tell them to complete the ad.

3. Read the ad aloud with the complete numbers.

4. Direct students' attention to the addition problem. Point out that the $1,100 comes from the first sentence in the ad. Have them transfer the other numbers to complete the problem. Tell them to work independently to solve the problem. Elicit and write the answer on the board. Ask: *How much do you pay in the first month for this apartment?* [$2,600]

Answers
1. 1,100 + 1,100 + 400 = 2,600 ($2,600)

> **MULTILEVEL STRATEGIES**
>
> • **Pre-level** If you have students who have difficulty doing mental addition, show them how to line up the numbers vertically and count to solve the problem.

2 Practice your pronunciation

Pronunciation Extension
10–15 minutes

A 🔊 **3-34** 1. Say: *Now we're going to practice the pronunciation of stressed syllables.* Write *bedroom* on the board. Use gestures and exaggerated pronunciation to demonstrate that a stressed syllable is longer and higher than a non-stressed syllable.

2. Play the audio. Tell students to listen silently and pay attention to the stress.

B 🔊 **3-35** Play the audio. Tell students to listen and underline the stressed syllables.

Answers	
1. <u>bath</u>room	4. No<u>vem</u>ber
2. four<u>teen</u>	5. <u>fur</u>niture
3. a<u>larm</u>	6. <u>so</u>fa

C 🔊 **3-35** Replay the audio one item at a time. Tell students to check their answers. Write the answers on the board. Have students repeat each word.

3 Make conversation: ask about a home for rent

Presentation
5–10 minutes

A 1. Direct students to look at the pictures. Draw students' attention to the *For Rent* sign. Elicit the meaning of the sign. Have students say and repeat *manager*. Elicit the duties of a manager [call plumbers, repair people, and gardeners; rent apartments; collect rent].

2. Direct students to read the conversation silently. Elicit any questions.

B 🔊 **3-36** Play the audio. Have students read the conversation silently.

Guided Practice
5–10 minutes

 1. Play the audio again and have students repeat the conversation.

2. Do a choral reading of the conversation in 3B. Divide the class in half. Have one side be Diana and one side be the manager, and then have the sides switch roles.

Communicative Practice and Application
15–20 minutes

 1. Model the conversation with a volunteer. Then switch roles and model it with another volunteer using a substitution from the *Need help?* box.

2. Elicit other ways to complete the conversation.

3. Set a time limit (five minutes). Tell students to practice the conversation with several partners. Encourage pantomime and improvisation.

4. Ask volunteer pairs to present their conversations to the class.

> **MULTILEVEL STRATEGIES**
>
> For 3D, adapt the practice to the level of your students.
>
> • **Pre-level** While other students are practicing the conversation, have these students complete page 80 in the *Literacy Reproducible Activities Unit 10*.
>
> • **Higher-level** Give these students more questions to practice: *How much is the deposit? Do I pay the first and last month's rent?*

Evaluation
5 minutes

TEST YOURSELF

Model the activity with a volunteer. Set a time limit (three minutes). Have students practice with several partners. Monitor and provide feedback.

> **EXTENSION ACTIVITY**
>
> **Discuss Local Prices**
>
> 1. Write on the board: *1-bedroom apartment, 2-bedroom apartment, 2-bedroom house,* and *3-bedroom house.*
>
> 2. Tell students to come up with a high and a low price for each of the apartment rents and home prices for your area. Give them a couple of minutes to confer with a partner. Tell them not to look online. Have the partners write their ideas on a slip of paper. Call on individuals to read the numbers.
>
> 3. Check a real estate site online to see how realistic their guesses were.

LESSON 5 READING

Lesson Overview

MULTILEVEL OBJECTIVES

On- and Higher-level: Identify types of housing and read housing ads

Pre-level: Recognize types of housing and read housing ads

LANGUAGE FOCUS

Grammar: Present tense *(The apartment has two bedrooms.)*

Vocabulary: *Condo, mobile home, townhouse*

For vocabulary expansion, see this **Oxford Picture Dictionary** topic: Different Places to Live, page 52

STRATEGY FOCUS

Interpret abbreviations.

READINESS CONNECTION

In this lesson, students interpret classified housing ads.

PACING

To compress this lesson: Assign 2B as homework or conduct it as a whole-class activity.

To extend this lesson: Have students write a housing ad. (See end of lesson.)

And/or have students complete **Workbook Introductory Level page 70** and **Multilevel Activities Introductory Level Unit 10 page 112.**

Lesson Notes

CORRELATIONS

CCRS: R.1.A Ask and answer questions about key details in the text.

R.7.A Use the illustrations and details in a text to describe its key ideas (e.g., maps, charts, photographs, political cartoons, etc.).

SL.2.A Confirm understanding of a text read aloud or information presented orally or through other media by asking and answering questions about key details and requesting clarification if something is not understood.

ELPS: 1. An ELL can construct meaning from oral presentations and literary and informational text through level-appropriate listening, reading, and viewing. 8. An ELL can determine the meaning of words and phrases in oral presentations and informational text.

Warm-up and Review
10–15 minutes (books closed)

Show students several pictures of houses and apartments. Ask them how many bedrooms and bathrooms they think each has and how much they think the rent would be.

Introduction
5 minutes

1. Ask students where they look when they need to find a home.

2. State the objective: *Today we'll learn about types of housing and read a housing ad.*

1 Get ready to read

Presentation I
10–15 minutes

 3-37 1. Tell students to look at the pictures and listen to the words.

2. Ask which of these places would be the most expensive and which would be the cheapest. Elicit the location of any mobile home parks or condo/townhouse complexes in your area.

3. Replay the audio and tell students to listen and repeat.

Guided Practice I
10–15 minutes

B **3-38** 1. Play number 1. Ask students what they heard [condo].

2. Play the rest of the audio and have students listen and circle *a* or *b*.

3. Call on volunteers for the answers. Write them on the board.

Answers
1. a
2. b
3. a
4. b
5. b

> **MULTILEVEL STRATEGIES**
>
> Replay the audio from 1B to allow pre-level students to catch up while you provide a challenge for on- and higher-level students.
>
> • **Pre-level** Have these students listen again to circle the correct answer.
>
> • **On- and Higher-level** Ask these students to listen again and write the sentences in number 1 and number 3.

Presentation II
5–10 minutes

 1. Direct students to look at the pictures. Say and have students repeat the words.

2. Write descriptions on the board: *Big apt. 3BR, 2BA*; *Sunny apt. 2BR, 1BA*. Ask students to read the descriptions aloud, pronouncing the words (not the abbreviations).

D Direct students to work individually to complete the sentence frame. Tell students what kind of home you live in.

2 Read housing ads

Guided Practice II
15–20 minutes

 1. Direct students to look at the ads. Ask them to identify the kind of home in each ad [apartment, mobile home, condo, townhouse].

2. Read the *Reading Note* aloud and ask students to look quickly through the ads for an example of *a month* [$1,100 a month, $800 a month, $1,900 a month].

3. Give students a couple of minutes to read the ads silently. Ask if there are any questions about the housing ads.

4. Check comprehension. Ask: *Where is the apartment?* [on Grant Street] *How many bedrooms does the condo have?* [3]

 1. Read number 1. Show students where to find the answer in the housing ads.

2. Have students work independently to circle *True* and *False*.

Answers
1. True
2. True
3. True
4. False
5. False
6. False

> **MULTILEVEL STRATEGIES**
>
> Adapt 2A and 2B for your pre-level students.
>
> • **Pre-level** While other students are completing 2A and 2B, work with these students. Say and ask them to circle the types of homes in 2A. Have them read the words back to you. Give them time to copy the answers to 2B off the board.

> **TIP**
>
> After your go over 2B, tell students to correct the false sentences. [4. The mobile home rent is $800 a month; 5. The room for rent is $450 a month; 6. The condominium is on Second Street.]

Application
5–10 minutes

> **TIP**
>
> Before assigning *Bring It to Life,* have students practice looking at real housing ads. Print out a page of housing ads from the Internet. Distribute the ads to students and ask them to locate and circle specific ads. For example, *Circle all of the two-bedroom apartments.* Elicit additional information about the ads students have circled.

BRING IT TO LIFE

Give students the URL for a real estate/rental site. Provide instructions for searching for housing in your area (for example, by entering the zip code).

> **TIP**
>
> In preparation for *Teamwork & Language Review*, have students review the unit vocabulary. Provide them with pictures you have collected or use the Picture Cards on pages 113–114 of *Multilevel Activities Introductory Level Unit 10*. Pair students and have them use the pictures as flashcards for recognition practice, dictation, or sentence writing.

EXTENSION ACTIVITY

Housing Ad

1. Seat students in mixed-level groups and provide each group with a large sheet of paper. Tell students they are going to write a housing ad like the ones in 2A, but the ad is for a fantastic house. Elicit some of their ideas about the perfect home and write them on the board.

2. Assign roles: secretary, reporter, editor, and manager, and have the students write their ad. Set a time limit (five minutes). Call "time" and have groups post their ads on the wall.

3. Have reporters read the ads for the class. Discuss which home students would like the best.

TEAMWORK & LANGUAGE REVIEW

Lesson Overview

MULTILEVEL OBJECTIVES
On-, Pre-, and Higher-level: Expand upon and review unit language and content

LANGUAGE FOCUS
Grammar: Possessive 's (*Marco's bedroom is small.*); prepositions of location (*The table is under the window.*)

Vocabulary: Housing

For vocabulary expansion, see these **Oxford Picture Dictionary** topics: A Bedroom, page 58; A Kitchen, page 54; A Living Room, page 56; A Bathroom, page 57

STRATEGY FOCUS
Use teamwork to reinforce and expand vocabulary.

READINESS CONNECTION
In this review, students work in a team to practice writing and decide what to do when the power is out.

PACING
To extend this review: Have students complete **Workbook Introductory Level page 71**, **Multilevel Activities Introductory Level Unit 10 pages 113–116**, and **Multilevel Grammar Exercises Introductory Level Unit 10**.

Lesson Notes

CORRELATIONS

CCRS: L.6.A Use words and phrases acquired through conversations, reading and being read to, and responding to texts, including using frequently occurring conjunctions to signal simple relationships (e.g., *because*).

R.7.A Use the illustrations and details in a text to describe its key ideas (e.g., maps, charts, photographs, political cartoons, etc.).

SL.1.A Participate in collaborative conversations with diverse partners in small and larger groups.

SL.4.A Describe people, places, things, and events with relevant details, expressing ideas and feelings clearly.

SL.6.A Speak audibly and express thoughts, feelings, and ideas clearly. Produce complete sentences when appropriate to task and situation.

ELPS: 2. An ELL can participate in level-appropriate oral and written exchanges of information, ideas, and analyses, in various social and academic contexts, responding to peer, audience, or reader comments and questions.

Warm-up and Review
5–10 minutes (books closed)

1. Review the *Bring It to Life* assignment from Lesson 5.

2. Ask students who brought in a housing ad to share some of the information. Call on other students to answer questions about what they heard: *How many bedrooms are there?*

Introduction and Presentation
5 minutes

1. Ask students questions about their homes. Write statements about them: *Jin's kitchen is yellow. Eugenia's sofa is next to the door.* Elicit the meaning of the possessive *'s*.

2. State the objective: *Today we're going to review possessive 's and prepositions.*

Communicative Practice
15–20 minutes

A 1. Tell students to take turns naming one thing they see in the picture. Have three volunteers help you model turn-taking.

2. Tell students to put their pencils down and listen to each other so that they don't repeat ideas. Direct them to go around the group until they have run out of ideas.

B 1. Have students work in the same groups from A. Assign roles: secretary, reporter, editor, and manager. Write the roles on the board. As you explain each role, pantomime the duties you expect the person taking that role to perform. Explain that students work with their groups to write the words. Verify comprehension of the roles.

2. Set a time limit (five minutes) to complete the chart. Circulate and answer any questions.

3. Call on the reporters from each group to say the words from their chart. Write the words on the board. Go around the class until there are no more ideas.

Possible Answers		
Parts of the house	**Furniture**	**Other**
window	bed	refrigerator
floor	dresser	sink
living room	sofa	stove
garage	table	lamp
bathroom		car
bedroom		shirt
kitchen		TV

C 1. Have the groups identify new words from the board and to look them up in a picture dictionary or a bilingual dictionary.

2. Tell students to add three new words to their chart. [New words might include: *chimney, drawer, fireplace, rug, shower*.]

MULTILEVEL STRATEGIES

For A–C, use mixed-level groups.

• **Pre-level** Assign these students the role of manager.

• **On-level** Assign these students the role of secretary or reporter.

• **Higher-level** Assign these students the role of editor.

D 1. Read number 1 aloud. Point out Mark's blue shirt in the picture. Tell students to work independently to complete the sentences.

2. Call on volunteers to read the completed sentences aloud.

Answers
1. on
2. in
3. under
4. on
5. next to
6. between
7. in
8. over

PROBLEM SOLVING
15–20 minutes

A **3-39** 1. Tell students the pictures in A tell a story about a husband and wife named Mr. and Mrs. Kolda. They have a problem at home.

2. Direct students to look at the pictures. Ask: *Where are they?* [at home] *What happened?* [The lights/electricity went off.]

3. Play the audio and have students listen and look at the pictures. Check comprehension. Ask: *Did the lights go off in their house?* [yes] *Did the lights go off on their street?* [yes] Ask students if this has happened in your area recently. Talk about how they feel when the lights go off.

B 1. Tell students to look at the pictures. Read the captions and talk about them. For choice *a*, say and have students repeat *candle*. Pantomime lighting a candle.

2. Tell students that this time one of the answers is wrong. Elicit the wrong answer. [Call 911.]

3. Elicit students' ideas for option *d*. Possibilities include going to bed, using the flashlight for light, and going out for dinner.

4. Ask for a show of hands to see which solution the class likes best. Emphasize that there can be more than one correct answer.

Evaluation
20–25 minutes

To test students' understanding of the unit language and content, have them take the Unit 10 Test, available on the Teacher Resource Center.

UNIT 11 Where's the Bank?

Unit Overview

This unit explores places in the community, the present continuous to describe everyday actions, work activities, asking about locations, and reading a city services website.

KEY OBJECTIVES

Lesson 1	Identify places in the community
Lesson 2	Describe locations and actions of family and friends
Lesson 3	Use the present continuous to describe common actions
Lesson 4	Ask for and give locations
Lesson 5	Use a city services website
Teamwork & Language Review	Review unit language

UNIT FEATURES

Academic Vocabulary	*Department of Motor Vehicles (DMV), paragraph*
Employability Skills	• Speak so others can understand • Understand teamwork • Communicate information • Work with others • Communicate verbally • Listen actively • Cooperate with others • Ask for and give directions • Distinguish between emergencies and non-emergencies • Decide what to do with noisy neighbors

Resources	**Class Audio** CD3, Tracks 40–57
	Workbook Unit 11, pages 72–78
	Teacher Resource Center
	    Literacy Reproducible Activities Unit 11
	    Multilevel Activities Introductory Level Unit 11
	    Multilevel Grammar Exercises Introductory Level Unit 11
	    Unit 11 Test
	Oxford Picture Dictionary City Streets, Emergencies and Natural Disasters, Job Skills

LESSON 1 VOCABULARY

Lesson Overview

MULTILEVEL OBJECTIVES
On-level: Identify places in the community
Pre-level: Recognize places in the community
Higher-level: Talk about places in the community

LANGUAGE FOCUS
Grammar: Questions with *Where is (Where is he?)*
Vocabulary: *Bakery, bank, bookstore, bus station, drugstore, gas station, gym, restaurant, supermarket*
For vocabulary expansion, see this **Oxford Picture Dictionary** topic: City Streets, pages 128–129

STRATEGY FOCUS
Remember vocabulary by talking about how it relates to you.

READINESS CONNECTION
In this lesson, students communicate verbally about places in the community.

PACING
To compress this lesson: Conduct 2A as a whole-class activity.
To extend this lesson: Conduct a class discussion about your community. (See end of lesson.)
And/or have students complete **Workbook Introductory Level page 72** and **Multilevel Activities Introductory Level Unit 11 page 118**.

Lesson Notes

CORRELATIONS

CCRS: L.6.A Use words and phrases acquired through conversations, reading and being read to, and responding to texts, including using frequently occurring conjunctions to signal simple relationships (e.g., *because*).
SL.1.A Participate in collaborative conversations with diverse partners in small and larger groups.

ELPS: 1. An ELL can construct meaning from oral presentations and literary and informational text through level-appropriate listening, reading, and viewing.

Warm-up and Review
10–15 minutes (books closed)

Write *Places in the Community* on the board. Show or draw pictures of the community places students learned in Unit 3: a clothing store, a school, a library, and a clinic. Elicit and write the name of each place. Ask students why they go to each place. Restate their ideas: *When I need clothes, I go to the store. When I need a book, I go to the library. When I need an English class, I go to school. When I need a doctor, I go to the clinic.*

Introduction
5 minutes

1. Draw or show a picture of an apple, a bottle of medicine, a stamp, and some money on the board. Elicit and write the name of each item. Say: *Where do I go when I need these things?*

2. State the objective: *Today we're going to learn more places in the community.*

1 Learn places in the community

Presentation
20–25 minutes

A Direct students to look at the pictures. Ask them to name things they see in the pictures.

B 🔊 3-40 1. Play the audio. Tell students to point to the correct picture as they listen. Circulate and monitor.

2. Check comprehension. Point to each picture and ask: *Is this the (bank)?* Have students hold their thumbs up (*yes*) or thumbs down (*no*) in order to get a nonverbal response.

C 🔊 3-40 1. Tell students to listen and repeat the words.

2. Write the words on the board and help students sound out and pronounce each one. Clap out the syllables. Point out the stress on the first syllable in all of the multi-syllable words in this list.

3. Call out the numbers out of order and ask students to say the words.

Guided Practice I
15–20 minutes

D Direct students to take turns reading the words with a partner.

E 1. Model the activity with two volunteers. Direct one partner to point to the pictures or say the numbers. Have the other partner cover the words in 1C and identify the pictures from memory.

2. Have students practice in pairs.

> **TIP**
>
> For additional vocabulary practice after 1E, have students draw a nine-square Bingo grid and write the words in 1C in a random order in the grid. Play Bingo twice. Then group the students, assigning a Bingo caller for each group. When the first caller finishes, have a second caller take over. Alternatively, have partners use Picture Cards 11.1–11.9 on page 123 of *Multilevel Activities Introductory Level Unit 11* as flashcards.

2 Talk about places in the community

Guided Practice II
15–20 minutes

A 1. Direct students to look at the picture. Call out the numbers and ask students to identify the places.

2. Copy number 1 on the board and have students spell *gym* aloud. Demonstrate how to write one letter on each line.

3. Tell students to work individually to complete the words.

4. Ask volunteers to spell the completed words aloud. Write the answers on the board. Read and have students repeat the words.

Answers	
1. g-y-m	6. b-o-o-k-s-t-o-r-e
2. b-a-n-k	7. r-e-s-t-a-u-r-a-n-t
3. s-u-p-e-r-m-a-r-k-e-t	8. d-r-u-g-s-t-o-r-e
4. b-u-s s-t-a-t-i-o-n	9. g-a-s s-t-a-t-i-o-n
5. b-a-k-e-r-y	

B Give students time to copy the words into their notebooks. Monitor and check their writing.

C 🔊 3-41 1. Play the audio. Have students read along silently.

2. Play the audio again. Tell students to listen and repeat.

Communicative Practice and Application
10–15 minutes

D 1. Conduct a choral reading of the examples. Tell the students to point to the picture in 2A for the places. They can use their imaginations about the people.

2. Set a time limit (five minutes) and have partners practice in both roles. Encourage students to use all of the words from 2A. Circulate and monitor. Provide feedback.

E 1. Model the conversation with a volunteer. Then have two volunteers model it.

2. Tell students to talk to three classmates to find out where they go every week.

3. Invite students to report back to the class. Ask students to identify which places most people go to every week.

Evaluation

10–15 minutes

TEST YOURSELF

1. Give students five to ten minutes to test themselves by writing the words they recall from the lesson.

2. Call "time" and have students check their spelling in the unit or in a dictionary. Circulate and provide feedback.

MULTILEVEL STRATEGIES

Target the *Test Yourself* to the level of your students.

- **Pre-level** Display or distribute to these students four pictures of the places listed in 1C. Have students open their books to page 144, identify the correct words to match the pictures, and copy them.

- **Higher-level** Direct these students to close their books and write as many places as they can remember. Challenge them to include words not presented in the unit.

EXTENSION ACTIVITY

Discuss Your Community

Find out how much students know about the places in your community. For example, brainstorm the names of bookstores, where they are located, and what you can buy there (besides books). As students brainstorm, write the information on poster paper. Have students make and display a poster for *drugstore*, *bakery*, *bank*, and *supermarket*.

LESSON 2 WRITING

Lesson Overview

MULTILEVEL OBJECTIVES

On- and Higher-level: Read and write about locations in the community

Pre-level: Recognize location words

LANGUAGE FOCUS

Grammar: Present continuous *(A woman is walking in the park.)*

Vocabulary: *Buy, drink, eat, exercise, play, use, walk, wash*

For vocabulary expansion, see this **Oxford Picture Dictionary** topic: City Streets, pages 128–129

STRATEGY FOCUS

Use paragraph formatting.

READINESS CONNECTION

In this lesson, students communicate information about people's actions.

PACING

To compress this lesson: Assign the *Test Yourself* for homework.

To extend this lesson: Play charades. (See end of lesson.)

And/or have students complete **Workbook Introductory Level page 73** and **Multilevel Activities Introductory Level Unit 11 page 119**.

Lesson Notes

CORRELATIONS

CCRS: L.6.A Use words and phrases acquired through conversations, reading and being read to, and responding to texts, including using frequently occurring conjunctions to signal simple relationships (e.g., *because*).

R.1.A Ask and answer questions about key details in the text.

R.7.A Use the illustrations and details in a text to describe its key ideas (e.g., maps, charts, photographs, political cartoons, etc.).

SL.1.A Participate in collaborative conversations with diverse partners in small and larger groups.

SL.2.A Confirm understanding of a text read aloud or information presented orally or through other media by asking and answering questions about key details and requesting clarification if something is not understood.

ELPS: 1. An ELL can construct meaning from oral presentations and literary and informational text through level-appropriate listening, reading, and viewing. 9. An ELL can create clear and coherent level-appropriate speech and text.

Warm-up and Review
10–15 minutes (books closed)

Pantomime several activities, such as eating, pushing a shopping cart, filling a gas tank, waiting for a bus, and lifting weights. Ask students to guess where you are. Write the places on the board.

Introduction
5 minutes

1. Tell the class what you do in each place: *At a restaurant, I eat. At a supermarket, I shop.*

2. State the objective: *Today we're going to read and write about things we do in different places.*

1 Learn about activities

Presentation
15–20 minutes

A Direct students to look at the picture. Ask them to name the places they see [gas station, park, laundromat, restaurant/coffee shop, bank/ATM].

B 🔊 3-42 1. Play the audio. Have students read along silently.

2. Check comprehension. Direct students to cover the words and look at the picture. Say the words out of order and have students call out the correct numbers. Then say the numbers and have students call out the words.

3. Replay the audio and tell students to repeat the words.

4. Pantomime the actions and ask students to call out the verbs.

Guided Practice I
5–10 minutes

C 1. Read and have students repeat the words in the box.

2. Read number 1 and have students find the couple walking in the park in 2A. Draw students' attention to the meaning of the present continuous. *In this picture, they are walking right now.*

3. Direct students to work independently to complete the sentences.

4. Have students read the completed sentences with a partner. Call on volunteers to read them aloud.

Answers	
1. walking	5. washing
2. eating	6. using
3. exercising	7. buying
4. drinking	8. playing

2 Prepare to write

Guided Practice II
20–25 minutes

A 🔊 3-43 1. Direct students to look at the pictures. Elicit the names of the places [restaurant, bakery, gym, park].

2. Play the audio. Tell students to number the places. Go over the answers as a class.

Answers
2, 1
4, 3

B 1. Read number 1 aloud. Tell students to work independently to complete the sentences.

2. Have students compare their answers with a partner.

Answers
1. bakery
2. restaurant
3. park, eating
4. gym, exercising

C 🔊 3-43 Replay the audio and have students check their answers.

D 🔊 3-44 1. Read the instructions aloud. Have students point to Pia in the picture in 1A.

2. Play the audio. Have students read along silently.

3. Draw students' attention to the *Writer's Note*. Point to the sentences in 2D. Ask: *What's the title?* [My Saturday] *Is this a paragraph?* [yes] Point out how the first line is indented.

E 🔊 3-45 Direct students to look at the picture. Say and have them repeat *Rob*. Play the audio. Ask where Rob's wife is. [She's at the supermarket.]

F Tell students to read the words in the box and copy them into the correct space in the paragraph. Have them work independently and then compare their answers with a partner.

Answers
Wednesday, supermarket, buying, work, washing

G 🔊 3-45 1. Replay the audio so students can check their work. Go over the answers as a class.

2. Conduct a choral reading of the paragraph.

3 Write

Communicative Practice
10–15 minutes

A 1. Introduce the new activity: *Now we are going to write about people's actions.*

2. Tell students to copy the sentence frames in their notebooks and to work individually to complete the paragraph. Remind them to add a title and use the paragraph form.

3. Tell students to review their sentences for periods and capital letters.

B Have students read their paragraph aloud to a partner. When they finish, ask them to read it to a new partner.

> **MULTILEVEL STRATEGIES**
>
> Adapt 3A and 3B to the level of your students.
>
> • **Pre-level** While on- and higher-level students are completing 3A and 3B, work with these students in a group, or have them complete page 84 of the *Literacy Reproducible Activities Unit 11.*

 AT WORK

Job duties
5–10 minutes

🔊 3-46 1. Write *job duty* on the board. Explain that a job duty is a thing you do for work. Tell the students about your job duties: *I teach the class. I correct papers. I take attendance.*

2. Point to the people in the pictures. Elicit the places [office, building, store].

3. Play the audio and have students read along silently.

4. Ask students if they do or use the same things at work: *He's making copies. He's using a photocopier. Do you use a photocopier at work?*

Evaluation
10 minutes

TEST YOURSELF

1. Model the activity by drawing a quick stick-figure picture of yourself, for example, at a table with a pen. Point to the picture. Say: *I'm at school. I'm reading students' papers.*

2. Tell students to draw a quick picture of themselves in the community, at work, or at school.

3. Have students copy and complete the sentence frames.

4. Collect and correct students' work.

> **EXTENSION ACTIVITY**
>
> **Charades**
>
> Play charades with the community words. Pass out cards with community places written on them. Tell students to pantomime the actions they do at each of the places (eating, pushing a shopping cart, etc.). Have the class guess the places and the actions.

LESSON 3 GRAMMAR

Lesson Overview

MULTILEVEL OBJECTIVES

On- and Higher-level: Explore present continuous verbs
Pre-level: Recognize present continuous verbs

LANGUAGE FOCUS

Grammar: Present continuous statements *(He's drinking coffee.)*; present continuous information questions *(What is he doing?)*

Vocabulary: Common verbs

For vocabulary expansion, see this **Oxford Picture Dictionary** topic: Job Skills, page 176

STRATEGY FOCUS

Remember to use *where* to ask about locations and *what* to ask about actions.

READINESS CONNECTION

In this lesson, students work with others to discuss what people are doing.

PACING

To compress this lesson: Conduct 2B and 3B as whole-class activities.

To extend this lesson: Do a memory circle. (See end of lesson.)

And/or have students complete **Workbook Introductory Level pages 74–75, Multilevel Activities Introductory Level Unit 11 page 120,** and **Multilevel Grammar Exercises Introductory Level Unit 11.**

Lesson Notes

CORRELATIONS

CCRS: L.1.A Demonstrate command of the conventions of standard English grammar and usage when writing or speaking. e. Use verbs to convey a sense of past, present, and future (e.g., *Yesterday I walked home; Today I walk home; Tomorrow I will walk home.*). k. Understand and use question words (interrogatives) (e.g., *who, what, where, when, why, how*).

SL.1.A Participate in collaborative conversations with diverse partners in small and larger groups.

R.1.A Ask and answer questions about key details in the text.

R.7.A Use the illustrations and details in a text to describe its key ideas (e.g., maps, charts, photographs, political cartoons, etc.).

ELPS: 10. An ELL can demonstrate command of the conventions of standard English to communicate in level-appropriate speech and writing.

Warm-up and Review
10–15 minutes (books closed)

Pantomime some of the actions that students are familiar with, for example, reading, walking, eating, drinking, playing, and writing. Elicit the words and write them on the board in the base form [read, walk, eat, drink, play, write].

Introduction
5–10 minutes

1. Read each word on the board and then make present continuous statements while repeating your pantomime: *Read. Right now I'm reading.*

2. State the objective: *Today we're going to use the present continuous to talk about actions.*

1 Explore present continuous verbs

Presentation I
20–25 minutes

A  1. Play the audio. Tell students to read the captions and look at the pictures.

2. Copy the sentences on the board. Underline the complete verb in each sentence. Say: *For present continuous, we use am, is, or are and a verb + ing. This is how we talk about what people are doing right now.*

B 1. Play the audio. Tell students to read the chart and repeat the verbs. Ask if there are any questions about the meaning of the verbs.

2. Draw students' attention to the verbs in the third column. Ask what they notice about the spelling. [They all end in *e*.] Point out that we drop the *e* when we add *ing*.

Guided Practice I
15–20 minutes

C Model the activity with a volunteer. Have students practice spelling the *ing* forms in pairs. Tell them to look away from the book and try to spell from memory.

D 1. Model how to make new sentences by reading one word from each column, for example: *I am buying bread.*

2. Tell students to work in pairs. Call on individuals to make sentences for the class.

> **MULTILEVEL STRATEGIES**
>
> For 1C and 1D, seat pre-level students together.
>
> • **Pre-level** Sit with these students. Pantomime actions and ask them to find the words in the chart in 1B.

2 Practice: present continuous questions and answers

Presentation II
10–15 minutes

A 1. Direct students to look at the pictures. Ask: *Where are they working?* [at a restaurant]

2. Tell students to read the questions and answers. Then read them aloud and have students repeat.

3. Have students underline the complete verb in the questions and answers. Point out the question word order.

Guided Practice II
10–15 minutes

B 1. Tell students to work independently to complete the questions.

2. Call on individuals to read the completed questions aloud.

Answers
1. b
2. b
3. a
4. a

C Have students ask and answer the questions with a partner.

3 Ask and answer questions with *What* and *Where*

Communicative Practice and Application
20–25 minutes

A 1. Direct students' attention to the picture. Ask: *Where are they?* [at work/the office] *What does the company make?* [lamps]

2. Play the audio. Tell students to listen and read silently.

B Have students work independently to complete the questions and answers.

Answers
1. is she, She's, is she, She's using
2. are they, They're, are they, They're writing

C 1. Set a time limit (five minutes). Have students read their completed questions and answers with a partner. Tell them to make up new questions and answers for the people in 3A, for example: *What is Mia doing? She's talking on the telephone. Where is Jill? She's at work./She's sitting at her desk.*

2. Call on pairs to read the completed conversations aloud. Start with the conversations in 3B and then call on volunteers to make a new conversation about 3A.

> **MULTILEVEL STRATEGIES**
>
> Adapt 3B and 3C for your pre- and higher-level students.
>
> • **Pre-level** Provide these students with the answers to 3B and have them practice reading the conversations.
>
> • **Higher-level** When these students have finished, tell them to ask and answer questions about the people in the picture on page 146.

Evaluation
10–15 minutes

TEST YOURSELF

1. Have students choose a picture on page 144 and write two questions and two answers.

2. Collect and correct their work.

> **EXTENSION ACTIVITY**
>
> **Memory Circle**
>
> Have students stand in a circle. (If you have a large class, model the activity with one circle and then create two or three more large circles.) The first student makes a statement and acts it out: *I'm drinking coffee.* The second student says: *She's drinking coffee* and then pantomimes a new action and makes an *I* statement, such as *I'm washing clothes.* The third student says: *She's drinking coffee; he's washing clothes; I'm _____* (pantomiming a new action). Continue as such around the circle.

> **TIP**
>
> Start the extension activity with pre-level students. Put higher-level students toward the "end" of the circle.

LESSON 4 EVERYDAY CONVERSATION

Lesson Overview

MULTILEVEL OBJECTIVES
On- and Higher-level: Ask for and give locations
Pre-level: Ask for locations

LANGUAGE FOCUS
Grammar: Prepositions *(It's next to the bookstore.)*
Vocabulary: Community places
For vocabulary expansion, see this **Oxford Picture Dictionary** topic: City Streets, pages 128–129

STRATEGY FOCUS
Use *Excuse me* to get someone's attention.

READINESS CONNECTION
In this lesson, students listen actively for locations of places in the community.

PACING
To compress this lesson: Have students practice 3D with only one partner.
To extend this lesson: Practice asking about locations in a picture. (See end of lesson.)
And/or have students complete **Workbook Introductory Level page 76** and **Multilevel Activities Introductory Level Unit 11 page 121.**

CORRELATIONS

CCRS: SL.1.A Participate in collaborative conversations with diverse partners in small and larger groups.
SL.2.A Confirm understanding of a text read aloud or information presented orally or through other media by asking and answering questions about key details and requesting clarification if something is not understood.
RF.2.A Demonstrate understanding of spoken words, syllables, and sounds (phonemes).

ELPS: 2. An ELL can participate in level-appropriate oral and written exchanges of information, ideas, and analyses, in various social and academic contexts, responding to peer, audience, or reader comments and questions. 9. An ELL can create clear and coherent level-appropriate speech and text.

Lesson Notes

Warm-up and Review
5 minutes (books closed)

Draw a simple one-street map on the board with squares to represent buildings. Label the street and the buildings. Call on individuals to make statements about the map, for example: *The bookstore is next to the school.*

Introduction
5 minutes

1. Write *Where* on the board. Say and have students repeat it. Say: *Where is the bookstore? It's next to the school. Where is the bank? It's on First Street.*

2. State the objective: *Today we're going to learn how to ask for and give locations.*

1 Listen for locations

Listening Extension
15–20 minutes

A 🔊 3-50 1. Direct students to look at the pictures. Ask them to name the places they see [supermarket, restaurant, post office, bookstore, clothing store, elementary school, high school].

2. Play the audio and have students point to the places.

B 1. Direct students to ask and answer the questions with a partner, using the answers in the box.

2. Call on pairs to say a question and answer for the class.

Answers
1. It's next to the restaurant.
2. They're on Ash Street.
3. It's on Oak Street./It's between the post office and the clothing store.

2 Practice your pronunciation

Pronunciation Extension
10–15 minutes

A 🔊 3-51 Play the audio and tell students to read along silently.

B 🔊 3-52 Play the audio. Tell students to write the words in the correct list in 2A. Elicit the answers.

Answers	
these	three
they	

C 🔊 3-53 Show students how the two sounds have the same mouth position but sound different because of the way they are voiced. Replay the audio from 2A and 2B. Stop after each item and have students repeat.

> **TIP**
>
> Demonstrate the difference between the voiced and voiceless sound by holding a small piece of paper loosely in front of your mouth while you pronounce the words in the chart. Show them how the paper moves when you pronounce voiceless *th* because you are blowing out a puff of air with the sound. Distribute small pieces of paper to the class and have the students try it.

3 Make conversation: talk about locations

Presentation
5–10 minutes

A 1. Direct students to look at the pictures. Ask: *What is Mario wearing?* [a white shirt, yellow pants, a brown belt] *Who is wearing a jacket?* [Phu] *What places do you see?* [laundromat, bookstore, drugstore, bank]

2. Have students read the conversation silently. Elicit any questions.

Guided Practice
5–10 minutes

B 🔊 3-54 Play the audio. Have students read the conversation silently. Ask: *What is Mario looking for?* [a drugstore] *Does Phu help him?* [yes]

C 🔊 3-54 1. Play the audio again and have students repeat the conversation.

2. Do a choral reading of the conversation in 3B. Divide the class in half. Have one side be Mario and one side be Phu, and then have the sides switch roles.

Communicative Practice and Application
15–20 minutes

D 1. Model the conversation with a volunteer. Use one of the other places from the picture in 3A (laundromat or bank).

2. Elicit other ways to complete the conversation. Model polite pronunciation of *Excuse me.*

3. Set a time limit (five minutes). Tell students to practice the conversation with several partners. Encourage pantomime and improvisation.

4. Ask volunteer pairs to present their conversations to the class.

> **MULTILEVEL STRATEGIES**
>
> For 3D, seat pre-level students together.
>
> • **Pre-level** While other students are practicing the conversation, have these students complete page 86 in the *Literacy Reproducible Activities Unit 11*.
>
> • **Higher-level** Teach these students *across from*. Have them ask and answer questions about the locations in the picture on page 146.

Evaluation
5 minutes

TEST YOURSELF

1. Elicit the names of nearby places and write them on the board.

2. Model the activity with a volunteer, using one of the places from the board.

3. Set a time limit (three minutes). Have students practice with a partner. Then have them switch partners and repeat.

> **EXTENSION ACTIVITY**
>
> **Picture Practice**
>
> Have the students look at the picture on page 145, 2A. Tell them the horizontal street is 1st Street and the other street is Oak Ave. Put them in groups. Have them take turns around the group asking and answering about the locations of the places. Tell them not to repeat a question that another team member has asked.

LESSON 5 READING

Lesson Overview

MULTILEVEL OBJECTIVES
On- and Higher-level: Identify community services and read a city services website
Pre-level: Recognize community services and read a city services website

LANGUAGE FOCUS
Grammar: Simple present of *be* (*The hospital is on First Street.*)

Vocabulary: *Ambulance, courthouse, directory, Department of Motor Vehicles (DMV), email address, emergency, fire station, hospital, non-emergency, police station, services*

For vocabulary expansion, see this **Oxford Picture Dictionary** topic: City Streets, pages 128–129

STRATEGY FOCUS
Use website tabs to find information.

READINESS CONNECTION
In this lesson, students distinguish between emergencies and non-emergencies.

PACING
To compress this lesson: Assign 2B as homework or conduct it as a whole-class activity.

To extend this lesson: Practice with city information. (See end of lesson.)

And/or have students complete **Workbook Introductory Level page 77** and **Multilevel Activities Introductory Level Unit 11 page 122**.

Lesson Notes

CORRELATIONS

CCRS: L.6.A Use words and phrases acquired through conversations, reading and being read to, and responding to texts, including using frequently occurring conjunctions to signal simple relationships (e.g., *because*).

R.1.A Ask and answer questions about key details in the text.

R.7.A Use the illustrations and details in a text to describe its key ideas (e.g., maps, charts, photographs, political cartoons, etc.).

SL.6.A Speak audibly and express thoughts, feelings, and ideas clearly. Produce complete sentences when appropriate to task and situation.

ELPS: 1. An ELL can construct meaning from oral presentations and literary and informational text through level-appropriate listening, reading, and viewing. 8. An ELL can determine the meaning of words and phrases in oral presentations and informational text.

Warm-up and Review
10–15 minutes (books closed)

Review places in the community. Call on students to brainstorm every community place name that they remember. Write the words on the board.

Introduction
5 minutes

1. Write the word *services* on the board. Say: *We go to the supermarket, the drugstore, and the bookstore to buy things. But we don't buy things at the clinic or the library. We go there for services.*

2. State the objective: *Today we're going read about more community services and read a directory.*

1 Get ready to read

Presentation I
10–15 minutes

 A 🔊 3-55 1. Tell students to look at the pictures and listen to the words.

2. Replay the audio and tell students to listen and repeat.

3. Check comprehension of the words. Elicit where the nearest hospital, DMV, etc. is in your area.

Guided Practice I
10–15 minutes

B 🔊 3-56 1. Direct students to look at pictures *a* and *b* in number 1. Elicit the meaning of each picture.

2. Play the entire audio once. Tell students to put their pencils down and point to each location as they hear it mentioned.

3. Replay the audio. Tell students to work individually to circle the correct answer. Go over the answers as a class and write them on the board.

Answers
1. a
2. a
3. a
4. b

Presentation II
10–15 minutes

 C 1. Direct students to look at the pictures. Say and have students repeat the words.

2. Go over each word as follows: For the house on fire and the cat in the tree, ask: *Is this a problem? Is it an emergency?* For *email address*, ask students if they have email addresses. Tell them your email address. For *website*, write a URL on the board or pull up a website on a computer screen that can be projected or that students can see.

D Direct students to look at the pictures. Ask: *Emergency or non-emergency?*

Answers
1. emergency
2. non-emergency
3. non-emergency

TIP

For more practice with emergencies versus non-emergencies after 1D, show or draw pictures of medical emergencies (choking, heart attack, a person who has drunk poison). Ask students if these are emergencies [yes]. Show some non-emergency problems (the power is out, you are lost, the heater isn't working). Ask students if these are emergencies [no]. You can find suitable pictures in the Emergencies and Natural Disasters and Household Problems and Repairs topics in *The Oxford Picture Dictionary*.

2 Read a city services website

Guided Practice II
15–20 minutes

 A 1. Ask students to look at the website in 2A. Ask: *How many non-emergency phone numbers do you see?* [5]

2. Call students' attention to the *Reading Note*. Ask: *What information will you see if you click on these tabs?* [Calendar and Jobs]

3. Ask students to read the city services website silently. Ask if there are any questions about the reading.

4. Check students' comprehension. Ask: *What is the emergency number?* [911] *Is (505) 555-9111 an emergency number?* [no]

 B 1. Read number 1 aloud. Have students locate the answer on the city services website.

2. Tell students to work individually to complete the exercise.

3. Call on volunteers for the answers and write them on the board.

Answers
1. a
2. b
3. b
4. a

TIP

After 2B, use a discussion of local city services as an opportunity to help your students recognize and pronounce local street names. Write the street names on the board. Sound each name out. Number the names and have students tell you which one you are saying. Ask *yes/no* questions about the names, for example: *Is there a hospital on Pioneer Boulevard?*

Application
5–10 minutes

BRING IT TO LIFE

Provide students with the URL for your city's website. Tell them to search for the number for the police station and any other community service numbers that might interest them.

TIP

In preparation for *Teamwork & Language Review*, have students review the unit vocabulary. Provide them with pictures you have collected or use the Picture Cards on pages 123–124 of *Multilevel Activities Introductory Level Unit 11*. Pair students and have them use the pictures as flashcards for recognition practice, dictation, or sentence writing.

EXTENSION ACTIVITY

City Information

1. Print a page from your city's website and distribute it to the students in groups. If you can project the website, tell students to name the features they have learned [menu, links, and tabs].

2. Give the groups four pieces of information to look for (or at least one piece of information per group member, for example, the library's address, phone number, fax number, and hours). Tell the group members to take turns finding the information.

3. Go over the answers as a class.

TEAMWORK & LANGUAGE REVIEW

Lesson Overview

MULTILEVEL OBJECTIVES

On-, Pre-, and Higher-level: Expand upon and review unit language and content

LANGUAGE FOCUS

Grammar: Questions with *Where* and *What*; present continuous *(Where is he? He's at the park. What's he doing? He's playing.)*

Vocabulary: Community places

For vocabulary expansion, see this **Oxford Picture Dictionary** topic: City Streets, pages 128–129

STRATEGY FOCUS

Use teamwork to reinforce and expand vocabulary.

READINESS CONNECTION

In this review, students work in a team to practice categorization, writing, and problem-solving skills by determining what do with noisy neighbors.

PACING

To extend this review: Have students complete **Workbook Introductory Level page 78**, **Multilevel Activities Introductory Level Unit 11 pages 123–126**, and **Multilevel Grammar Exercises Introductory Level Unit 11**.

Lesson Notes

CORRELATIONS

CCRS: L.6.A Use words and phrases acquired through conversations, reading and being read to, and responding to texts, including using frequently occurring conjunctions to signal simple relationships (e.g., *because*).

R.7.A Use the illustrations and details in a text to describe its key ideas (e.g., maps, charts, photographs, political cartoons, etc.).

SL.1.A Participate in collaborative conversations with diverse partners in small and larger groups.

SL.4.A Describe people, places, things, and events with relevant details, expressing ideas and feelings clearly.

SL.6.A Speak audibly and express thoughts, feelings, and ideas clearly. Produce complete sentences when appropriate to task and situation.

ELPS: 2. An ELL can participate in level-appropriate oral and written exchanges of information, ideas, and analyses, in various social and academic contexts, responding to peer, audience, or reader comments and questions.

Warm-up and Review
5–10 minutes (books closed)

1. Review the *Bring It to Life* assignment from Lesson 5.

2. Have students who found a phone number say the number for the class. Write the number(s) on the board. Write *courthouse, police station, hospital,* and *DMV* on the board, and write the phone number for each. Have students say the phone numbers aloud.

3. Ask students if these are emergency or non-emergency numbers [non-emergency].

Introduction and Presentation
5 minutes

1. Write on the board: *Marco is at school. He's studying English.*

2. State the objective: *Today we're going to review unit vocabulary and talk about where people are and what they are doing.*

Communicative Practice
15–20 minutes

A 1. Tell students to take turns naming one thing they see in the picture. Have three volunteers help you model turn-taking.

2. Tell students to put their pencils down and listen to each other so that they don't repeat ideas. Direct them to go around the group until they have run out of ideas.

B 1. Have students work in the same groups from A. Assign roles: secretary, reporter, editor, and manager. Write the roles on the board. As you explain each role, pantomime the duties you expect the person taking that role to perform. Explain that students work with their groups to write the words. Verify comprehension of the roles.

2. Set a time limit (five minutes) to complete the chart. Circulate and answer any questions.

3. Call on the reporters from each group to say the words from their chart. Write the words on the board. Go around the class until there are no more ideas.

Possible Answers		
Places	**Actions**	**Other**
park	play	children
restaurant	eat	music
hospital	clean	lunch
office building	exercise	table
street	listen	window
	help	car
	wash	coffee

C 1. Have the groups identify new words from the board and to look them up in a picture dictionary or a bilingual dictionary.

2. Tell students to add three new words to their chart. [New words might include: *bench, wheelchair, street light, trash/garbage can, stretch.*]

> **MULTILEVEL STRATEGIES**
>
> For A–C, use mixed-level groups.
> • **Pre-level** Assign these students the role of manager.
> • **On-level** Assign these students the role of secretary or reporter.
> • **Higher-level** Assign these students the role of editor.

D 1. Read number 1 aloud. Point to Ken in the picture. Tell students to work independently to complete the questions and answers.

2. Call on volunteers to read the completed questions and answers aloud. Write the answers on the board.

Answers
1. Where's, park, What's he, He's exercising
2. Where are, are in the park, What are they, are playing

E 1. Read the example conversation with a volunteer. Have students ask and answer questions with a partner.

2. Call on pairs to ask and answer questions for the class.

> **MULTILEVEL STRATEGIES**
>
> Adapt D and E to the level of your students.
> • **Pre-level** Have these students sit with on- or higher-level students. Direct the pre-level students to answer questions that their partners ask.

PROBLEM SOLVING
15–20 minutes

A 🔊 3-57 1. Ask: *Do you live in a house or an apartment?* Using pantomime or drawing to get the idea across, ask: *Who lives next to you? Do you hear their music? Their dog?* Tell students the picture in A tells a story about a woman named Elena. She has a problem at home.

2. Direct students to look at the picture. Ask: *Does Elena live in a house or an apartment?* [an apartment] *What is she doing?* [studying/working] *What is happening in the next apartment?* [a party]

3. Play the audio and have students listen and look at the picture. Check comprehension. Ask: *What time is it?* [11:00 p.m.] *Is Elena a teacher or a student?* [a student] *Is Elena happy?* [no]

B 1. Tell students to look at the pictures. Read the captions and talk about them. For choice *a*, ask students if this is an emergency or non-emergency situation [non-emergency]. Ask: *Should Elena call 911 or call the police station?* [no] For choice *b*, elicit ideas about where Elena could go at 11:00 at night [a restaurant, a friend's house, etc.]. For choice *c*, discuss what kind of music might be good for studying [quiet, no singing, etc.].

2. Elicit students' ideas for option *d*. Possibilities include talking to the neighbor, going to the party, calling the landlord, studying tomorrow, and using earplugs.

3. Have the class vote on the best idea. Emphasize that there can be more than one correct answer.

Evaluation
20–25 minutes

To test students' understanding of the unit language and content, have them take the Unit 11 Test, available on the Teacher Resource Center.

> **TIP**
> Encourage students to reflect on what they have learned in this unit. Write these topics in a list on the board and elicit words, phrases, and sentences that students learned for each topic: *a) Places in the community; b) Locations; c) Present continuous; d) Asking for and giving locations; e) Community services.* Congratulate students on their progress.

UNIT 12 Yes, I Can!

Unit Overview

This unit explores common occupations, job duties, interview skills, job skills, and reading a job ad.

KEY OBJECTIVES	
Lesson 1	Identify common occupations
Lesson 2	Describe jobs and duties; describe interview skills
Lesson 3	Use *can* and *can't* to describe job skills
Lesson 4	Respond to questions about abilities
Lesson 5	Interpret a job ad
Teamwork & Language Review	Review unit language

UNIT FEATURES	
Academic Vocabulary	*construction worker, dental assistant, dress appropriately, driver's license, use a computer*
Employability Skills	• Understand teamwork • Communicate information • Listen actively • Work with others • Communicate verbally • Interpret help-wanted ads • Determine how to handle a conflict between social and work obligations

Resources	**Class Audio** CD3, Tracks 58–72
	Workbook Unit 12, pages 79–85
	Teacher Resource Center
	    Literacy Reproducible Activities Unit 12
	    Multilevel Activities Introductory Level Unit 12
	    Multilevel Grammar Exercises Introductory Level Unit 12
	    Unit 12 Test
	Oxford Picture Dictionary Jobs and Occupations, Job Skills, Job Search

LESSON 1 VOCABULARY

Lesson Overview

MULTILEVEL OBJECTIVES

On-level: Identify jobs
Pre-level: Recognize jobs
Higher-level: Talk about jobs

LANGUAGE FOCUS

Grammar: The verb *be* (*Is he a gardener? Yes, he is.*)

Vocabulary: *Cashier, gardener, hairdresser, housekeeper, mechanic, painter, salesperson, secretary, truck driver*

For vocabulary expansion, see this **Oxford Picture Dictionary** topic: Jobs and Occupations, pages 170–173

STRATEGY FOCUS

Identify vocabulary in different contexts to increase retention.

READINESS CONNECTION

In this lesson, students communicate verbally about common occupations.

PACING

To compress this lesson: Practice the conversation in 2E with only one partner.

To extend this lesson: Discuss and categorize occupations. (See end of lesson.)

And/or have students complete **Workbook Introductory Level page 79** and **Multilevel Activities Introductory Level Unit 12 page 128.**

CORRELATIONS

CCRS: L.6.A Use words and phrases acquired through conversations, reading and being read to, and responding to texts, including using frequently occurring conjunctions to signal simple relationships (e.g., *because*).

SL.1.A Participate in collaborative conversations with diverse partners in small and larger groups.

ELPS: 1. An ELL can construct meaning from oral presentations and literary and informational text through level-appropriate listening, reading, and viewing.

Lesson Notes

Warm-up and Review
10–15 minutes (books closed)

Write *teacher, student, clerk, salesperson,* and *apartment manager* on the board. Ask where each person works [school, school, store, store, apartment building]. Elicit any other jobs that students can name and write them on the board.

Introduction
5 minutes

1. Say and have students repeat the words on the board. Write the word *Jobs* above them.

2. State the objective: *Today we'll learn the names of jobs.*

1 Learn the names of jobs

Presentation
20–25 minutes

A Direct students to look at the pictures. Ask them to say the job words they know.

B 🔊 3-58 1. Play the audio. Tell students to point to the correct picture as they listen. Circulate and monitor.

2. Check comprehension by asking *yes/no* questions. Point to each picture and ask, for example: *Is she a mechanic?* Have students use thumbs up (*yes*) or thumbs down (*no*) to respond.

C 🔊 3-58 1. Tell students to listen and repeat the words.

2. Call out the numbers out of order and ask students to say the words.

Guided Practice I
10–15 minutes

D Direct students to take turns reading the words with a partner.

E 1. Model the activity with two volunteers. Direct one partner to point to the pictures or say the numbers. Have the other partner cover the words in 1C and identify the pictures from memory.

2. Have students practice in pairs.

> **MULTILEVEL STRATEGIES**
>
> For 1E, pair same-level students together.
>
> • **Pre-level** Tell these students to practice together by pointing to the pictures in 1B and saying the correct words.
>
> • **Higher-level** Tell these students to dictate the words to each other.

2 Talk about jobs

Guided Practice II
20–25 minutes

A 1. Direct students to look at the picture. Call out job titles and ask students to say the numbers.

2. Copy number 1 on the board and have students spell *hairdresser* aloud. Demonstrate how to write one letter on each line.

3. Tell students to work individually to complete the words.

4. Ask volunteers to spell the completed words aloud. Write the answers on the board. Read and have students repeat the words.

Answers	
1. h-a-i-r-d-r-e-s-s-e-r	6. p-a-i-n-t-e-r
2. c-a-s-h-i-e-r	7. s-a-l-e-s-p-e-r-s-o-n
3. h-o-u-s-e-k-e-e-p-e-r	8. m-e-c-h-a-n-i-c
4. g-a-r-d-e-n-e-r	9. t-r-u-c-k d-r-i-v-e-r
5. s-e-c-r-e-t-a-r-y	

B Give students time to copy the words into their notebooks. Monitor and check their writing.

> **TIP**
>
> For more practice with the vocabulary after 2B, play charades. Pass out picture cards. (See Picture Cards 12.1–12.9 on page 133 of *Multilevel Activities Introductory Level Unit 12*.) Ask a student to pantomime doing the job on their card. Call on other students to guess the job.

C 🔊 3-59 1. Play the audio. Have students read along silently.

2. Play the audio again. Tell students to listen and repeat.

Communicative Practice and Application
10–15 minutes

D 1. Model the conversations with a volunteer. Show students how to use the picture in 2A. Switch roles and model the conversations with another volunteer.

2. Pair students. Have one pair model the conversations.

3. Set a time limit (five minutes) and have the partners practice the conversations in both roles. Encourage students to use all of the words. Circulate and monitor. Provide feedback.

E 1. Direct students to stand and circulate. Tell them to ask at least three classmates: *What is your job?*

2. Circulate and help students with the names of their jobs. Write the new words on the board.

Evaluation
10–15 minutes

TEST YOURSELF

1. Have students work independently to write the words they remember.

2. Have students open their books and check their spelling.

> **MULTILEVEL STRATEGIES**
>
> Target the *Test Yourself* to the level of your students.
>
> • **Pre-level** Give these students 3–4 pictures representing the occupations. Tell them to look at page 158 and write the correct word for each picture.
>
> • **Higher-level** Challenge these students to include words not presented in the lesson. Have them check their answers in a picture dictionary.

> **EXTENSION ACTIVITY**
>
> **Categorize Occupations**
>
> 1. Hold a class discussion about the occupations in this lesson. Ask students who works outside; who wears a uniform; and who has the most difficult, most boring, most interesting, or best-paying job.
>
> 2. As you elicit the students' ideas, draw charts on the board to help everyone follow along. For example, draw a dollar sign, a uniform, a sun, a happy face, a frustrated face, and a tired face for column headings and write jobs underneath them. If students disagree about whether a job is interesting, boring, or difficult, write the job in every category to reflect students' opinions.

LESSON 2 WRITING

Lesson Overview

MULTILEVEL OBJECTIVES
On- and Higher-level: Read and write about job skills
Pre-level: Recognize job skills

LANGUAGE FOCUS
Grammar: Can (He can fix cars.)
Vocabulary: Clean, cut hair, drive trucks, fix cars, paint houses, sell clothes, take care of plants, use a computer
For vocabulary expansion, see this **Oxford Picture Dictionary** topic: Job Skills, page 176

STRATEGY FOCUS
Use capital letters in a story title.

READINESS CONNECTION
In this lesson, students communicate information about their job skills.

PACING
To compress this lesson: Assign the Test Yourself for homework.
To extend this lesson: Match occupations and skills. (See end of lesson.)
And/or have students complete **Workbook Introductory Level page 80** and **Multilevel Activities Introductory Level Unit 12 page 129.**

Lesson Notes

CORRELATIONS

CCRS: L.6.A Use words and phrases acquired through conversations, reading and being read to, and responding to texts, including using frequently occurring conjunctions to signal simple relationships (e.g., because).

R.1.A Ask and answer questions about key details in the text.

R.7.A Use the illustrations and details in a text to describe its key ideas (e.g., maps, charts, photographs, political cartoons, etc.).

SL.1.A Participate in collaborative conversations with diverse partners in small and larger groups.

SL.2.A Confirm understanding of a text read aloud or information presented orally or through other media by asking and answering questions about key details and requesting clarification if something is not understood.

SL.6.A Speak audibly and express thoughts, feelings, and ideas clearly. Produce complete sentences when appropriate to task and situation.

ELPS: 1. An ELL can construct meaning from oral presentations and literary and informational text through level-appropriate listening, reading, and viewing. 9. An ELL can create clear and coherent level-appropriate speech and text.

Warm-up and Review
10–15 minutes (books closed)

Pantomime cutting hair, fixing a car, driving a truck, painting, gardening, and cleaning. Have students call out the associated job for each. Tell volunteers to write the job names on the board [hairdresser, mechanic, truck driver, painter, gardener, housekeeper].

Introduction
5 minutes

1. Make statements about the jobs on the board: *A housekeeper cleans rooms. A truck driver drives a truck. These are their job skills.*

2. State the objective: *Today we'll read and write about job skills.*

1 Learn about job skills

Presentation I
15–20 minutes

A Have students look at the pictures. Ask students to name the jobs they see [hairdresser, mechanic, truck driver, painter, janitor, salesperson/clerk, gardener, secretary/office worker].

B 🔊 3-60 1. Play the audio. Have students read along silently.

2. Check comprehension. Say the words out of order and have students call out the correct numbers.

3. Replay the audio and ask students to repeat the words.

4. Say the numbers and have students call out the words.

Guided Practice I
5–10 minutes

C 1. Read the instructions aloud. Tell students to work independently to complete the sentences.

2. Have students read their completed sentences with a partner. Remind them to pronounce the *s* at the end of the verbs. Call on individuals for the answers and write them on the board.

Answers	
1. cuts	5. sells
2. paints	6. uses
3. drives	7. fixes
4. takes care of	8. cleans

2 Prepare to write

Presentation II
25–30 minutes

A 🔊 3-61 Direct students to look at the job applications. Ask: *Can Lily use a computer?* [yes]

2. Play the audio. Have students listen silently and look at the job applications. Tell them to check the skills they hear.

Answers
Lily Ng: use a computer, speak English
Gabriela Valdez: other: cut hair
Paul Fields: drive a car, speak English, other: drive a truck

B 1. Tell students to look at the job application. Explain that *current* means *now*. Point out the information in the *Need help?* box.

2. Tell students to work independently to complete the applications. Circulate and provide feedback.

C 🔊 3-62 1. Have students identify Nick in the picture in 1A. Explain that this is his story. Tell students to listen and read along silently.

2. Check comprehension. Ask: *What does Nick's brother do?* [He's a mechanic.] *What does his friend do?* [She's a truck driver.] *Is Nick a mechanic?* [No, he isn't.]

3. Draw students' attention to the *Writer's Note*. Tell them to look at the unit title on page 158 and notice that it also uses capital letters.

> **MULTILEVEL STRATEGIES**
>
> For 2C, seat students in mixed-level groups. After the whole-group practice, ask students to take turns reading the sentences aloud. Demonstrate turn-taking, with the first student reading number 1, the second number 2, and so on.
>
> • **Pre-level** Tell students who don't want to read aloud to listen to their classmates and follow along silently.

Guided Practice II
10–15 minutes

D 🔊 3-63 1. Direct students to look at the picture in 2E. Say and have them repeat *Nora*. Read the instructions aloud.

2. Play the audio. Ask students what Nora can do.

Answer
Nora can take care of plants.

E 1. Have students work independently to write the words in the paragraph.

2. Tell them to compare their answers with a partner.

Answers
painter, secretary, types, paint, letters, take care of

F 1. Replay the audio so students can check their work. Go over the answers as a class.

2. Conduct a choral reading of the paragraph.

3 Write

Communicative Practice
10–15 minutes

A 1. Introduce the new activity: *Now you are going to write about your job skills and other people's job skills.*

2. Call on volunteers to complete the sentences aloud.

3. Tell students to work individually to complete the sentences with their own information.

4. Remind students to give their story a title and to capitalize the words.

B 1. Have students read their paragraph aloud to a partner. Tell them to correct any mistakes they notice. When they finish, ask them to read the stories to a new partner.

2. Have students copy their paragraph into their notebooks.

> **MULTILEVEL STRATEGIES**
>
> Adapt 3A and 3B to the level of your students.
>
> • **Pre-level** While on- and higher-level students are completing 3A and 3B, work with these students in a group, or have them complete page 90 of the *Literacy Reproducible Activities Unit 12.*

AT WORK

Job interview skills
10–15 minutes

A 1. Direct students to look at the pictures. Ask what the man is wearing [shirt, tie, pants, belt, shoes].

2. Play the audio and tell students to read along silently.

3. Check comprehension. Review the meaning of *on time*. For example, say: *I come to class at 9:00. Am I on time?* Clap out the syllables and help students pronounce *appropriately*. Model a good, firm handshake and have students practice with a partner.

B Read the directions aloud and elicit students' answers to the questions. Write their ideas on the board.

Evaluation
10 minutes

TEST YOURSELF

1. Have students copy the sentence frames into their notebooks. Tell them to look at the pictures on page 158 and complete the sentences.

3. Collect and correct students' work.

> **EXTENSION ACTIVITY**
>
> **Match Occupations with Skills**
>
> 1. Write a list of occupations on the board and tell students to copy it, for example: *gardener, hairdresser, salesperson, secretary, mechanic,* and *housekeeper.*
>
> 2. Make statements about job skills and have students write the number next to the correct job. For example: *Number 1 can take care of plants. Number 2 can cut hair.*
>
> 3. Call on volunteers for the answers. Then re-state the sentences using the job titles: *A gardener can take of plants. A hairdresser can cut hair.*

LESSON 3 GRAMMAR

Lesson Overview

MULTILEVEL OBJECTIVES
On- and Higher-level: Use *can* and *can't*
Pre-level: Recognize *can* and *can't*

LANGUAGE FOCUS
Grammar: Statements with *can* (I can drive.); yes/no questions with *can* (Can you drive?)
Vocabulary: Job skills
For vocabulary expansion, see this **Oxford Picture Dictionary** topic: Job Skills, page 176

STRATEGY FOCUS
To talk about your schedule, use *can* or *can't* to express whether or not you're free, or available, to do something.

READINESS CONNECTION
In this lesson, students work with others to talk about job schedules.

PACING
To compress this lesson: Conduct 1C as a whole-class activity. Assign 1D for homework.
To extend this lesson: Conduct a circle practice. (See end of lesson.)
And/or have students complete **Workbook Introductory Level pages 81–82**, **Multilevel Activities Introductory Level Unit 12 page 130**, and **Multilevel Grammar Exercises Introductory Level Unit 12**.

Lesson Notes

CORRELATIONS

CCRS: L.6.A Use words and phrases acquired through conversations, reading and being read to, and responding to texts, including using frequently occurring conjunctions to signal simple relationships (e.g., *because*).

R.1.A Ask and answer questions about key details in the text.

R.7.A Use the illustrations and details in a text to describe its key ideas (e.g., maps, charts, photographs, political cartoons, etc.).

SL.1.A Participate in collaborative conversations with diverse partners in small and larger groups.

SL.2.A Confirm understanding of a text read aloud or information presented orally or through other media by asking and answering questions about key details and requesting clarification if something is not understood.

ELPS: 10. An ELL can demonstrate command of the conventions of standard English to communicate in level-appropriate speech and writing.

Warm-up and Review
10–15 minutes (books closed)

Pass out pictures of the job skills from Lesson 2. (See Picture Cards 12.10–12.17 on pages 133–134 of *Multilevel Activities Introductory Level Unit 12*.) Tell students to pantomime the actions on the cards. Have other students write the actions on the board.

Introduction
5–10 minutes

1. Make *can* statements about yourself using the words on the board: *I can drive. I can't fix cars.*

2. State the objective: *Today we'll learn to use* can *and* can't.

1 Learn about *can* and *can't*

Presentation I
20–25 minutes

 A 🔊 3-65 1. Play the audio and ask students to read the captions.

2. Check comprehension, using gestures as necessary to make your meaning clear: *Is his typing good?* [yes] *Is her job fixing computers?* [yes] *Is his job cooking?* (or *Are his cookies good?*) [no] *Is she good at driving?* [no]

B Give students a couple of minutes to study the chart. Ask if they have any questions.

Guided Practice I
15–20 minutes

C 1. Model how to make new sentences by reading one word from each column, for example: *He can use a cash register.*

2. Tell students to work in pairs. Set a time limit (two minutes).

3. Call on individuals to make sentences for the class.

> **MULTILEVEL STRATEGIES**
>
> Adapt 1C for your pre-level students.
>
> • **Pre-level** Seat these students with an on- or higher-level pair. Tell them to point to the correct words in each column and repeat the sentences their partners say.

D Direct students to look at the pictures and complete the sentences with *can* or *can't*. Go over the answers as a class.

Answers
1. can't
2. can
3. can't
4. can

Communicative Practice I
5–10 minutes

E Direct students to take turns telling a partner about the things they can and can't do using the pictures in 1A and 1D on page 163. Set a time limit (two minutes).

2 Practice: *yes/no* questions with *can* and *can't*

Presentation II
10–15 minutes

 A 1. Direct students to look at the pictures. Say: *These people are at a job interview.*

2. Read the conversations and have students repeat them.

B Give students a minute to study the charts. Elicit any questions.

Guided Practice II
10–15 minutes

 C 1. Read number 1 aloud. Point out that students will need to write two words in some of the blanks.

2. Tell students to work independently to complete the questions and answers.

3. Have students read their completed questions and answers with a partner. Call on pairs to read them aloud for the class.

Answers
1. Can she
2. Can he
3. Can they
4. can't
5. can
6. can't

Communicative Practice II

 D 1. Read the example conversations with volunteers, encouraging them to provide their own answers.

2. Tell pairs to ask and answer questions about the pictures on page 163. Set a time limit (two minutes).

3 Use *can* to talk about a schedule

Presentation III
10–15 minutes

 1. Direct students' attention to the schedules. Point out the names below. Ask: *What time is Kara's class?* [from 6 p.m. to 9 p.m.] Play the audio and tell students to listen and look at the schedules.

2. Check comprehension of the schedules. Ask: *Can Todd work on Sunday?* [No, he can't.]

 1. Tell students to work independently to answer the questions.

2. Play the audio and have students check their answers. Tell them to read the completed questions and answers with a partner.

Answers
1. Yes, she can. / No, she can't.
2. Yes, he can. / No, he can't.

Communicative Practice II
15–20 minutes

 1. Model the activity with a volunteer. Demonstrate the substitution with a different name and words from the box. Tell students to refer to the schedules in 3A for the answers.

2. Have students practice asking and answering the questions in pairs. Encourage them to use all of the times in the box.

3. Call on pairs to say questions and answers for the class.

Evaluation
10–15 minutes

TEST YOURSELF

Read the example questions. Have students circulate and talk to at least three partners. Circulate and provide feedback.

> **MULTILEVEL STRATEGIES**
>
> Target the *Test Yourself* to the level of your students.
>
> • **Pre-level** While other students circulate for the *Test Yourself*, sit with these students and ask them questions about their schedules. Tell them to respond with *Yes, I can* or *No, I can't*.

EXTENSION ACTIVITY

Circle Practice

1. Have students stand in a circle.
2. Write this sequence on the board:
   1. I can/can't _____.
   2. Can he/she _____?
   3. Yes, he/she can. No, he/she can't.
3. Ask a student to make a statement using the frame in number 1. Have the next student ask a question about the first student, and have the third student answer the question. The fourth student begins the cycle again with number 1. Go through several rounds until students have the pattern down. If you have a very large class, break the circle into smaller circles at this point. Avoid multiples of three so that students have a different kind of sentence to practice every time their turn comes along.

LESSON 4 EVERYDAY CONVERSATION

Lesson Overview

MULTILEVEL OBJECTIVES

On-, Pre-, and Higher-level: Respond to job interview questions and interpret a work schedule

LANGUAGE FOCUS

Grammar: Yes/no questions and answers with *can* (*Can you use a computer?*)

Vocabulary: Job skills

For vocabulary expansion, see these **Oxford Picture Dictionary** topics: Job Skills, page 176; Job Search, pages 168–169

STRATEGY FOCUS

To talk about a range of consecutive days when you are or aren't available, use *to*: *I'm busy (from) Monday to Wednesday.* = *I'm busy Monday, Tuesday, and Wednesday.*

READINESS CONNECTION

In this lesson, students listen actively for information about a schedule.

PACING

To compress this lesson: Conduct 1B as a whole-class activity.

To extend this lesson: Dictate sentences. (See end of lesson.)

And/or have students complete **Workbook Introductory Level page 83** and **Multilevel Activities Introductory Level Unit 12 page 131**.

Lesson Notes

CORRELATIONS

CCRS: R.1.A Ask and answer questions about key details in the text.

R.7.A Use the illustrations and details in a text to describe its key ideas (e.g., maps, charts, photographs, political cartoons, etc.).

SL.1.A Participate in collaborative conversations with diverse partners in small and larger groups.

SL.2.A Confirm understanding of a text read aloud or information presented orally or through other media by asking and answering questions about key details and requesting clarification if something is not understood.

RF.2.A Demonstrate understanding of spoken words, syllables, and sounds (phonemes).

ELPS: 2. An ELL can participate in level-appropriate oral and written exchanges of information, ideas, and analyses, in various social and academic contexts, responding to peer, audience, or reader comments and questions. 9. An ELL can create clear and coherent level-appropriate speech and text.

Warm-up and Review
5 minutes (books closed)

Write *Can you _____?* on the board. Call on volunteers to complete the question. Call on other students to answer.

Introduction
5 minutes

1. Tell students that when they are looking for a job, the interviewer might ask them questions with *can*.

2. State the objective: *Today we'll learn to answer job-interview questions.*

1 Listen for schedule information

Listening Extension
20–25 minutes

A Direct students to look at the schedule and identify the days and times of the classes.

B 🔊 3-67 1. Play the audio and have students work independently to circle the answers.

2. Tell them to compare their answers with a partner.

Answers
1. a
2. b
3. b
4. a

C 🔊 3-67 Replay the audio one item at a time and have students check their answers.

2 Practice your pronunciation

Pronunciation Extension
10–15 minutes

A 🔊 3-68 1. Say: *Now we're going to practice the pronunciation of* can *and* can't.

2. Play the audio. Tell students to listen silently. Focus their attention on the difference in the sentence stress. (*Can* is unstressed, but *can't* is about equally stressed with the verb.)

B 🔊 3-69 Play the audio. Tell students to listen and check the correct column.

Answers	1.	2.	3.	4.	5.	6.
can	✓		✓			✓
can't		✓		✓	✓	

C 🔊 3-69 Replay the audio one item at a time. Tell students to check their answers. Write the answers on the board. Have students repeat each sentence.

TIP

After 2C, have students try the activity with a partner. Tell them to make a *can/can't* chart with four rows in their notebooks. Write these sentences on the board: *I can work. I can't work. I can drive. I can't drive. I can go. I can't go. I can fix cars. I can't fix cars.* Tell students to choose four of the sentences to say to their partners. The partner should check off *can* or *can't* in the chart. Have partners check the results and then switch roles.

Tell students that *can* and *can't* are easy to misunderstand. Encourage them to practice confirming information by saying: *I'm sorry, can or can't?*

3 Make conversation: answer job interview questions

Presentation
5–10 minutes

A 1. Direct students to look at the pictures. Ask: *Who is looking for a job?* [Silvia] *Who is the interviewer?* [Patrick]

2. Direct students to read the conversation silently. Elicit any questions.

B 🔊 3-70 Play the audio. Have students read the conversation silently.

Guided Practice
5–10 minutes

C 🔊 3-70 1. Play the audio again and have students repeat the conversation.

2. Do a choral reading of the conversation in 3B. Divide the class in half. Have one side be Patrick and one side be Silvia, and then have the sides switch roles.

Communicative Practice and Application
15–20 minutes

D 1. Draw students' attention to the *Need help?* box. Point out the difference between *to* and *and* to connect dates. Check comprehension: *Is our class Monday to Friday or Monday and Friday?*

2. Model the conversation with a volunteer.

3. Elicit other ways to complete the conversation.

4. Set a time limit (five minutes). Tell students to practice the conversation with several partners. Encourage pantomime and improvisation.

5. Ask volunteer pairs to present their conversations to the class.

> **MULTILEVEL STRATEGIES**
>
> For 3D, adapt the practice to the level of your students.
>
> • **Pre-level** While other students are practicing the conversation, have these students complete page 92 in the *Literacy Reproducible Activities Unit 12*.
>
> • **Higher-level** Give these students more questions to practice: *What is your job now? Can you work nights? Weekends?*

Evaluation
5 minutes

TEST YOURSELF

Model the activity with a volunteer. Set a time limit (three minutes). Have students practice with several partners. Monitor and provide feedback.

> **EXTENSION ACTIVITY**
>
> **Dictation**
>
> Dictate sentences with *can* and *can't*. Use the sentences from the *Tip* after 2C, choosing two negative and two affirmative statements. Have volunteers check off the answers on the board.

LESSON 5 READING

Lesson Overview

MULTILEVEL OBJECTIVES
On- and Higher-level: Identify job titles and read a job ad
Pre-level: Recognize job titles and read a job ad

LANGUAGE FOCUS
Grammar: Present tense (*He builds houses.*)
Vocabulary: *Babysitter, classroom aide, construction worker, dental assistant, driver's license, full time, part time*
For vocabulary expansion, see these **Oxford Picture Dictionary** topics: Jobs and Occupations, pages 170–173; Job Search, pages 168–169; Job Skills, page 176

STRATEGY FOCUS
Interpret a website menu.

READINESS CONNECTION
In this lesson, students interpret help-wanted ads.

PACING
To compress this lesson: Assign 2B as homework or conduct it as a whole-class activity.
To extend this lesson: Discuss job salaries. (See end of lesson.)
And/or have students complete **Workbook Introductory Level page 84** and **Multilevel Activities Introductory Level Unit 12 page 132**.

Lesson Notes

CORRELATIONS

CCRS: L.6.A Use words and phrases acquired through conversations, reading and being read to, and responding to texts, including using frequently occurring conjunctions to signal simple relationships (e.g., *because*).
R.1.A Ask and answer questions about key details in the text.
R.7.A Use the illustrations and details in a text to describe its key ideas (e.g., maps, charts, photographs, political cartoons, etc.).

ELPS: 1. An ELL can construct meaning from oral presentations and literary and informational text through level-appropriate listening, reading, and viewing. 8. An ELL can determine the meaning of words and phrases in oral presentations and informational text.

Warm-up and Review
10–15 minutes (books closed)

Write letters on the board: *c, g, h, m, p, t, s*. Tell students they are the first letters of job titles. Give them a couple of minutes to recall or look up the spelling of the jobs. Then ask volunteers to write the jobs on the board [cashier, gardener, hairdresser/housekeeper, mechanic, painter, truck driver/teacher, secretary/salesperson].

Introduction
5 minutes

1. Elicit a skill for each of the jobs on the board, for example: *mechanic—fix cars*.

2. State the objective: *Today we'll learn about more jobs and read some job ads.*

1 Get ready to read

Presentation I
10–15 minutes

 1. Tell students to look at the pictures and listen to the words.

2. Check comprehension of the words. Ask: *Who works at a school?* [classroom aide] *Who works in a house?* [babysitter] *Who works outside?* [construction worker] *Who works in a dentist's office?* [dental assistant] Find out if any of your students have ever done one of these jobs.

3. Replay the audio and tell students to listen and repeat.

4. Say and have students repeat the verbs *help* and *build*. Act out other examples of *help* and *build*, for example, a teacher helping students or someone building a piece of furniture.

Guided Practice I
10–15 minutes

B 1. Read number 1 aloud. Tell students to work individually to match the jobs with the sentences.

2. Call on volunteers for the answers. Write them on the board.

Answers
1. d
2. a
3. c
4. b

Presentation II
5–10 minutes

 Direct students to look at the pictures. Say and have students repeat the words. Tell students if you work part or full time. Show them your driver's license.

D Have students work individually to circle *yes* and *no*. Find out how many students have a driver's license (from this country or from their native country), how many students work full time, and how many work part time.

2 Read job ads

Guided Practice II
15–20 minutes

1. Direct students to look at the ads. Ask them to say the job titles.

2. Read the *Reading Note*. Have students identify the menu in the realia. Discuss the meaning of *hire, job seeker,* and *employer.* Ask: *For which job do you have to speak Spanish?* [classroom aide]

3. Give students a couple of minutes to read the ads silently. Ask if there are any questions.

4. Check comprehension. Ask: *Is the construction worker job full time or part time?* [part time]

5. Show students how to find the answer to number 1 in the ads. Have students work independently to check the answers. Go over the answers as a class.

Answers	Ad 1	Ad 2	Ad 3	Ad 4
1. work on Saturdays	✓	✓		
2. work in the summer			✓	
3. use a computer	✓			✓
4. work full time	✓			
5. have a driver's license		✓		
6. work in the evening	✓	✓		

MULTILEVEL STRATEGIES

Adapt the reading for your pre-level students.

• **Pre-level** While other students are completing the activity, work with these students. Say and ask them to circle familiar words in job ads, for example: *evenings, mornings, nights, June, school, FT, Friday.* Have them read the words back to you. Give them time to copy the answers off the board.

Application
5–10 minutes

> **TIP**
>
> Before assigning *Bring It to Life*, have students practice looking at real job ads. Print out a page of job ads from the Internet. (The "Now hiring" section of a retail chain can be a good source of different kinds of jobs on the same page.) Distribute the ads and tell students to locate and circle specific ads. For example, *Circle all of the part-time jobs.* Then have students read you the titles of those jobs.

BRING IT TO LIFE

Provide students with a URL for job ads on the Internet. Show them how to search the site for location or job category.

> **TIP**
>
> In preparation for *Teamwork & Language Review*, have students review the unit vocabulary. Provide them with pictures you have collected or use the Picture Cards on pages 133–134 of *Multilevel Activities Introductory Level Unit 12*. Pair students and have them use the pictures as flashcards for recognition practice, dictation, or sentence writing.

EXTENSION ACTIVITY

Guess Salaries

Have students guess the salaries of the jobs they have studied in this unit.

1. Write several job titles on the board. Tell students to work with a partner to guess an average monthly salary for each one. Tell them to write the guesses.

2. Provide them with the real answers. You can find this information in the *Department of Labor's Occupational Outlook Handbook*, or just type "average salary for a [job title]" into a search engine.

3. After you read each salary, have students indicate whether their guesses were accurate by pointing up for "too high," down for "too low," or making the "so-so" hand sign for "pretty close."

TEAMWORK & LANGUAGE REVIEW

Lesson Overview

MULTILEVEL OBJECTIVES

On-, Pre-, and Higher-level: Expand upon and review unit language and content

LANGUAGE FOCUS

Grammar: Statements with *can* (*I can drive a truck.*); yes/no questions with *can* (*Can you fix cars?*)

Vocabulary: Jobs and job skills

For vocabulary expansion, see these **Oxford Picture Dictionary** topics: Jobs and Occupations, pages 170–173; Job Skills, page 176

STRATEGY FOCUS

Use teamwork to reinforce and expand vocabulary.

READINESS CONNECTION

In this review, students work as a team to practice writing and problem-solving skills by determining how to handle a conflict between social and work obligations.

PACING

To extend this review: Have students complete **Workbook Introductory Level page 85**, **Multilevel Activities Introductory Level Unit 12 pages 133–136**, and **Multilevel Grammar Exercises Introductory Level Unit 12**.

CORRELATIONS

CCRS: L.6.A Use words and phrases acquired through conversations, reading and being read to, and responding to texts, including using frequently occurring conjunctions to signal simple relationships (e.g., *because*).

R.7.A Use the illustrations and details in a text to describe its key ideas (e.g., maps, charts, photographs, political cartoons, etc.).

SL.1.A Participate in collaborative conversations with diverse partners in small and larger groups.

SL.4.A Describe people, places, things, and events with relevant details, expressing ideas and feelings clearly.

SL.6.A Speak audibly and express thoughts, feelings, and ideas clearly.

ELPS: 2. An ELL can participate in level-appropriate oral and written exchanges of information, ideas, and analyses, in various social and academic contexts, responding to peer, audience, or reader comments and questions.

Warm-up and Review
5–10 minutes (books closed)

1. Review the *Bring It to Life* assignment from Lesson 5.

2. Ask students what job ads they saw. Write the job titles on the board. Ask the class to say any related job skills.

Introduction and Presentation
5 minutes

1. Write some statements about job skills on the board: *A mechanic can fix cars. A construction worker can build houses. A classroom aide can work with students.* Ask students related questions with *can you*: *Can you fix cars? Can you build houses?*

2. State the objective: *Today we're going to review unit vocabulary and* can *and* can't.

Communicative Practice
15–20 minutes

A 1. Tell students to take turns naming one thing they see in the pictures. Have three volunteers help you model turn-taking.

2. Tell students to put their pencils down and listen to each other so that they don't repeat ideas. Direct them to go around the group until they have run out of ideas.

B 1. Have students work in the same groups from A. Assign roles: secretary, reporter, editor, and manager. Write the roles on the board. As you explain each role, pantomime the duties you expect the person taking that role to perform. Explain that students work with their groups to write the words. Verify comprehension of the roles.

2. Set a time limit (five minutes) to complete the chart. Circulate and answer any questions.

3. Call on the reporters from each group to say the words from their chart. Write the words on the board. Go around the class until there are no more ideas.

Possible Answers		
Job	**Job Skill**	**Other**
cashier	use a cash	store
cook	register	kitchen
truck driver	cook	stove
secretary	drive a truck	hat
babysitter	type	uniform
	take care of	office
	children	desk
	speak … (a	
	language)	
	use a computer	

C 1. Have the groups identify new words from the board and to look them up in a picture dictionary or a bilingual dictionary.

2. Tell students to add three new words to their chart. [New words might include: *toy, keyboard, utensils, scanner, apron, uniform.*]

D 1. Read the instructions aloud and give students time to make a blank T-chart in their notebooks. Explain that when they finish, there will be three names in the "Name" column and the skills should be across from the right person's name.

2. Make a T-chart and have a volunteer model the activity with you. Tell the volunteer to take the part of speaker A. Encourage him/her to ask you for the spelling of your name and write it in the chart on the board. Tell them to note your answers to the question as well.

3. Set a time limit (five minutes). Have students talk to three partners and take notes in their charts.

MULTILEVEL STRATEGIES

Adapt D for your pre-level students.

- **Pre-level** While other students are interviewing partners, sit with these students in a group. Have them answer the question "What are your job skills?" Pass a paper around and have them take turns writing *I can* sentences as answers. Correct them together.

E 1. Copy the chart on the board. Include the headings, but not the example entries.

2. Call on students to make *I can* statements to help you complete the chart with their skills. For the last column, elicit other things they can do, for example: *sew, play soccer,* and *take care of children*. Congratulate the class on their accomplishments.

PROBLEM SOLVING
15–20 minutes

A 🔊 3-72 1. Tell students the pictures in A tell a story about a woman named Adriana. She has a problem at work.

2. Direct students to look at the pictures. Say and have students repeat the word *wedding*. Ask if a friend's wedding is important.

3. Play the audio and have students listen and look at the pictures. Check comprehension. Ask: *When is the wedding?* [Saturday] *What is Adriana doing on Saturday?* [working]

B 1. Tell students to look at the pictures. Read the captions and talk about them. For choice *b*, ask students if Adriana is really sick. Ask how Adriana feels about choice *c*.

2. Elicit students' ideas for option *d*. Possibilities include asking to work a different day, quitting the job, telling the boss there's an emergency, telling the friend she'll come to the reception, but not the wedding, etc.

3. Ask for a show of hands to see which solution the class likes best. Emphasize that there can be more than one correct answer.

Evaluation
20–25 minutes

To test students' understanding of the unit language and content, have them take the Unit 12 Test, available on the Teacher Resource Center.

> **TIP**
> Encourage students to reflect on what they have learned in this unit. Write these topics in a list on the board and elicit words, phrases, and sentences that students learned for each topic: *a) Jobs; b) Job skills; c) Can and can't; d) Job ads.* Congratulate students on their progress and on completing *Step Forward Introductory Level!*